A BUNDLE OF MEMORIES

A
BUNDLE OF MEMORIES

BY

HENRY SCOTT HOLLAND, D.D., D.Litt.,

REGIUS PROFESSOR OF DIVINITY IN THE UNIVERSITY OF OXFORD,
AND CANON OF CHRIST CHURCH

LONDON:

WELLS GARDNER, DARTON & CO., LTD.

3 & 4, PATERNOSTER BUILDINGS, E.C.

AND 44, VICTORIA STREET, S.W.

1915

Second Impression

PUBLISHERS' NOTE.

Since this book was put into the hands of the printer, as month by month the national anxiety has deepened, Dr. Holland felt that its publication would appear sadly incongruous in the face of the present realities. The chapters were, however, all written and the book planned long before the war; and, as many readers were already expecting the volume, the Publishers—believing that the memory of the quiet dead may help to relieve the strain of living—have obtained Dr. Holland's consent to issue the book with this note.

PREFACE

THIS little book may win forgiveness if its preventive and prohibitive purpose be fully recognized. It makes it finally impossible for me to write a volume of Reminiscences. It is wise to guard against this in time. For the period of anecdotage is fast drawing in upon me. And at any moment of weakness I might yield to a publisher's bribe, and the worst would have happened. It is the last dotty years that do all the mischief. Old age affords a fatal leisure: and, then, the devil gets busy with one's idle hands. So, now, I have taken steps to forestall a lapse. I have scrapped the materials that might have been of service. The Public is saved. And it may, therefore, be the better inclined to tolerate kindly this casual gleaning out of the memories that lie behind me.

I have to thank my friend, Mr. G. W. Wardman, for the trouble that he has taken to bring the fragments together.

HENRY SCOTT HOLLAND

CHRIST CHURCH, OXFORD
May 1, 1915

CONTENTS

vii

A BUNDLE OF MEMORIES

I

ALGERNON CHARLES SWINBURNE

Never again shall we see that strange figure, working its fixed way along the edge of Wimbledon Common, to and fro, from the hideous villa at the bottom of Putney Hill to the Rose and Crown and the bottle of stout, and back again. Time after time I have caught sight of it—twitching zealously along, with odd jerky motions, the head thrown far back, the long back rigidly set, the long arms reaching to the knees, like Buddha's, with the hands wagging and out-splayed, and the very short legs, and the short crumpled trousers, ending somehow above the funny boots. Everything was queer and rather uncanny, until you were close enough to catch sight of the fine grave eyes above the elusive chin, and the splendid brow. No one could ever induce him to speak a word. If adventurous people asked him the time of day, he would silently hold out his watch for them to see. In silence he passed into the Rose and Crown : in silence drank his fixed amount : in silence deposited the charge : and in silence emerged to work his way home. He always moved as if engaged on a strenuous

B

task. Only now and then a baby in a perambulator, with its rose-leaf face, would arrest him : and he would turn to feast on the sight that he loved. Now and again it would disappoint him by shrinking into a scream of fright at its worshipper.

So for thirty years and more he had lived out his life, trying to obey the French novelist who said that a poet should " live like a bourgeois and think like a God." Did ever such a house hold for thirty years such a poet ? Could anything more commonplace, more formal, more Philistine, more hopelessly suburban be imagined than that semi-detached villa, with its stucco porch and its Victorian meanness ? It was a squat denial that there had ever been such a thing as romance, or music, or song in the world. If there ever had been, obviously, it could not have been built. Yet there it stood, in blind protest. And there he lived in peace and content—living out days that were regular and uneventful and humdrum to a degree that surprised even the humdrum monotony of a suburb. Something very domestic and quiet there was, after all, in his nature. He asked for so little to make him happy, if he had his books and his thoughts. We know how intense his home affections were—how deep was his love for his mother and his sister ; how strong his attachment to home memories, to Bonchurch, to Northumberland ; how passionate his adoration of childhood and babies. All this recalls to me the verdict of Bishop Stubbs, to whose country vicarage Swinburne retired for six months in order, according to our Balliol legend, to learn where Ramoth-Gilead was, for ignorance of which he had been ploughed in " Divinity." There he sat on the ground at Mrs. Stubbs's feet, and read to her " Queen Mary," to her great dislike and astonishment. The Bishop judged him to be not a man of strong or vehement passions, but of intense intellectual imagination. It was an intellectual interest which prompted him to imagine morbid sensual situations from which real passion would have recoiled, disgusted. For him it was an imaginative feat ; and the more repellent the situation, therefore, the more exciting the feat. This agrees with what he once said to an Oxford friend, I believe—that he wrote best about what he had never personally experienced. This would explain much that shocked in the famous volume of Poems and Ballads

For the thirty years at Putney he had ceased to have any helpful message to give. His politics became at last an acrid scream. So he no longer counted among the forces at work upon us. But since he has gone the old memories have stirred again, and we have been haunted again by that amazing magical music which swept us all off our feet so long ago. Never, surely, was there such magic given to our English tongue. Who could have imagined that it held in it the splendour, and the motion, and the cadence, and lilt of those enthralling refrains ?

> " Dream that the lips once breathless
>   Can quicken if they would :
>   Say that the soul is deathless :
>   Dream that the Gods are good.

" Say March may wed September,
    And time divorce regret :
But not that you remember
    And not that I forget ! "

We sang them : we shouted them : we flung them
about, to the skies and to the winds. It was like
becoming possessed of a new sense. And then the
wonder of recognizing that that astonishing Bible of
ours was the quarry from which he had dug ! The
finest lilt of all that he wrote was the lilt of the
Prophets and the Psalms. The most vibrant music
was the music of the Song of Solomon : and the passion
and the melancholy were but echoes of the Son of
Sirach.

" We have seen thee, O Love, thou art fair : Thou art goodly, O Love !
    Thy wings make light in the air, as the wings of a Dove.
    Thy feet are as winds that divide the stream of the sea :
    Earth is thy covering to hide thee, the garment of thee :
    Thou art swift and subtle and blind as a flame of fire.
    Before thee the laughter, behind thee the tears of desire."

Biblical England pricked up its ears at the strange
translation of its familiar language. It was troubled
at this bold spoiling of the Hebrews by the Egyptians,
as it saw its finest jewels prostituted to the service of
the goddesses of mud and slime. Yet the secret
sway of this new song over our souls came from out
of this reverberation in it of ancient vibrant melodious
refrains which belonged to the deepest experiences of
the spirit. That sway over the lilt of delicate refrains
Swinburne never lost : but at last it ceased to disguise
the fact that he had nothing much to say to us.

Beyond the sweet sorrow at the passing of beautiful things he had no motive, no theme on which to dwell.

> " We know not whether death be good :
> But life at least it will not be :
> Men will stand saddening as we stood,
> Watch the same fields and skies as we—
> And the same sea."

He could shout glorious hymns of praise to the sea, or to the heroes whom he delighted to honour. But these high lyrics only told us that he loved the sea, and loved great men : and that it was worth while to love, in spite of all that death could do. A good theme, but it could not bear the strain of all this majestic rhetoric for ever. And there was nothing more. So it is still the wonderful musical cadences that came to us as a new revelation of what words could be made to do, when first he let them loose upon our hearts—it is still only these that we can recall or care for. They were his peculiar gift to us. He could but repeat them over and over again. He had no other gift to give. The music of these phrases will never be forgotten. For the elemental emotion at the simple thought that fair things perish, they will remain as the most perfect and delicate expression ever given to it. And there it ends.

> " Time takes them home that we loved, fair names and famous,
> To the soft long sleep, to the broad sweet bosom of death :
> But the flower of their souls he shall not take away to shame us,
> Nor the lips lack song for ever that now lack breath.
> For with us shall the music and perfume that die not dwell,
> Though the dead to our dead bid welcome, and we farewell."

II

GEORGE MEREDITH

It was a month after Swinburne had been laid by the sea that he loved in Bonchurch churchyard that the very last of the old Victorian guard was buried under his beloved Surrey hill, after the honour of a Memorial Service in Westminster Abbey. It was well that George Meredith should be so honoured. He belonged to the high race : and he lived his life out in simple devotion to the work given him to do. Once again, as Swinburne's death set us shouting again the brave rhymes that had fired us long ago, so we crooned over the wonderful words in which Meredith swayed our souls. We all read over again the idyllic scene in the river meadows where Richard Feverel passed into the magic land. There has been no such love scene as that since Shakespeare dreamed of Ferdinand and Miranda. How deep a pathos the death of the man, who gave life to man and maid in that mystic hour, infused into the familiar words ! And there are certain poems that we read over again —since he has gone—with a deeper touch at the heart. The charm and movement of " Love in the Valley," put out their old haunting power.

> " When her mother tends her before the laughing mirror,
>   Tying up her laces, looping up her hair,
>   Often she thinks, were this wild thing wedded,
>   More love should I have, and much less care.

6

When her mother tends her before the lighted mirror,
  Loosening her laces, combing down her curls,
Often she thinks, were this wild thing wedded,
  I should miss but one for many boys and girls.

. . . . . .

" Stepping down the hill with her fair companions,
  Arm in arm, all against the raying West,
Boldly she sings, to the merry tune she marches,
  Brave is her shape, and sweeter unpossessed.
Sweeter, for she is what my heart first awaking
  Whispered the world was ; morning light is she.
Love that so desires would fain keep her changeless ;
  Fain would fling the net, and fain have her free.

. . . . . .

" When at dawn she sighs, and like an infant to the window
  Turns grave eyes craving light, released from dreams,
Beautiful she looks, like a white water-lily
  Bursting out of bud in havens of the streams.
When from bed she rises clothed from neck to ankle
  In her long nightgown sweet as boughs of May,
Beautiful she looks, like a tall garden lily
  Pure from the night, and splendid for the day.

. . . . . .

" Could I find a place to be alone with heaven,
  I would speak my heart out : heaven is my need
Every woodland tree is flushing like the dogwood,
  Flashing like the whitebeam, swaying like the reed.
Flushing like the dogwood crimson in October ;
  Streaming like the flag-reed South-West blown ;
Flashing as in gusts the sudden-lighted whitebeam :
  All seem to know what is for heaven alone."

How beautiful the swing and joy of it all! And over against it we may put that sonnet of " Dreadful Night " in which the " Modern Love " opens:—

> " By this he knew she wept with waking eyes :
>   That, at his hand's light quiver by her head,
>   The strange low sobs that shook their common bed,
>   Were called into her with a sharp surprise,
>   And strangled mute, like little gaping snakes,
>   Dreadfully venomous to him. She lay
>   Stone-still, and the long darkness flowed away
>   With muffled pulses. Then, as midnight makes
>   Her giant heart of Memory and Tears
>   Drink the pale drug of silence, and so beat
>   Sleep's heavy measure, they from head to feet
>   Were moveless, looking through their dead black years,
>   By vain regret scrawled over the blank wall.
>   Like sculptured effigies they might be seen
>   Upon their marriage-tomb, the sword between ;
>   Each wishing for the sword that severs all."

And to relieve the terror of the depression, we will recall the tender lyrical fall of " Dirge in Woods " :—

> " A wind sways the pines
>   And below
>   Not a breath of wild air ;
>   Still as the mosses that glow
>   On the flooring and over the lines
>   Of the roots here and there.
>   The pine-tree drops its dead ;
>   They are quiet as under the sea.
>   Overhead, overhead
>   Rushes life in a race,
>   As the clouds the clouds chase :

And we go,
And we drop like the fruits of the tree,
Even we,
Even so."

All these quotations show how great was the beauty that Meredith could throw into words. Yet he and Browning will still remain to us, as the men, who, over against the perfect melodiousness of Tennyson, flung up tempestuous defiance against all that was smooth and conventional and easy and limpid in literature. Carlyle, too, was storming his way through: but his heated vehemence sprang from indignation at the follies of men rather than from an artistic impulse. The other two definitely set themselves to forge a novel armoury. Romance was aflame in them both: and romance asked for new worlds to conquer. How was it to be done? What new worlds in the domain of language had classicalism left unperfected? Oddly enough, both of them attempted to answer this question by the same method. Classicalism had attained its effects by selection, exclusion, simplicity, purity: it worked on aristocratic lines. It pruned off all that obscured the prime result. It shed all excess: it elided the incidental: it cut down to the core: it purged the dross. So it offered men the flawless expression of a perfect thought. It secured its result by elimination: and the product was a jewel.

But for Meredith and Browning thought was a living growth. It grew in a context. It was in touch with thousand-fold accidents. It belonged to a

mind: and that mind was rich with possibilities.
The thought that finally emerged was the triumphant
residue of all that went to its making. It was only
intelligible in its triumph, by virtue of all that through
which it triumphantly forced its way to the front.
It carried traces of all that it has survived: it arrived,
bedraggled by all that was caught in it, in the way, to
tangle it and to withstand it. You must know what
it has scraped through, if you would estimate its
value. You must throw into it the complex materials
out of which it has built itself together. Let anyone
look at one of his own imaginations or decisions.
Even as he holds it up for inspection, half a hundred
irrelevant fancies have crossed his mind: endless
suggestions have all but over-topped it: cross-currents
of thought have flashed, and passed, and disappeared:
a dozen alternatives have come and gone. And all
this hubbub curls and whirls round the main matter:
and it is in contrast with all this ferment, that its
own permanence is tested, and its own value
appraised.

So they saw. So they said. Therefore, their
method is inclusive. It prunes nothing away. It
drags all in. It is democratic: it knocks the dominant
idea up against a whole mob of competitive wranglers.
In order to exhibit their meaning, these two bring in
as much half-alive matter as they can: not as little.
There is no allusion, or hint, or parody, or paraphrase,
or counter-fancy, or illustration that may not serve
their need in elucidating the main thesis. So they
go off at a tangent: they bring in the contingent:

they fly off in parenthesis: they fling in cross-lights:
they take up anything and everything that the mind
may have dropped upon: for all this tangled noise
goes to the making of the one loud dominant hum
that holds the ear spell-bound. The by-products
of the central thought are all included in the process.
They come and go, helter-skelter: the only hope of
understanding is to read on very fast, refusing to be
arrested in the details. For these details do not bear
fixing or defining, any more than you can fix or define
the varying sights and sounds and smells that vaguely
accompany all mental activity.

So the leading theme arrives, thronged about with
compromise. And the artistic result is not like Venus
rising from the sea, stark and sweet, in clean fine naked
outline: but rather like Glaucus, as Plato pictures
him, dragging himself to shore, a human thing, but
still meshed in a tangle of shells and seaweed, to show
whence he has emerged. Sometimes our two writers
will even like to make us aware of that ·effort that
went to the production—of the whirling wheels of
the machinery, as if this too could not be left out of
the full account. So the music of the organ is all the
more impressive because it works its way out into
beautiful sound through the noise of straining pipes
and pedals. And even in the finest tone that soars
away into high space from the violin, we should still
value it all the more because we are kept aware of
the physical rasp of the horse-hair against the catgut.

Thus it was that Meredith and Browning arrived
at their characteristic styles. And whenever the

imagination is strong enough at work to fuse, with its heat, the whole complicated mass of the materials, the effect is overwhelming. The danger is lest the fine ardour should slacken: and then the weight of material imperils the result. They have chosen to dare a great risk, which demands that they should ever be at their highest level. And both have justified the risk by the splendour of their best.

III

THE CENTENARY OF ROBERT BROWNING

A HUNDRED years ago! Impossible! How can he have been born so far back behind everything, before the boom of the guns at Waterloo had, " on that loud Sabbath," shaken the spoiler down—before the finest and worst gentleman in Europe had come to the throne—before the flood-gates had burst and modern life had begun? Born, then; and certainly alive to-day: walking at our side: level with our hopes and fears: speaking to our hearts: a vital voice that tells of active companionship, and daily intimacy, and quick give-and-take, and all the immediate efficacy of a life shared and understood. It is amazing to think that he should be still with us, keeping step, giving utterance to our souls, unjaded and alert. He is still so fresh-aired: so spontaneous: so alive. We hear him talking: we feel him in move-ment: he and we live together. Nothing has yet thrown him behind: or come between: or divided him off from actual present speech on life's affairs as they occur. He is not relegated to a distinguished sanctuary into which we withdraw. He takes part with us in the breathing, seething, boisterous Present. We and he are of one date.

Now, this is startling, if he really was born a hundred years ago. He ought to have taken on, by this time,

a reverential dignity, a touch of seclusion. He ought
to be showing signs of becoming a Classic. We should
be taking him down from our shelves, and dusting
him with a pocket-handkerchief, and giving him
sonorous utterance, to the restrained horror of a
younger generation. But nothing of the kind. He
still belongs to the hour. He is with us, not above us.
He is our mate : he tips us the word that we want.
He is at hand, ready at need, to interpret our actual
experience as it grows. This is the wonder.

The skilled gentry of " The Times Literary Sup-
plement " say that this is only true of the Browning
who took life for its own sake in the spirit of the
intuitionalist and the emotionalist : but not of the
Browning who set himself to justify the ways of God
to man, and to argue out a moral creed. The true
Browning stands with Shakespeare, not with Milton
or Æschylus. His deliberate intellectuality may all
be dropped out. It came to little. He never went
to the bottom of the problem. And he let argumentation ruin his work. Let all this go, they now
tell us ; and be content that you have the poems of
the Bells and Pomegranate type, and the " Men and
Women ": the splendid colour and passion and force
of the Bishop ordering his tomb, and of the Lost
Duchess, and all the glowing, glorious splendours
caught from out of the heart of the Italian Renaissance.

These are wonders and delights, indeed. But dare
we drive this dreadful cleavage ? Dare we sever our
babe in twain ? Surely, the lines cross. The greatest
work of all that he gave us involves the fusion of the

intellectual with the imaginative.   What about "A Death in the Desert"?   What about the Pope in "The Ring and the Book"?   Can we refuse to poems of this order the recognition that places them at the very top of Browning's poems?   Has he not here given us the work by which the final verdict stands?   Did he ever rise higher?   Can you pretend to estimate his position as a poet, and drop them out of account?   Yet in them the intellectualism is pronounced and emphatic.   He throws into them all his familiar argument, all his formal Creed.   His Apologetic for Christianity finds, in these poems, its finest and fullest form.

We cannot then exclude from his supreme moments as a poet his capacity as a thinker.   How can the two sides be reconciled?   We must remember that he himself foresaw and discounted the difficulties involved in the fusion.

First, he himself chaffed the attempt to wring poetry out of metaphysic, in "Transcendentalism: a Poem in twelve books."

> "Stop playing, poet! May a brother speak?
> 'Tis you speak, that's your error. Song's our art:
> Whereas you please to speak these naked thoughts
> Instead of draping them in sights and sounds."

He wants the poet to do the magic trick so that " in there breaks " not words about roses but

> " the very rose herself,
> Over us, under, round us every side,
> Buries us with a glory, young once more,
> Pouring heaven into this shut house of life.

"So come, the harp back to your heart again !
You are a poem, though your poem's naught.
The best of all you showed before, believe,
Was your own boy-face o'er the finer chords
Bent, following the cherub at the top
That points to God with his paired half-moon wings."

So much for argumentation: and then, again, in
"Pacchiarotto," he indignantly and scornfully derides
the introduction of the private personality of the
poet into the domain of his art. He will not be a
Byron, who uses his poetic gift to tell the wide world
that he has quarrelled with his wife. The poet's
views on life, the poet's conduct at home, are matters
with which the outside world which reads his poetry
has no concern whatever. Only the unnatural horror
of an earthquake reveals, by destroying the outer
walls of the poet's house, how he lived inside with his
wife. It is the sin of sins to try and get round to that
other secret side of the moon which the poet reserves
from his art, and keeps for his love.

We ought not to want to know what Browning,
the man, thought about his religion. Yes ! But,
then, he *did* let us know. We could not mistake him.
He told it us over and over again. We cannot read
"Easter Day" and "Christmas Eve" or the
"Epilogue," and yet declare that these are but
dramatic studies, and tell us no secrets about the soul
of the poet. If Shakespeare disclosed himself in the
Sonnets, and unlocked the key of his heart to us,
"the less Shakespeare he." Well, but Browning does
unlock his heart : there is no denying it. He himself,

then, broke his own canon. He allowed his poetic
art to tell us what he himself thought, and how he
argued for it. Was the result poetry ? Did it justify
itself from the point of view of Art ?

I think that he saved it as Art by his insistence on
choice, on decision, as the sole material of artistic
interest. The spiritual and emotional significance of
life lies in Decision. So he believed. We are here on
earth to make a judgment. Heaven and Hell are at
stake. We choose. And that choice is life. Poem
after poem preached the high Gospel. We all know
it. Its triumph is sung in " At the Fireside." Its
failure is read out defiantly in " Dis Aliter Visum "
and " Youth and Art " :—

> " Now I may speak : you fool, for all
>   Your lore ! Who made things plain in vain ?
> What was the sea for ? What, the grey
>   Sad church, that solitary day,
> Crosses and graves and swallows' call ?
>
> " Was there naught better than to enjoy ?
>   No feat which, done, would make time break,
> And let us pent-up creatures through
>   Into eternity, our due ?
> No forcing earth teach heaven's employ ?
>
> " No wise beginning, here and now,
>   What cannot grow complete (earth's feat)
> And heaven must finish, there and then ? .
>   No tasting earth's true food for men,
> Its sweet in sad, its sad in sweet ? "

c

" It once might have been, once only :
    We lodged in a street together,
You, a sparrow on the housetop lonely,
    I, a lone she-bird of his feather.

" Why did not you pinch a flower
    In a pellet of clay and fling it ?
Why did not I put a power
    Of thanks in a look, or sing it ?

" Each life unfulfilled, you see ;
    It hangs still, patchy and scrappy :
We have not sighed deep, laughed free,
    Starved, feasted, despaired,—been happy.

" And nobody calls you a dunce,
    And people suppose me clever :
This could but have happened once,
    And we missed it, lost it for ever."

And fiercely in the " Statue and the Bust." Its
glory fills the world in " The Flight of the Duchess."
And its trumpet-blast is blown in "Childe Roland ":—

" There they stood, ranged along the hill-sides, met
    To view the last of me, a living frame
    For one more picture ! in a sheet of flame
I saw them and I knew them all. And yet
Dauntless the slug-horn to my lips I set,
    And blew ' *Childe Roland to the Dark Tower came.*' "

It is the real motive and secret of " Christmas Eve "
and " Easter Day."

Now, the excitement of making a choice allows for
the introduction of a mass of argumentation. You

can discuss the pros and the cons without stint. You can indulge in endless apologetics. You can go behind the choice, and let yourself loose on all the infinite intellectual process by which decision was reached. And yet, with the concrete, emotional, dramatic act of choice as the determinate throughout, as the resultant climax, all this intellectual business will fall within the poetic motive. It will belong to the imaginative impulse. It will minister to the artistic crisis. It is not a mere argument that it is there: but an argument which exalts the spiritual excitement—argument which holds the issue in breathless suspense. So used, in service to the gathering storm-pressure, it is fused with real passion, and becomes true material for poetry. The poetic element lies wholly in the agony of the decision that has to be made: and, swept into this stress of critical judgment which will determine the character of a life and decide between heaven and hell, the most prolonged logomachy may be filled with rapturous thrill. This is how Browning contrives to make his speculative apologetics justifiable. They serve to heighten and intensify the passion that is engaged in coming to a vital decision.

And, again, is it not this emphasis on decision, as the vital significance of life, which accounts for the gross amount of clumsy stuff, which his poetic current carries along with it? The final choice is his real poetic subject. The choice is a growth: a result. To appreciate a choice, you must know what lies behind it: you must be aware of the hidden processes through which it arrived at itself. You must feel the rough-and-tumble antecedents—the wild tumult of the warring forces. The beauty of the ultimate decision turns on the ugliness of the preliminary conditions. The honour of the choice wrung out of unfavourable auspices cannot be recognized unless the ghastly possibilities have been fitly felt. So Browning must force us back, behind the actual decision of which he sings the praise or the blame, on to the noises, the clamour, the stupidities, the meannesses, which were doing their utmost to pervert it. He must bring in a whole mob of ugly matters, into order, to justify his passionate interest in the strange and eventful outcome. His poetry cannot tell of the fair and beautiful fruit of life, without taking us below ground to see the grim root at work in the dark, among the insects and the worms.

That is why his wonderful verse which, at its best, is so exquisite in form and sound, is like the music of a great organ which is all the more effective because it carries with it the clatter of the valves, and the groan of the tubes, and the creaks and noises of the pedals. An enormous process is to be heard at its work. The music is simply the top event of a tumultuous movement underlying it. And the tumult of the tumbled movement is essential to the white rare radiance of the event.

Yet music there certainly is. Radiance he most certainly gave us. Our life braces itself under the call, the inspiration. We rise and follow our leader, who moved through this crowded and tired world of ours with step alert, and back straight, and head erect, and eyes set forward : and who told us of hope, and joy, and the glory of strength, and the glow of victory, and the peace that comes after the storm, and the infinite value of love.

> " Oh heart ! oh blood that freezes, blood that burns !
>   Earth's returns
> For whole Centuries of folly, noise, and sin !
>   Shut them in.
>   Love is best."

IV

GEORGE AUGUSTUS SELWYN

It was in the very heart of the great war with France, under the pressure and strain of that dreadful struggle, that we had a superb output of great men. The babes born in that distressful hour were singularly virile, and momentous. The personalities that emerged were massive, weighty, vital. How curiously different from that nervous, feverish, distraught generation which, according to Alfred de Musset's brilliant picture, was born in the days when their fathers looked hurriedly in at home, to snatch a kiss from wife and child in the swift intervals of war, with the smoke of the battle still reeking upon them, with the heat of the fray driving them on in the frenzy of adventure ! Here the concentrated force of the determination to carry the terrible strife through at any cost issued in this sturdy and impressive result. Gladstone, Tennyson, and a dozen others stand out to us, as the giants born in those days. And Selwyn was not unworthy to take rank among them. He had the same splendid physical vigour, the same impressive type of build, with remarkable beauty in the strong features, large-hearted, large-brained, forceful. He had a certain magic in his presence which told, as much as his dauntless courage, upon the imagination of his Maoris and Melanesians.

" It was only his quick-sighted reading of character and gesture, his habits of order and forethought, besides his calmness and courage, which enabled him to walk unscathed when others would be in danger.

" He would not allow a weapon in his boat. His wonderful presence of mind and dignified bearing, and a certain something quite indefinable, had such influence over the savage mind, that the natives never seemed to contemplate the possibility of his molesting them.

" The enterprise undertaken by the Bishop was one of no little risk. It required the perfect presence of mind and dignified bearing of Bishop Selwyn, which seemed never to fail in impressing these savages with a feeling of superiority, to render such an act one of safety and prudence.

" We weighed and ran out of the roads, admiring, as we passed and waved our adieu to the *Undine*, the commanding figure of the truly gallant Bishop of New Zealand, as, steering his own little vessel, he stood, surrounded by the black heads of his disciples."

This quick-sighted reading of character, combined with pluck, was never better illustrated than when he broke up a Native war by singing the Lady-Bird Song. How vividly would Bishop Abraham tell the full story, showing as it did the brilliant oratorical gift of the Maori, on which he loved to enlarge. The Bishop had gone to face a " third party " in the war—the Sons of the Red Ditch was, I think, their name. The other two tribes engaged had a quarrel of their own. The Bishop said that he could understand that. At the worst they must fight it out. " But you, Sons of the Red Ditch, have no part in that quarrel. You have nothing to fight about. Why are you here ? "

Unanswerable, you would think. But the Chief of the Red Ditch Sons rose and said : " We understand that there is a war in Europe between two nations who have a quarrel—the Russians and the Turks. That is all right. They must fight it out. But what are you English doing in that business ? Why are you there ? " The Bishop was done. It was no use to try and parry the home thrust. And then it was that, throwing his argument to the winds, he danced out and sang :—

" Ka tangi te ronniko."
" Lady-bird, Lady-bird, fly away home ! "

until all the Sons of the Red Ditch were singing it too : and, in singing it, sang themselves home.

The wonderful thing about Selwyn was his power of practical prophecy. A little paper, admirably drawn up by Canon Abraham for the commemoration of the Selwyn Centenary, gave amazing evidence of this. Who could have believed that in the dry hard years 1837–1838, he could have anticipated the full power of voluntary work of which the C.E.M.S. is giving such rich proof ?

" As long as the service rendered is purely voluntary, numbers of tradesmen and others will be willing to devote their spare time to the Christian work of helping to better the condition of their neighbours. There are many who are willing to work for the pure love of God."

Or that he should have bravely grasped all the possibilities which Kelham and Mirfield are now verifying ?

" Let the Church take root downward ; let every peasant in the country have an interest in the Church's ministry. We have the best materials for the formation of a ministry from the people that ever were possessed by any nation—trained in religious principles by a sound and scriptural course of instruction. Collect the élite of our schools, carry on their teaching in the parishes up to eighteen, and then determine which shall be sent on to the University with a view to future ordination.

" Many a rustic mother will bless the Church which has adopted her son into her service ; men who, by their talents and virtues, have proved themselves worthy of a higher vocation."

Or again, is it not surprising that in 1841 he should have felt all that we are now discussing as to the right way in which the call to work should be made ?

" It has never seemed to me to lie in the power of an individual to choose the field of labour most suited to his own powers. Those who are the eyes of the Church are the best judges.

" Whether it be at home or abroad is a consideration which, as regards the work to be done, must rest with those who best know what that work is, and how many and of what kind are the labourers.

" The only course seems to be to undertake it at the bidding of the proper authority, and to endeavour to execute it with all faithfulness.

" I looked upon this as the first exercise of the Church's lawful authority, and I asked myself, What is the duty of every priest ? There could be but one reply—to obey. To test this I put to myself what seemed of all to be the most improbable case, that I should ever be called upon to go, and the answer could be but this—I am ready. Are you ready to go wherever you may be sent ? Are you ready to go even to the centre of Africa ? I thought that if I refused to go, the bones of those who fell in Walcheren would rise up in judgment against me. . . . Should any soldier of Christ refuse to go to support a cause to which he has been pledged by a far more solemn engagement ? "

"A high official of S.P.G. was going down to Eton to 'sound' Selwyn on the subject of New Zealand Bishopric. He met a friend, who dissuaded him. 'Let the offer be from authority in the Church.' The Bishop of London and the Archbishop of Canterbury wrote, making the call, and were immediately answered in the following terms :—

"' Whatever part in the work of the ministry the Church of England, as represented by her Archbishops and Bishops, may call upon me to undertake, I trust I shall be willing to accept with all obedience and humility.' "

His direct prophetic insight may be noted on two special points. First, while flinging behind him all the conventionalism of an Establishment with un-hesitating audacity, and offering to the Colony the picture of a Bishop who could swim rivers, dive under his ship, sail her in any seas, dig, live on roots, knock about in any quarters, carry his own luggage, and wash his own house out, he, nevertheless, far from sitting loose to ancient Church Order, set himself to revive it. It had, indeed, deadened itself into fossilized forms in the old country: but this was due, not to lack of purpose, but to lack of use. Forms were not obsolete survivals, involved in an Establishment. Nay ! They were the muscles and sinews of the living Body of Christ, which Establishment had atrophied by disuse. Out here, in the open Colonial workaday world, the Body will revive in its native reality ; and all true forms will reveal themselves as active functions of a living organism, essential to its health and its efficiency. So he believed in the 'Forties. As those at home were discovering in theological theory, so out there, under practical pressure, he rediscovered the significance that underlay the ecclesiastical structure. The Church revealed itself to him as the one organ of efficient activity. So he set to work to revive Synodal action. So he saw what Cathedrals really meant.

" They stand to secure the effectual organization which the Clergy are in need of—supplementary to the parochial system—a bank of supply on which the Church may draw for assistance in all her work.

1. For aid in parishes insufficiently worked.
2. For the training of the Ministry in Cathedral Colleges.
3. For the training of Teachers for Church Schools.
4. To educate and develop the spiritual energies of the nation : standing open all day for private prayer, by the appeal of art and music, by the glory of the daily services, by intercession.
5. From them should go forth the conquerors of the unconverted at home and abroad. Centres for missionary activity, and the training of preachers.
6. A spiritual heart to a Diocese, diffusing life and warmth.
7. A central office for assistance and employment, aiding those in need. Taking the lead in Church extension and building in Diocese.
8. Centre of learning and knowledge. Libraries for Clergy."

So, again, he saw clearly what a Bishop was meant to be, and what a properly organized Province would involve.

" From 1841, for fourteen years, Selwyn laboured single-handed as Bishop of New Zealand, but never lost sight of the need of division, if only it might be had. The foundation of the Diocese of Christchurch for the care of the Southern Island was delayed till 1855; Wellington and Nelson were formed in 1858 ; Waiapu, the Maori Diocese, in 1859; the missionary Diocese of Melanesia in 1862; and Dunedin in 1866. Meantime Australia had been beforehand—the one Diocese of Sydney was divided, and the Sees of Melbourne, Adelaide, and Newcastle constituted in 1848. ' Some time or other I suppose my turn will come to be relieved.'

" With the Bishops of Australia and Tasmania Selwyn took every chance that offered of conference and co-operation, uniting in Synod with the five other Bishops, ' the first fore-shadowing of that Provincial organization' which has since obtained, and strengthened Church life, not only in Australia and New Zealand, but in Canada, South Africa, and India, etc. Relations with sister Churches, the forging of links and the binding fast by the strong bonds of knowledge and sympathy the scattered members of the body, were ever in his mind, and led afterwards to his two visits to the Churches of the United States of America and Canada."

So determined was he to get his new Bishops consecrated that when the lawyers, as usual, invented every conceivable difficulty as to what could be done within the territory of the Queen, he declared that he would take his men out in a ship and consecrate them on the high seas, if so alone he could escape from out of the legal meshes. Thus, in a hundred ways, he detected the lines of the living Church, hidden behind the dead cumber of centuries.

And, secondly, he saw, at a glance, what it has taken us such long years to recognize, that Christianity is a Life ; that it cannot therefore be transmitted by book, or handed over the counter, or merely preached ; it has to be lived. It is transmitted only by the touch of life on life. Our Lord trusted to no book to convey what He taught, but only to the hearts of living men. Christianity has only one way of spreading—i.e. from heart to heart, from soul to soul. Therefore, in order to reach a native people, it must come to them in a native form. The Native, alone, can teach the Native. The white man will never, therefore, bring the full message home to a people, except through men of that people whom he has had the opportunity of inoculating with the very life so that it has passed into their blood. Native boys, passed under a white man's care at an early impressionable age, and then slowly and laboriously re-created into the new manhood, are the only organs and instruments by which their own races can effectively be reached. And the life that is to be put into them must be built up from the very ground : it must fashion anew their innermost instincts and habits : it must cover the entire mass of their humanity. It is no mere doctrine to be taught : no mere gospel to be read in a book. It is the occupation and possession of the manhood itself by a new transfiguration.

So he planned Norfolk Island, to which home he brought boys to be adequately trained, who should then be replanted. And of their training he wrote :—

"I doubt whether converts are edified, whether the foundation is secure, whether they do not rest still upon the personal character of their English teachers ; and this support will tend to fall off when other fields of fresher interest absorb the zeal of the rising generation, and carry it off to Central Africa, to China, to Japan. There is a downward tendency in the secondary stage of a mission. The only remedy is a native ministry.

"I need men of the right stamp to conduct the central organization of a system which will require.an entire devotion in a spirit of the most single-minded love, of every faculty of body and mind, to duties apparently of the humblest kind, to the most petty and wearisome details of domestic life, and to the simplest rudiments of teaching ; but all sanctified by the object in view, which is to take wild and native savages from among every untamed and lawless people, and to teach them to sit at the feet of Christ, ' clothed and in their right mind.' Religion, civilization, and sound learning—all, in short, that is needful for a man, seem to be meant by those three changes : the feet of Christ, the clothing, and the right mind.

"Our natives are most willing to be employed, but have no order or method in anything that they do except under superintendence.

"It needs minute and careful arrangement, without which no barbarous people, I am sure, can ever be thoroughly Christianized.

"Throughout the whole mission the delusion has prevailed that the Gospel will give habits as well as teach principles. My conviction is that habits uncorrected will be the thorns which will choke the good seed, and make it unfruitful.

"In England religious principle is rarely strongly developed without orderly habits.

" We are apt to forget the laborious processes by which we acquired the routine duties of cleanliness, order, method, and punctuality. We expect to find ready-made in a native people the qualities we ourselves learnt with difficulty . . . the unfavourable tendency of native habits is every day dragging back into sin many who seemed to have escaped."

To appreciate this depth and thoroughness of view we must remember that it was taken at the very hour when the influence represented by Lord Macaulay was at its height, and we were framing an Educational System for India in the belief that Western culture could be transplanted to the East through the medium of Academic Text-Books and a scheme of Competitive Examination. From that disastrous superficiality we are suffering woefully to-day.

A big man, this, charged with imaginative fire, force, and faith. No wonder that his departure to the derided mission field shook his generation with unwonted emotion—so that Dr. Keate, the famous Flogger, is recorded in Mrs. Gladstone's diary to have been seen at the farewell Eton luncheon, amid sobbing men and women, crying like a child, with his face buried in his pocket-handkerchief, as Selwyn spoke. Yet the secret of this enthralment which he exercised over all his contemporaries was due, not merely to his muscular Christianity, to " his massive and gracious presence, his courage, gaiety, humour, tenderness, or to the electric effect of his personality, or to the attractive charm of his strength and his goodness ": though all this was his : but, rather, to the profound reality, behind all his gifts, of that surrender of the soul to Christ the Redeemer, which alone can trans-figure humanity into an organ of power. It is revealed in that noble story told by Bishop Montgomery, of his answer to the fervid salutation which reached him from his far home, saying that all the mountains and waters of New Zealand spoke to them of him. " Give God the glory," he wired back. " As for this man, we know that he is a sinner."

V

JAMES MOZLEY

*Fellow of Magdalen College, Regius Professor of Divinity,
and Canon of Christ Church*

CAN it be that the memory and reputation of James
Mozley are passing away ? Is he really forgotten and
unread ? Yet he was a man who, according to Mr.
Gladstone's enthusiastic verdict, combined the clear
form of Cardinal Newman with the profundity of
Bishop Butler. Pretty strong, that ! And some may
remark the solemn passages at the close of Dean
Church's book on the Oxford Movement, in which he
tells how, amid the panic that followed Newman's
conversion to Rome, one man rose to his full strength
under the blow, and headed the rally, and stemmed the
flight. That man was James Mozley. Church,
evidently, felt that there was no one to whom he
looked more confidently in the black hour. With him,
and with Frederick Rogers, he felt that the Cause was
not lost, but that, now, for the first time he, and these
two, went behind their old fighting ground, and dug
their way down to a deeper foundation. They saw
the peril of pitting the Roman Ideal against the mixed,
concrete confusions of Anglicanism. They, now,
went behind the Roman Ideal. They read all History
in its concrete reality : and they learned how intricate
was the confusion that beclouded every case, Rome's

D   33

as much as Canterbury's. The man who would read History as it is, must be prepared for a heavy strain on his Faith. Nobody who appeals to History can ride off on a cocksure hobby-horse. You must be able to get down behind the confusion. You must touch deeper things. So alone will you stand. And as Church set himself to his own task on the historical field, he felt that he had in James Mozley the one dauntless champion who could bring a strong philosophy into play, adequate for the work set them, and sufficient to bear the strain of life. Newman's departure " left wrecks on every shore," as Mr. Gladstone used to be fond of saying : and, especially, it broke those who had been his intimates. But here was one as intimate as any, within the inner circle of friends, knit by relationship to Newman's family : and he, far from breaking, rose again the stronger man : and found his full power.

A curious incident made me aware of Mozley's greatness earlier than I should, otherwise, have learned news of it. For while Mozley was buried in the vicarage of Shoreham, unknown to the younger University, some of us undergraduates at Balliol who were worshipping at the shrine of T. H. Green, noticed, with amazement and awe, that our guide, philosopher and friend would go off on a very rare visit to St. Mary's whenever a certain clergyman of the name of Mozley was preaching a 'Varsity Sermon. Drawn by this strange spectacle, we thought that we would go too, and see why it was that Green made this unwonted effort. We found

a nearly empty church : and a very odd old gentleman, blinking rather helplessly through his glasses,
reading his MS. monotonously with a very thin voice,
blowing his nose in the middle of a sentence, stopping
to sniff at unexpected moments, and performing
generally every feat that a preacher ought not to
perform if he expects to be heard. Still, we noticed
that the group of Dons, who had joined Green in
making up the scanty congregation, represented the
talent of Oxford, and were of those who knew. So we
listened on in faith. And thus it was that I happened
to hear most of those brilliant and masterly Sermons
which make up his first volume.

When, at last, he reappeared at Oxford, as Regius
Professor of Divinity, we, younger Dons, were all
ready to sit at his feet. We knew, now, all about the
early Littlemore days with Newman ; and we had
read not only his University Sermons, but, also, those
fascinating Essays which represented the fruitage of
the days when he was editing the chief Tractarian
Review, and doing an immense deal of the literary
warfare by which the Movement had won its way.
And there were the Bamptons, too, which Mill and
Huxley had felt to be a criticism that must be recognized. We venerated, therefore. We knew that we
had a seer among us. He was a man to whom you
could take problems that asked for a philosophic
answer. Liddon happily described the process of
consulting the oracle which he himself adopted. He
used, whenever he had a problem on his mind, to take
Mozley a walk, and, at the opening, after the weather

had been dealt with, he would insert the problem in at the slot, as it were. He would, then, wait in silence while certain contortions went on, and, at last, by a violent motion, Mozley would thrust his stick into the hedge. Liddon would then inquire the result : and would obtain his problem exactly reversed. That meant that the process was only half completed. So he passed on in silence, till there came another thrust of the stick into the hedge, and, on inquiry, he obtained his proper answer. He, then, proceeded to insert another problem, with the like happy result.

Now, this was all very well for Liddon : but what about the unhappy Undergraduates ? They were compelled, if they were going to take Orders, to attend his lectures. They had no tradition, by which to discount the oddities of speech. He blinked : he sniffed : he blew his nose. They had no notion that they were in the presence of a Master. They read their novels. They were hopeless. How was this dreadful wastage to be arrested ? Could not we induce him to lecture to us, and then we might convey to those poor innocents his milk out of our bottles ? So we schemed. And we asked him to dine with us. And he was immensely pleased. And, after dinner, in full flutter of success, we propounded our plan. He professed to accept it with enthusiasm : but always in the form of *our* reading papers, while he sat in the Chair. In vain, we pleaded over and over again, " No ! You will read the paper. We will do the questions and talk." " Exactly," he still repeated. " Capital. Three meetings a term : and I will take the Chair :

and you will read the paper." So he smiled: and
blinked: and beamed. Finally, we screwed out the
desperate compromise that, at two of the three
meetings, we should read papers to him: if at the
third he would read a paper to us. So it happened.
And our scheming produced those papers of our own,
by which we bought, as with our blood, the final
reward.

Still, in old buried notebooks in my cupboards, I
have a suspicion that two or three of these efforts of
my own could be found. And if anyone, after my
death, drops on them, and cries aloud, " What rot is
this ?": he should be told, " Yes; pure rot! But it
was the price paid for Mozley's book on Old Testament Morality." For that volume was the result of
the papers that we forced the dear old man to produce. It is a volume exceedingly characteristic: full of
strong positions that can never be forgotten: full of
impossible and paradoxical positions which, nevertheless, are supported by strangely stimulating work.

He was very cordial to the advances of the younger
men. Once, when we wanted Liddon to do something
that we knew he would not like, we asked Mozley to
approach him deftly. He was delighted at undertaking the character of the arch-diplomatist: and
took Liddon out for a walk. On our keen inquiries
as to how he had fared, he only blinked, and said:
" Well! you know; there are subjects at which Liddon, you know, shies! Yes! Liddon shies! Shies
like a horse! Yes! Just like a horse!" We knew well
what the illuminative picture meant. Liddon's quick

eyes had detected, at once, from afar, the object of
this cautious and diplomatic approach: and had
absolutely refused to be drawn anywhere near it. "He
shies—shies like a horse!" That catches the very
gleam that we knew so well in Liddon's eyes, as his
nose scented danger.

Dr. Mozley used to ask us to dinner, in his kindly
way, and would lead us up in the general direction of
four nice interesting nieces, daughters of Observer
Johnson at whose house Newman had spent his last
days of farewell to Oxford, who lay crouching like
fawns in the window. "My niece," he would say.
"My niece, Amy. You will take her down to dinner."
And so he would leave us anxiously smiling towards
the white mass of calico fluff, until some one portion
of it would detach itself from the rest, and assure us
that it was the specified Amy.

He was stricken down, some time before his death,
and was afflicted with a certain aphasia. But his mind
was evidently hard at work, behind the hindrance.
He could not recall the name, one day, of a certain
great Finance Minister. So he called him. He rejected all suggestions. Gladstone? No! No!
Goschen? No! Great Finance Reformer! Was it
something about Egypt made those round him try
"Disraeli" and the Suez Canal shares? Oh no!
Not at all. Great Land Reformer! Who was it?
A niece, by inspiration, said "Joseph." Exactly!
That was it. Joseph! So, in the freshness of his
intelligence, he was vivifying the old biblical problems.

There are, perhaps, three stages of interest in his

writings. First, the Essays written during the heat of
the fierce fight for the Movement. These are young :
somewhat audacious, but exceedingly brilliant. They
are rare good reading, even though the judgments
given bear the mark of being written for a living
Cause, and would sound a bit one-sided, read in cold
blood. There is the famous one on Laud and Strafford,
one of the first attempts to present the Policy of
" Thorough " in the light which commended it to
its author. Mozley makes one feel the keen passion of
Strafford for good Government, for Law and Order :
and his readiness to use any instrument of power, and
especially the Crown, just to get a country well
governed, and corruption and rottenness and obstruction swept out of the way. Then, there is the
naughty one on Dr. Arnold, who had this one irritating
fault—that he was too optimistic : too happy with
this world. It was positively " juicy." He was like
a dog whose tail was always wagging. It was in contrast
to Dr. Arnold that he drew his splendid picture of
that other type of character, of which Hurrell Froude
had been for him the fascinating embodiment.

" Arnold, gushing with the richness of domestic life, the
darling of nature, and overflowing receptacle and enjoyer,
with strong healthy gusto, of all her endearments and sweets
—Arnold, the representative of high, joyous Lutheranism, is
describable—Mr. Froude hardly. His intercourse with earth
and nature seemed to cut through them, like uncongenial
steel, rather than mix and mingle with them. Yet the polished
blade smiled as it went through. The grace and spirit with
which he adorned this outward world, and seemed to an

undiscerning eye to love it, were but something analogous in him to the easy tone of men in high life, whose good-nature to inferiors is the result either of their disinterested benevolence or sublime unconcern. In him the severe sweetness of the life divine not so much rejected as disarmed those potent glows and attractions of the life natural ; a high good temper civilly evaded and disowned them. The monk by nature, the born aristocrat of the Christian sphere, passed them clean by with inimitable ease ; marked his line and shot clear beyond them, into the serene ether, toward the far-off light, toward that needle's point on which ten thousand angels and all heaven move."

Mozley wrote a very fine palinode long afterwards : in the form of a beautiful sermon on Arnold's real influence. Again, in his rather truculent review of Carlyle, there is the comparison of Cromwell's speeches to the pink folds of a hippopotamus's mouth, into which, if you place a pebble, it disappears, and then emerges for a moment, only to disappear again, as the vast arrangement of jaws and gums rolls it up and down and over and over. So it was with the real intention with which the great Protector spoke. The speech rolled and shook in helpless involutions, amid which a wary eye could just now and again detect what it was at which he was driving.

Then, in mid-life, following this literary period, came his stronger and more deliberate work. There was his very serious and rather heavy book on Baptism, which had the effect of severing him, a little, from his old companions, the typical Tractarian leaders. He rode off on a tack of his own : and showed himself to be an independent thinker. After this came the

Bampton Lectures on the Miracles, in which he took up the average sceptical position of the Experientialists of the day, and, with extraordinary acuteness, exhibited its weakness and its lack of logical authority. It was a serious attempt to explode John Stuart Mill's prevailing ascendancy from within. It is a remarkable instance of Mozley's power to stimulate and charm, even when you are least of all in agreement with his case.

Then, in his later years, as Professor, he put together the great volume of University Sermons, followed by another volume of general Sermons, in which he showed himself to be one of the masters of his generation, whose power of thought and of expression were surpassed by very few. He is not, indeed, to be credited with a Philosophy. He had not an organized system of thought to which the high name could be applied. But he brought to bear upon the deep problems of life the remarkable intellectual energy to which he was singularly ready to give himself away. He would allow it perfectly free and frank play: and would let it carry him whither it would, in the true Socratic spirit. This is why he often takes perilous directions and discharges himself down very doubtful tracks: he is prepared to try any road that reason suggests. His thought works like a hound after a lost scent, picking up any cue that might help, making brave experiments, knocking round until it hits the right road. His quick intellectual courage makes him, often, just as good reading when he is right as when he is wrong. He is always sincere: suggestive: unhampered: illuminative: and bold.

Let us take a sample of his finest work. Here is the opening of the famous Sermon on Nature :—

" Nature has two great revelations,—that of use and that of beauty ; and the first thing we observe about these two characteristics of her is, that they are bound together, and tied to each other. It would not be true, indeed, to say that use was universally accompanied by beauty ; still, upon that immense scale upon which nature is beautiful, she is beautiful by the selfsame material and laws by which she is useful. The beauty of nature is not, as it were, a fortunate accident, which can be separated from her use ; there is no difference in the tenure upon which these two characteristics stand ; the beauty is just as much a part of nature as the use ; they are only different aspects of the selfsame facts. Take a gorgeous sunset ; what is the substance of it ? only a combination of atmospheric laws and laws of light and heat ; the same laws by which we are enabled to live, see, and breathe. But the solid means of life constitute also a rich sight ; the usefulness on one side is on the other beauty. It is not that the mechanism is painted over, in order to disguise the deformity of machinery, but the machinery is itself the painting ; the useful laws compose the spectacle. All the colours of the landscape, the tints of spring and autumn, the hues of twilight and the dawn —all that might seem the superfluities of Nature, are only her most necessary operations under another view ; her ornament is but another aspect of her work ; and in the very act of labouring as a machine, she also sleeps as a picture " (" University and Other Sermons," pp. 138, 139).

That last sentence used to haunt us, like a refrain. We murmured it to ourselves when out on a walk : we repeated it in our sermons. " Nature, in the act of labouring at her work, sleeps as a picture." Let anyone read the Sermon on the Reversal of Human

Judgment: or on our Duty to Equals: and they will understand why Mr. Gladstone spoke of the temper of Butler combined with the form of Newman. Still, for quotation, we may perhaps find most reward from out of the earlier writings. There is, for instance, the historic passage, from the book on Newman's Theory of Development, which every English Churchman, troubled by antinomies, ought to wear as a charm next his skin. It contrasts the Roman claim for logic with the Anglican confession of opposites. And finds, in the first, the note of all Heresies.

" Be logical, said the Sabellian: God is one, and therefore cannot be three. Be logical, said the Manichean: evil is not derived from God, and therefore must be an original substance independent of Him. Be logical, said the Gnostic: an infinite Deity cannot really assume a finite body. Be logical, said the Novatian: there is only one baptism for the remission of sins; there is therefore no remission for sin after baptism. Be logical, to come to later times, said the Calvinist: God predestinates, and therefore man has not free will. Be logical, said the Anabaptist: the Gospel bids us to communicate our goods, and therefore does not sanction property in them. Be logical, says the Quaker: the Gospel enjoins meekness, and therefore forbids war. Be logical, says every sect and school: you admit our premises; you do not admit our conclusions. You are inconsistent. You go a certain way, and then arbitrarily stop. You admit a truth, but do not push it to its legitimate consequences. You are superficial; you want depth. Thus on every kind of question in religion has human logic from the first imposed imperially its own conclusions; and encountered equally imperial counter ones. The truth is that human reason is liable to error; and to make logic infallible we must have an infallible logician."

" To the intellectual imagination of the great heresiarchs of the early ages, the doctrine of our Lord's nature took boldly some one line, and developed continuously and straightforwardly some one idea ; it demanded unity and consistency. The creed of the Church, steering between extremes and uniting opposites, was a timid artificial creation, a work of diplomacy. In a sense they were right. The explanatory creed of the Church was a diplomatic work ; it was diplomatic because it was faithful. With a shrewdness and nicety like that of some ablest and most sustained course of statecraft and cabinet policy, it went on adhering to a complex original idea, and balancing one tendency in it by another. One heresiarch after another would have infused boldness into it ; they appealed to one element and another in it, which they wanted to be developed indefinitely. The creed kept its middle course, rigidly combining opposites ; and a mixed and balanced erection of dogmatic language arose. One can conceive the view which a great heretical mind, like that of Nestorius, e.g., would take of such a course ; the keen, bitter, and almost lofty contempt which,—with his logical view of our Lord inevitably deduced and clearly drawn out in his own mind,— he would cast upon that creed which obstinately shrank from the call, and seemed to prefer inconsistency, and refuse to carry out truth " (" The Theory of Development," pp. 43, 44).

And, to close this slight remembrance of this most remarkable man, let us recall the noble close to the article on Blanco White, in which he contrasts the tone of the man who enjoys the search for Truth, with the tone of him whom Truth seeks out and finds.

" Not as the function of his own activities, the triumph of his own penetration, the offspring of his mind, not in the subterranean regions, where Nature's fallen machinery and emulous exertion is at work, and the begrimed intellect

labours in its own smoke and exults in its difficulties, does the
disciple of Christ search for truth. He searches and he
penetrates, but not in this way. Truth penetrates into him,
rather than he into Truth ; Truth finds him out, and not he It.
He looks out for Its approach, waits for It, prepares himself
for Its reception. He knows the signs of Its approach, and can
tell Its features through the distance ; he is alive to the
slightest stir of the air, to a whisper, to a breath. But he
looks on It all the while as something without himself, as
something to advance and act upon him. The tender wax
expects its impress, the air its motion. Upon all his activities
sits an awful passiveness, and the mind adores with pure
devotion an Object above itself. From the invisible realm
above us a Form comes, too vast for our eyes' comprehension,
majestically slow the heavenly clouded weight descends, and
bears an impress with it. The soul awaits in stillness the
awful contact and embrace ; and while, with meekest pliable-
ness and unresisting faith and trust, she commits herself to it,
she fears it too. . . . Change is awful ; Truth changes us. It
is not a mere discovery, and then over and done with, a goal
reached, a prize won ; but a power that reacts and operates
upon ourselves. It is a new visitant that we are introduced
to ; we know it not at first ; we get to know it after we have
become acquainted with it. . . . This is an awful aspect which
Christian Truth has, and which mere intellectual truth has
not. Let those who make it a dead thing and a philosophical
reflection deal with it lightly. . . . He who really deifies Truth
cannot. He sees in it no plaything, no invention, no curiosity
of science, no mineral from the mine, but a living, Omnipotent
and Heavenly Form. All nature sobers at Its faintest step ; the
very skirt of Its robe turns all things cold ; the distant hills look
iron ; the horizon hardens, and repels the gaze ; nature is treacherous, her colour fades ; this blue concave is but a sepulchre ;
' the earth mourneth and languisheth, the world languisheth
and fadeth away, all the merry-hearted do sigh, the mirth of

tabrets ceaseth, the noise of them that rejoice endeth, the joy of the harp ceaseth.' The mighty form of Truth that the heavens just dimly disclose is spectral to our earthly eye, and a veil must be pierced through before we get within Its genial home and sanctuary. Sad and sepulchral in Its omnipotence, weak helpless nature fears Truth while she invokes It ; and as the mountain moves, and the overshadowing form bends over, and the arch of heaven closes in upon the human soul, she breathes, not without a touch of mortal tremor, her mute prayer : Oh ! Image Omnipotent, Eternal Pattern, fain would I love while I secretly dread Thee. . . . Come down upon me, and be my living Mould. Yet not without some tender condescension, some mercy and unutterable love, impress Thy awful stamp upon my poor and trembling being. I am weak, and Thou art mighty ; I am small, and Thou art Infinite. Crush me not by Thy force, Thy magnitude divine, but come in gentleness, in pity. For Thou art ' kind to man, steadfast, sure, free from care, having all power, overseeing all things, and going through all pure spirits—holy, one, only, manifold, subtle, lively, clear, undefiled. Thou being but one canst do all things, and remaining in Thyself, makest all things new ; and in all ages Thou enterest into holy souls, and makest them friends of God.' Thou hast appeared upon earth, and man has seen Thee in visible form ; and we know that Thou art the Way, the Truth, and the Life ; the Door and the Shepherd ; Thy sheep hear Thy Voice, and Thou gently leadest them, and carriest them in Thine arms. Thou didst suffer for them ; and now, being made higher than the heavens, intercedest for them ; an High Priest that art touched with the feeling of our infirmities, Jesus Christ our Lord " (" Essays Historical and Theological," Vol. II, pp. 146–8).

That is young : redundant : audacious. Yes ! But it reveals the exuberant capacities that were controlled and disciplined into the fine workmanship of the Sermons. And it was a joy to us, young things, in those days, to recognize how daring and excessive this dear old gentleman in the mild spectacles had been, before he became wholly wise. And it will be my comfort, in old age, if I have at all succeeded, through these brilliant passages, in persuading some men of a younger generation to turn again and recapture the rich heritage that is theirs in the fine and enkindling work of James Mozley.

VI

EDWARD KING, BISHOP OF LINCOLN

A LIGHT went out of our lives when Edward King passed out of our companionship. It was light that he carried with him—light that shone through him—light that flowed from him. The room was lit into which he entered. It was as if we had fallen under a streak of sunlight, that flickered, and danced, and laughed, and turned all to colour and to gold. Those eyes of his were an illumination. Even to recall him for an instant in the bare memory, was enough to set all the day alive and glittering.

> " My heart leaps up when I behold
> A rainbow in the sky."

So the heart ever leaped, as it caught sight of that dear face, that shone and quivered with the radiant hope that had made it its very own. Was there ever such a face, so gracious, so winning, so benignant, so tender ? Its beauty was utterly natural and native. It made no effort to be striking, or marked, or peculiar, or special. It possessed just the typical beauty that should, of right, belong to the human countenance. It seemed to say " This is what a face is meant to be. This is the face that a man would have, if he were, really, himself. This is the face that love would normally wear." We felt as if we had been waiting

48

for such a face to come and meet us—a face that would
simply reveal how deep is the goodness of which
humanity is capable. Oh! if all men could but be
just like that! So typical was its naturalness. Yet,
of course, this did not diminish its intense individuality.
It was only that this most vital individuality was so
whole and sound and normal and true, that it seemed
to be the perfect expression of what a man might be.

Throughout, one was conscious of this rounded
normality. There was nothing in him one-sided, or
excessive, or unbalanced. There was no side of his
character which wanted explanation, or was out of
perspective. Everything hung together. Everything
befitted. He never overshot his mark: or fell below
it. He knew what he could do: and did it. No note
was forced. No pose was taken. Where limits came,
they were instinctively accepted. His natural manhood always found itself, in whatever he did: and
showed itself complete and distinctive. And Grace
had so intimately mingled with his nature that it was
all of one piece. Grace itself had become natural.
Who could say which was which? Was it all Grace?
Was it all nature? Was it not all both? Anyhow,
the whole man moved altogether, in every word and
act. There were no separate compartments; and no
disturbing reserves. The soul of Edward King was
alive throughout his whole bodily frame and gifts
and capacities, so that the impact that he made upon
one was absolutely simple and undivided. The central
spirit tingled in every pressure of the hand, in every
turn of the voice, in every gleam of the eye. You had

E

the whole of him, whenever you touched him. That was one of the unique delights of his companionship.

And, always, this inner manhood of his, which so spontaneously and freely responded to your call, was sound as a bell: lucid as a brook: clear-eyed as a child. How wholesome it was to be near him! How open-aired, and unsophisticated, and simple-hearted, he was! The founts of his life were so unclouded, and unsoiled. You knew, at once, as he spoke, why it is that the earth is saved by the laughter of little children and the song of birds, and the wonder of flowers, and the sound of flowing waters.

This gracious beauty of his countenance lasted to the very end. Indeed, it had taken on a new charm: for the signals of old age in the wreathed wrinkles only gave an additional emphasis to the delicate rose-pink colouring of a face that was charged with the gaiety of an unconquerable gladness. You saw that he was alive with a spirit of good cheer which years could not damp, nor infirmities becloud. He thought better and better of the world every year that he lived. It was impossible to depress him. Those kindly grey eyes could, indeed, shine with a glint of steel: and the level brows, with their bushy eyebrows, could wear a look of sternness. For he was a soldier at heart: and knew the stress of battle: and had a sword that he could wield. This touch of severity was apt to come out in photographs. But he was still an undying optimist. He believed in everything being for the best. He saw goodness and wisdom everywhere manifest. He loved everybody and everything. He grew happier and happier. His eyes twinkled with daunt-less merriment: his presence brimmed over with joy. After all, the earth was a good place: and heaven would be better still. God be thanked !

I suppose that Cuddesdon men will always say that, whatever else came out at Christ Church and Lincoln, still there was never anything quite so full of thrill as the old days on the blessed Hill, when King was Principal. The whole place was alive with him. His look, his voice, his gaiety, his beauty, his charm, his holiness, filled it and possessed it. There was an air about it, a tone in it, a quality, a delicacy, a depth, which were his creation. He could draw love out of a stone: and there was not a man of any type or character that did not yield to his sway. Great burly chaps, arriving alarmed and unshaped, keeping their portmanteaux packed ready for a bolt, were at his feet before they knew where they were. There was nothing of the forcing-house, of the seminarist pose, as was popularly supposed. All was human, natural, free. " Here is one of my hot-house plants," I re-member him saying at one of the annual luncheons, as he laid his hand on the enormous shoulders of a man who had stroked the Oxford boat to victory for four years running on the Putney course. It is hope-less to try to tell the wonder of those old days. All over England there are men who look back to them, as to a heavenly vision—to which, by the infinite mercy of God, they have not been wholly disobedient.

One thing they certainly learned, apart from the secret of their own souls: and that was—belief in the poor. He loved the poor with a peculiar reverence and delight. He was their man. He knew them through and through. He felt as they felt. He could get at the heart of the very rough lads who were the bane of Wheatley and Cuddesdon.

Once, no doubt, this led to a mischance. His successor found a gang of them quite hopeless. They were the hooligans of the village : they pillaged his garden. In desperation, he sent off for a Sergeant from Cowley Barracks to come along and see what he could do. The Sergeant was eminently successful : and carried off three of the worst in triumph as recruits. But three mothers at once set out on foot. By nine o'clock they were kneeling on the carpet of the new Canon's study at Christ Church, weeping and wailing for their boys : and by twelve o'clock every boy had been bought out again by Dr. King, and had returned to the bosom of their families, and to the orchard of the unhappy Principal.

This was unlucky. It did not mean that King was not perfectly shrewd in his reading of the poor. He had no illusions. He had a very quick eye. He did not give himself away with the reckless " abandon " of Dr. Liddon. Perhaps it may be good to recall how anxious he was, lest—by signing the petition for pardon on behalf of the young sailor, condemned for murder, whom he visited in the prison at Lincoln —he should lower the man's sense of the justice of his condemnation. He desired to keep his conscience severely intact.

It was a real joy to him, as Bishop, to recover his

touch on the country poor, whom he loved so intimately at Cuddesdon. And, especially, he delighted in the confirmation of his beloved plough-boys. " So nice to smell the pomatum again ! " he exclaimed.

Here is an extract from a letter to me in 1877 and another in 1895 :—

" . . . The same is true of the Labour trouble, and the strikes. Political economy—the relation of Ethics to Politics, is becoming a practical question, and I very much hope some of your good people will bring out an edition of the ' Republic ' adapted for a ' Christian Ploughboy,' with notes in his language, and illustrated, not by arguments, but by stories. We have been worrying these poor boys with the Proverbs, and little narrow bits of personal ethics, and now they are beginning to feel there is a big world round about them, and lots of new powers, and hopes, and so they are dashing about. But we must put them upon the real principles, and then, after a bit, they will go on, and up, in order, dear things ! "

" . . . I still sometimes long to do a little in attaching the minds of the simple ones to the great Life-giving principles. I don't think the minds of the poor have been treated with sufficient loving, reverent, ability. We want a book, like Darwin on Worms, on the intellectual, moral, and spiritual capacities of the poor—*do* write it ?

" Good-bye. Many, many thanks. I feel I am less nuisance in an hotel, at least there is some sort of satisfaction in paying for the nuisance that one is.

" With my love and blessing,
" Always, always,
" Your most affectionate,
" E. Lincoln."

On his coming up to the Professorship at Oxford,

the University was, naturally, very patronizing. "A good holy man, no doubt: but without a pretence at Academic distinction." That is what each uplifted nose obviously suggested. But what we, who were nearest to him, came to discover was his excellent ability. He took great pains with himself, for one thing. He re-read his Aristotle, with great keenness. He worked at Italian: and made himself quite a good Dante scholar. He even went to Dr. Pusey's Hebrew Lectures: and told us amazing tales of how the dear old doctor pegged away, so deaf that he could not hear the passing waggons which entirely drowned whole sections of his lecture. Still, after each interval of thunder, he would be found still going on, as if nothing had happened, though all hope of discovering where he had got to was gone.

As the years went on, we got more and more to see that King's judgment on the intellectual interests of the hour went right home, and was best worth having. He could take a measure, or give an estimate, of the worth of things, with singular felicity. Once, we had all been rather swept off our feet by the vivacity of certain Bampton Lectures which were laid out on rather well-worn conventional lines. The material was old, no doubt: but, still, it was surprising how well they went. How was it ? What would King say of them ? "Well, it is wonderful," he said, "how good an old pair of trousers will come out, if you have laid them away for some time in a drawer." He had hit it exactly. The trousers were green, for all their apparent sheen.

A Bishop had been in St. Mary's pulpit, warning the undergraduates against everything that they were the least likely to commit—the use of the Confessional or Mariolatry, I think it was. " That sort of sermon," said King, " always reminds one of the useful notice-board sticking up out of the water in Magdalen meadow, when the floods are out—earnestly announcing that ' Trespassers will be prosecuted.' "

As for his own sermons, who can report their delicate perfection ? They were like nothing else in the world. They dropped out, in that level, low-toned quality of voice which was so dear and so characteristic to those who loved him. Brief little breaths of phrases fell on the heart like dew. Something there was of the traditional Tractarian restraint and reserve, in the manner of delivery. The bent figure kept one posture : and there was hardly any motion of hand or head. Only, now and again, the eyes were lifted, and opened : and the glory of the spirit flashed swiftly through.

Sometimes, the exquisite simplicity of the utterance led to misjudgments on the worth of what was said. He had preached one of these flawless sermons on one Sunday morning in Christ Church Cathedral : and I had rushed out, after it, all one thrill of rapture : and had gone to Frank Paget, then a tutor at the House, to pour out my emotions. I told him that it had been priceless : incomparable : a gem : such a sermon as no one else in the wide world could have given : and so on. Paget thought that he might improve the occasion, when the next undergraduate came to his room, and said: "So I hear that you had a good sermon in Cathedral this morning." The man looked up with an air of relief, and said: "Oh! I am so glad that you say that: because I thought so too: but the other chaps said that it was awful rot!"

Through all the Cuddesdon and most of the Oxford time, the most delightfully characteristic feature of his home was his mother. She had his gracious tender ways: and it was an infinite joy to him to play round her with his fun.

In the trial for libel which a strange clergyman brought against him for writing a letter which lost him a living, King's letters to Colonel Talbot, the Patron, were read out to an astonished Court. "It will be so nice to get to Wales, for then our mums will meet." "Their what?" asked the judge. "It appears to be, My Lord, a name by which they call their mothers."

One of the prettiest sights in the world was to watch him open the little side-door into their garden out of the Cathedral, and pass through with her, after service. In a later year, when a rasping, scarifying sermon had been preached, he said to Edward Talbot: "It is at such a time that I miss my dear mother." Talbot asked why. "Because, directly we were through the door, I should have turned to her and said: 'That was a *beastly* sermon'; and then it would all have been out: and I should have been sorry to have said it: and should have begun to apologize for the sermon: and to love the preacher. Now, the poison is in me all the week and I can't get rid of it."

We used to wonder how he would ever bear her departure. But, when the death came, we found that he had been preparing himself for years, and that he could retain all his wonderful serenity and gentleness and confidence and courage. I have hit on a letter written to me after it, so quiet and sure, recalling, in its tone, the spirit of his own death and the last words that he uttered before passing:—

" My great satisfaction is that the victory was so complete. I did not expect any fear, but there was not one word of anxiety or care about anything. Just the same trustful, bright, loving self she's always been; for the last two days she was not outwardly conscious, but all was perfectly calm. I think this is what I should have chosen before all things if I might have chosen, and it was given unasked in greater abundance. How to get on I do not quite see, but then I need not move just yet; I am sure the light will come. I have had so many kind letters speaking of her brightness, sympathy, wisdom, etc., and when I remember that she has been enabled to do all this in the days of her widowhood, it is a bright example for me, and gives me hope. Pray for me, dear friend, a little bit, that I may be guided. I am tempted to fear the loss of her wisdom almost more than the comfort of her brightness, but I know whence it came and it can come still.

" All blessings for the coming term; the angels are busy.

" Your most affectionate,

" E. KING."

In his message to me from his own death-bed, he just says " all is wisdom, goodness, and love." The last words of his letter show that it was the first night of Term when the Freshmen were pouring up in bustling cabs. He always pictured anxious and occupied Angels shepherding the boys in, for their first start: and I generally got a little word sent across from him, on such a night, to show where his thoughts and prayers lay.

All through the Oxford days, we younger men clung to him for the succour of his hopefulness under dark days. Liddon had given in to despair. The University was, for him, dead. It had lost, not only its ancient association with the Church of England, but even its Christian character. Everything was to be thrown open to any or to no Creed. There was to be no witness left to any positive Truth. Education was to abandon its claim to have any spiritual and religious significance. He poured out lamentations, and denunciation. He bade us fly to Zanzibar. He ridiculed any attempts to make the best of the situation left us. "I do not see any profitable use, dear friend," he would say, "in combing the hair of a corpse." But—we could not accept this counsel. Our very youth forbade us to be hopeless. We were all for saying: "Clear the ground: give us an open field. We can let the whole privileged position go. We are all the better for it. Let us trust no longer to prestige and authority: but go forward on purely voluntary lines, making free appeal to all or any who will hear." We did not desire to die in the last ditch: but to throw defences and ramparts behind us, and to charge with flags flying, and see what we could do with a clear field and no favour.

King was wholly with us. He was ready to take things gaily: to utilize all opportunities: to keep up heart: and to hope for the best. He bade us not despise the day of small things. He was quick to co-operate with all that was attempted. His presence was a perpetual godsend to us. I do not know how we should have fared through without him.

Sometimes, I think that there was only one event in his whole life that was " out of the picture." And that was his historic trial before the Archbishop. He was not meant for that episode, which was, somehow, forced upon him. He had nothing of the Ritualist in him. Nor were those precise liturgical minutiæ, however important in themselves, in the least congenial with his nature. They served to present him to the broad glare of the world in a form that was utterly alien to him. He may have felt that his " boys " who had gone out from his hands at Cuddesdon ought not to be left alone to fight the battle over these things: and that he was shrinking, under cover, from sharing their risks. I fancy that this spirit of gallantry did move him. But he was meant by God, surely, to be kept free from the dust and heat of legal turmoil, and from the cruel misunderstandings and crudities of a public trial. It was dreadful to think of him, in the trouble and roughness and indignity of such a situation. It gave him many miserable years: which he bore with his own noble sweetness. But it was a profound relief to all who loved him, when it was over, and he was released from this uncomfortable part, and given back to the tender amenities which formed his natural atmosphere.

He was English and Anglican down to the very

finger tips. There was nothing Roman about him.
His very look and instinct belonged to the Church of his
baptism. It was impossible to imagine him as anything else. He taught continuously the spiritual
value of the Anglican " You may," in contrast with
the Roman " You must." He revelled in the blend
of the appeal to authority and of the appeal to the
free personal conscience. He was steeped in the
typical traditions of our particular expression of
Catholic Christianity. You felt, as you looked at him,
that he must actually belong to the very build of an
English Country Parsonage, with some sweet church
tower looking in over the garden wall.

At Lincoln, he gave his whole soul to his Confirma-
tions. He did not attempt organization, beyond the
actual diocesan necessities. Nor did he take any active
part in the official councils of the Bishops. He left
all the " business " side of his office alone. Only, just
in his last years, he threw himself with eagerness into
the work of Church Extension in Grimsby. Otherwise, he was content to go up and down every corner
of the Diocese, and to take a whole day, on hopeless
side-lines, reaching some far village in the wolds, and
laying his hands on a half-dozen beloved plough-boys,
with the pomatum and all. He delighted in the far-
away look to be caught in the eyes of the shepherds
on the wolds, always steadying their faces to scrutinize
something seen approaching from out of the distance.
" Be you a beast, or be you a man ? " That is the
sort of gaze with which they greeted you. He loved
one of them, who had slowly learned that the candles on

the altar were lighted in broad daylight, because they
had no utilitarian purpose. They were not there to
give light, but to bear witness. " Eh ! Then yours is
a *Yon-side* Religion, I see, Sir." It appeals, he meant,
to something beyond this world. The porters loved
him. The villagers loved him. The town loved him.
Twice I went down to Lincoln fair with him, all
among the cocoa-nuts, and the ginger-bread, and the
fat women. It was a delicious experience, to note the
affection that followed him about. He drew out love,
as the sun draws fragrance from the flowers. He
moved in an atmosphere of love. And as we laid him
to rest in that beautiful Garth, in a grave heaped high
with flowers and carpeted with white lilies, the tears
in the voice, as we sang our last hymn over his body,
told of the deep passion of love which was following,
with its longing prayers, into the quiet place, him who
had shown us, as none other had ever done, what the
tender Grace of the love of Jesus could mean.

VII

FRANCIS PAGET, BISHOP OF OXFORD

IT was difficult, in later years, to persuade people
to believe the memories of the frolic and the fun that
were associated, in my mind, with the name of Francis
Paget in the early 'eighties. They looked at the sad
strained eyes, at the set face, they felt alarmed at the
careful and deliberate reserve of his manner: they
were aware of a certain over-wrought anxiety, of an
austerity of discipline, that gave a melancholy touch
of depression to the tone of his voice. Here was a
stricken man who took life seriously and even hardly.
That was plain. And how could they accept my
report that never had I laughed so long and so freely
as I had laughed with him in the first days of our
friendship, as I found him the leader of the little band
of scholars reading for Greats, when I went to Christ
Church as a student in 1870 ? Yet for me the memory
is always of evenings that were one continuous carousal,
in which we never stopped laughing. He was in the
full swing of that undergraduate time when words
are the toys that we play with. The delight is to
exercise all the swiftness of wits released from restraint
in making fun out of everything: in turning everything topsy-turvy: in tossing words about like balls: in
evoking and provoking the unexpected. A young Don,
free as yet of all responsibilities, and fresh from the

schools, is only an undergraduate writ large : and this rollicking logomachy was entirely to my mind. I enjoyed myself to my heart's bent with this young group. And there was no limit to Frank Paget's capacity of keeping up the game. He was charged with intellectual electricity. He had the wit that revels in surprises. He could let himself go. He was nimble, alert, spontaneous, with an infinite felicity of epigrammatic speech. He loved the play of happy companionship. He was a master in the art of personal chaff. And all was so clean, and delicate, and fastidious, and good-tempered. There was never a shadow upon our joy in being together. We had only to meet, and the merry business began at once.

And this joy of comradeship was carried on, with ever-deepening satisfaction, into endless reading parties, in spring and summer. Hidden away, with a half-dozen, or even a dozen, undergraduates, in some delicious retreat, far from madding crowds, perhaps on the coast of Brittany, or in a recess of the Vosges Hills, or in a green Alp hollow of the Oberland, or in a Devon combe, or by Dartmouth Harbour, or, again and again, amid the heather and the deep brown pools of North Wales, we spent the days that hold in them the promise and the fragrance of some earthly paradise. We always went together, and we lived in " the glory of flannels and shooting-jackets," climbing, bathing, reading—and always laughing. Life was all un-buttoned. We knew that we were doing our duty ; for did we not read, and read hard ? And, yet, it was all a joke : a holiday : a freak : from end to end.

There were no invading cares. There were no duties. There were no conventions. There were no social stupidities: there were no obligations to fulfil. We were complete in ourselves: we owed nothing to anybody: we were a band of friends who were sufficient for each other: and we wanted nothing more. Round us the loveliness of some selected fairy spot ringed us in. The hills waited upon us: the rivers ran for us: the great sea laughed as we plunged into its green Cornish waters. Nature was on our side: and we were one with it.

These were the magic hours, that fed our lips with honey-dew. To me they will be always the symbol and the expression of all that can make this earth the joyous home of health, and beauty, and friendship. And into them all came his dear presence: and in them all I hear still the sound of his gaiety and the play of his wit. And, through them all, our intimacy deepened, and the powers of the world beyond began to work, with fuller force, upon the lives that were now together committed to the ministry of the Spirit, and the service of Christ. Out of such days of companionship as these life receives its imperishable endowments, of which no after years, with their harsher obligations and uneasy troubles, can ever rob us.

After the ecstasy of the Reading Party, Paget would come on to the more sober felicities of what we ironically named "the Holy Party." It was simply the habit of a gang of us young Donlets to occupy some small country parish for a month, do the duty, read, discuss, say our offices and keep our hours to-

gether. Talbot, Gore, Illingworth, Richmond, Arthur
Lyttelton, J. H. Maude, Robert Moberly, would be
there—with Lock, or Cheyne, now and again.   We
would work, and play, and talk over the possibilities
of an Anglican Oratorian Community: and be
exceedingly happy. We would think whether anybody could be found to meet Dr. King's demand and
write a new " Summa Theologica." Who would do it ?
Perhaps Swallow, the learned Cuddesdon Chaplain ?
" No," said Paget, " not quite ! It is not every Swallow
that can make a Summa ! "

Or we would devise an Office to be said in term by
weary hard-run tutors. " Yes," said Paget, " and the
antiphon would be ' She tired her head.' "

So, in successive years, the friendship rooted itself
in the deeper ground. Only once did some friction
begin to appear. Frank Paget more and more surrendered himself to the pessimistic influence of
Liddon. He revelled in Liddon's brilliant aggressions
on the new situation. We others, who were struggling
to make the best of it, were told that we were but
fruitlessly engaged in " combing the hair of a corpse."
So Paget drew away a little from us. He became the
special lieutenant of Pusey and Liddon. " Who is
this reactionary young man, who writes such excellent
Latin ? " asked Mark Pattison after Paget had made
the Latin speech to the Bodleian Curators. He was
chosen to read from St. Mary's pulpit a sermon of
Dr. Pusey's, which the dear old man's throat forbade
him to attempt. A task to recoil from, Paget thought,
and pictured to Liddon the disgust of the University

F

as they looked for a mountain in labour, and only a
ridiculous mouse appeared. " On the contrary, dear
friend," said Liddon to cheer him, " they will see a
mouse go up into the pulpit, and there be delivered of
a very fine mountain." " Painful for the mouse, you
will allow," pleaded Paget. " Painful, no doubt,"
rejoined Liddon, " but glorious."

At this time Paget was stiffening up a little : the
academic crust was creeping over him. Oxford was
playing its evil part. When, just in the nick of time,
came a tremendous convulsion. He married : and
accepted the Cure of Bromsgrove. Three brimming
years of intense delight in the new experience of a
Parish Priest did their work, and when he came back
to Christ Church as Pastoral Professor he was a changed
man. The crust was broken. He was free, human,
elastic, sympathetic again. The warm friendship of a
man like Frederick York Powell was an index of how he
had won back the confidence of the Common Room.

I cannot speak about the marriage. It was one of
those marriages which are revelations of the excellence
which waits to be unsealed in our human nature. It
gave one a new standard of what the communion of
two lives might mean. He had a very deep and
diffident reserve, which would have always held him
back from his true liberty, if it had not been unlocked
and released through the mediation of this unqualified
intimacy of soul with soul. It meant everything in
the world to him, more especially as the responsibilities
and the conventions of public life made it more and
more difficult for him to commit himself. His

fastidious and tentative diffidence made him politely distrustful of others, in the rougher intercourse of affairs. He could only open out to a few: and he held himself in hand with a tight discipline, which took the outward form of an elaborate courtesy such as served to keep people back behind barriers of civility. It took them long to discover how profoundly sincere he was. Thus he built walls round himself. Only, within, there was ever and always the infinite peace of being absolutely understood in that delicious security of touch which only a perfect marriage can bring into play. So he lived, through his Professorship and Deanery, while six children were born to him. How he drew the divided elements of the House together, and how he broke for ever its old stupid tradition of rowdiness and swagger, is known to all who were inside the secret of that time, and recognized his admirable leadership.

Only, I have said enough to make it clear why, when the blow fell in his last year at the Deanery, and his wife was taken from him, he became the man who, in later years, carried with him, wherever he went, the look of one stricken by some woe that had no remedy. He took up his Bishopric in the following year. He was scrupulously devoted to his work. He laboured with a pertinacity and a thoroughness that were a perpetual reproach to us who dallied through our business with a lighter heart. He spent himself in endless trouble and pain. He had an iron strength of body, and could work far beyond our normal measure. He was quite unflinching in his determination to do everything himself, and to write his own letters, and plod through the grinding details. But he worked as bound by a rigid conscience to his task. " Are there not twelve hours to the day ? " He was set his job: and he would see it through. But he looked for no joy any more here. His eyes: his heart—these were elsewhere. The world had nothing in it by which to hold him. I never knew anyone in whom natural ambition was more obviously dead. It had been killed. He had no more of that instinct which comes from the desire to exercise gifts of which you are conscious. It had ceased to be even a temptation. And this was the more remarkable because he had inherited or acquired from his great father, Sir James Paget, an almost inordinate respect for the honour and dignity of established things. They wore for him a special significance. He saw in them the evidence of high worth. This had been his natural scale of valuation. But, though in some degree he retained the scale, the things themselves had totally ceased to affect him. His blood made no more response to their appeals than that of a corpse. He was, in this sense, actually " dead to the world." In this spirit, he went steadily through with the burden laid upon him. He treated himself hardly. He made his work so predominate over everything, that it hardly allowed for the free play of emotion. Grimly, he set himself to discharge his obligations, until the night, the blessed night, should come to give release.

In the meantime he told more and more on his colleagues, through his power of judgment, and his singular felicity of speech. He made a great im-

pression on the Ritual Commission. He was offered
Winchester, but would not go. And every year he
became more and more the chosen counsellor and
intimate friend of the Archbishop of Canterbury.

So he toiled at his oar, in the place set him, with
pathetic joylessness. This might have been the mood
which never yielded, before the end, so desired, should
arrive. But something happened, and it broke. A
year before the end he underwent a severe operation.
It was critical: it was only just in time: he was very
near to death: but he pulled through. And, after
six months he returned to the Diocese, to find a
warmth of welcome from every side, which was to
him a surprise and a revelation. It showed that he
had won the heart of the Diocese in a way that he
had not dreamed of. He himself found a joy in taking
up work again, from the very rebound of this joy
which greeted his home-coming. The glowing recognition gave him confidence and light. He went
through his last year with a springing step, taking his
work lightly and gaily, unencumbered and assured.
He gave himself more liberty: and was more open in
response. In spite of the cloud thrown over it by the
death of his second daughter, who had been most
happily married to his former chaplain and beloved
friend, Campbell Crum, a certain ease and brightness
were upon him such as he had not worn for years.
He gave a great gathering in Christ Church Hall to
his Diocese, a fortnight or so before his death, in which
this glad sympathetic intercourse with his clergy and
laity culminated.

He came once again to join the " old Gang " of his familiar Oxford allies at Longworth, just before the end. He had missed the annual gathering very often : and it was a peculiar delight to us all to have him back in something like his old gaiety of spirit. He was singularly well : and hopeful. He preached, in impressive simplicity, in the village church. He went off to wind up his last things before the holiday, to which he was looking forward with quite a boyish glee.

Then, the blow fell : and he was gone. He knew everything. He joined, with broken voice but concentrated energy, in the prayers of the last twenty minutes before the heart totally failed. He remembered everybody with a personal keenness. But his heart had already passed over. They spoke to him of the dead whom he would see again. " So soon ! " he said. He would know more of what life meant over there : and of what he had yet left unlearned here. His dear friend, the Archbishop, had given him the Sacrament. All was fair, and right, and clear, and clean. May God's own light and peace be his everlasting refreshment !

He had a gift of felicity in speech which at its best was quite perfect. It was inherited from his father, who was a born orator, of pure and noble style : and it is shared by his brother, the Bishop of Stepney, and by his sister, Miss Paget, one of the most gifted speakers that we have. But with him, it had all the fine polish of the trained scholar. It would appear in phrasing a resolution or a formula, as in the Ritual

Commission: or in an after-dinner speech in which he was not to be excelled, unless it were by the Master of Trinity: or in those exquisite Latin inscriptions which he would write for memorials of the dead. He was a real master in the use of that epigrammatic force to which the Latin tongue so supremely lends itself. It is difficult to read without tears the delicate words set on the quiet and beautiful tablet which commemorates his wife in Christ Church Cathedral.

With remarkable swiftness of wit and word he combined a strangely slow judgment. He took very long to come to a decision: and was apt to be over-weighted by his sense of responsibility. He, who could flick and flash with rapid insight, would, on serious occasions, speak with a slowness that was almost oppressive. This was the proof of the severity with which he disciplined his natural self.

Greatly as he enjoyed country sights and country folk, with whom he made close friendships, he was a " Cockney " to his finger-tips. He was steeped in London. He was always feeling with his feet for the beloved pavements. This was part of the fun of our old Reading Parties. He might walk, climb, bathe, with the best of us: but we always knew that Piccadilly held him as its own. The country was a pleasant adventure for him: a strange land. Animals were possessed of fearsome and unaccountable possibilities. He could never make himself look as if he really belonged to horse or cow. There was London in reserve, all the time.

He was a man of intense prayerfulness: he had his eyes set on the unseen. And this had, somehow, the effect of making one feel as if, in spite of home and friends, he was a very lonely man. There was a loneliness in his self-restraint and reserve, a loneliness in the tone that had come into his voice. He had his secret to himself, behind all the lighter moods. The last year of his life brought relief and light: and he rounded off his days with a very happy memory. But, after all, he was dead and his life was hid: and now he has passed to where, in Christ, his treasure had long lain.

VIII

GEORGE HOWARD WILKINSON

Bishop of Truro and St. Andrews

OUR personal intimacy was too dear for me to venture
on any critical review of a life that meant so much
for me. But I should like to record for those who did
not know the Bishop of St. Andrews, something of
that secret which gave him such amazing and unparalleled sway over souls.

What was it, in his character, which made him so
wonderful a channel through which the Spirit of
God could find its free way? For, most certainly, it
was the Spirit which came: it was the Spirit which
worked. There was no one who made one so entirely
and vitally aware of the moving Presence of a Spirit
not his own. This was the marvel of his preaching.
It brought the soul into the Presence. It possessed
the soul with the sense of a living Power at work upon
it. It brought the Invisible into full and urgent play.
Yet how was this done? Through what personal
and peculiar means? For the means were intensely
personal. It was the personality of the man that
brought it all about. It was not what he said: it was
not his particular message: for that was not special in
any precise sense. He delivered the old message, the
Gospel message, the message of Redemption, of
Pardon through the Blood, of salvation through

sacrifice, of the surrender of the soul in Faith to Him Who was its sole and prevailing Redeemer. It was the message of Jesus, man's Saviour from Sin. We had all heard it a hundred times. But it had never before come home to us like this. It had never before become charged with such compelling power, with such quickening efficacy. Never before had we felt it to be a living thing, that would lay hold, and change us, and regenerate and transfigure. The man made it tell. The personality of the man, in its most marked and unique and exceptional identity, was alive with its message, It was identified with its message. It was itself involved in the message. It was inseparable from it, in the passionate impression made upon us.

How was this ? What made the manhood of the messenger so effectually an organ of divine manifestation ? Well, I should say that it lay in the remarkable combination in him of the mystical and the practical temper. Mystical, of course, he was : everyone saw and felt that. He lived in direct and intimate touch with the Invisible world. For him, Spirit was the one real fact. It possessed the scene. It looked through the veil of material things. It could not be omitted, or excluded. He saw nothing between him and it, except what revealed it. Nature could not get itself taken seriously. It was merely a parable : an allegory. He could not rest in it, without the spiritual significance, that lay behind it, breaking through. Later on in life, when he sorely needed mental repose, we used to amuse ourselves with trying to teach him how to look on a sunset as a sunset, and how to enjoy

a beautiful view, without turning it into a text. And
he used, in his delightful, humble, child-like way, to
report any success that he had had in this way, with
the pleasure of a pupil who had learned his lesson. We
even induced him to be interested in people as people,
without any regard to their souls. But this was very
far on : and could only be attained with great effort.
So Earth appeared to him, shot through with the
illumination of the spiritual Drama which was the
supreme reality : and into that ever-living Drama he
continuously propelled his soul : and there he lived
in constant prayer, and intercession : and to it he
turned : and on it he leaned : and for it he ever felt :
and in its atmosphere he breathed freely : and his
talk was of it : and his behaviour assumed it : and all
else was a mere interlude, which withheld him from
it. So immediate, so intimate, so habitual, so in-
stinctive was his apprehension of it. This gave him
his extraordinary power in private prayer and in
public preaching. This gave to him his incomparable
mastery in a sick-room, by a bed of death, in a scene
of sorrow. Here he simply became at once at home,
as in his native place. He was perfectly sure of himself. It was his day : his moment. He understood
it all, as we understand sunlight. Everything that
belongs to such times of trial seemed to him natural,
suggestive, right. His whole being rose to it. He was
set free. There was no one like him.

But, then, together with this mystical mood,
involved in it, inseparable from it, was a shrewd
practical judgment that could hardly be surpassed.

Falling into a trance with his eyes open, he saw, at the same time, both what was farthest and what was nearest. He noted details with exactitude; he brought into play a precision that was military in its demands. Nothing escaped him. He had a relentless eye: and detected infirmities with singular keenness. He was sensitive to the tiniest minutiæ of behaviour. Characterized, as he was, by beautiful courtesy, his conscience was acutely alive to lapses of tone and breeding. He concealed all this sensitiveness by the power of grace: but it was natural to him: and, in close companionship with him, it would peep out in most unexpected ways. He was neat to a fault: a first-rate rider, he had about him the well-groomed, scrupulous niceties of the true sportsman. He could not tolerate anything loose or disorderly in dress. Every button was remembered. Each hair was in its place. All the little appliances of life had to be perfect and exact. Punctuality was a positive fine art with him. He could time a spiritual interview to a minute. Many were the tales that floated about St. Peter's in old days of this exactitude and regularity. He loved order. Method was a passion. Everything was noted down: planned: regulated. He was a master in the use of Note-books, References, Rules. His accounts were made up to the last penny. There was no loose cash. He was thoroughly business-like. He was an admirable Chairman. He could push business through with excellent practical skill. He kept things to the point. He used all his opportunities with decisive insight and quickness. He knew men: and never blundered over affairs : and made no mistakes : and took pains with little things : and ever kept his eyes on the business in hand. His grasp on practical possibilities was victoriously effective.

Now, is not that a remarkable power for a mystic to wield ? It was this which made him so amazing in his hold over the big laity of the West End. They would not have ventured to commit themselves so entirely to the mysterious emotion that he roused in them, if they had not learned to trust him, as a master, in the practical judgments which they could thoroughly appreciate. Here, on their own ground, he was obviously strong and sound. He understood them : they understood him. They had in this a pledge to give them confidence, when his burning language passed beyond their ken and his visionary fervour swept them off their feet. It was through this combination of contrasted tempers that he held together his Evangelical Gospel and his Catholic Creed. We have become more familiar in later days with such a combination through men like Body, and Stanton, and Dolling. But it was once very rare, and the Bishop made it noticeable. He had, himself, begun on the subjective side, working among his Durham miners in the force of an intense personal religion, preaching conversion, and developing extempore prayer. All this he retained : he left nothing of it behind : but his counter-temperament led him to add to it all the order, regularity, dignity, reverence, which were so eminently congenial to him and which came to him through the sacramental worship of the Church. Thus, he came to Confession through the door of his Evangelicalism. It was the consummation of personal conversion, and personal intercourse of soul with soul. But he used it in the full Catholic spirit. He had found pure gain in its formalities, in its regularity, in its solemnity, in its traditional validity, in its systematic thoroughness, in its methodical reality, in its unflinching sincerity. So he gave himself to its use, fully and freely. I remember well a little instance that will show how the old and the new tempers came together, without shock, at the time of the dedication of Truro Cathedral. He had been for weeks taking intense interest in every syllable of the Rubrics that were to determine the acts and movements of the Dedicatory Services. He had thought out every detail of the form. Yet he laughed with glee, because, by chance, going down to the Cathedral to see that all was ready, and finding the workmen still at it, he held an impromptu prayer-meeting, and so succeeded in making his first Prayer in the new Cathedral extempore.

His long and trying illnesses, by draining, as they so often did, the springs of his inward spiritual energy, drove him more and more to see the value of sacramental objectiveness. He was profoundly struck by finding that if, in hours of dark depression and deadness, he flung himself in trust upon the sheer authority of his office, it never once failed him. He always pulled through. All this experience intensified his Churchmanship, without reducing in the slightest degree his sympathy with the rich Evangelical internality.

The pathos of his last years lay in this, that God, Who had brought him so far through inward assurance and outward method, now would draw him on to further and higher levels of spiritual experience, which could only be won by leaving both method and assurance behind. His old familiar rules and recipes, by which he had won for so many souls their peace, were to fail him, in hours of direst need, in order that he might pass through them and beyond them, into the peace that passeth understanding. He was to learn the perfect discipline of his dear Lord and Master, Who might have, at times, to be denied, in the wilderness of His Temptation, the very Bread with which He fed the multitude on desert hills when they were starving. " Come up higher ! " That is the incessant call, which he still followed. " Come up high, by joyful aspiration, by glad assurance, by patient toil, by steady work at the holy craft. And, then, so trained and equipped, come up higher yet, without any glad emotion, without any sure footing, without any inviting light : in the night : under the cloud : not knowing whither you are being led."

" When thou art old, another shall gird thee : and carry thee whither thou wouldest not."

Yes ! And glad and inspiring as it is to gird oneself, it is this other girding that, in its divine severity, draws one up nearest to the Crucified Christ. That is what he, through whom so many have found their peace, now knows, in the blessed Rest of Paradise, in the Haven where he would be. He entered into rest, just as he would have most desired, in the act of delivering his witness, still proclaiming, with his very last breath, the power that lies in child-like prayer. He gave a sigh: and was gone. "Surely," writes a friend, "it was the very thinnest of veils through which he had to pass." He had, all his life, walked with God: and, now, he was not: for God took him.

IX

ROBERT GREGORY
Dean of St. Paul's

THE venerable figure, bowed under the white hair, moving with helping hands to and fro through the Cathedral to which he had given his life and love, had won for Robert Gregory a romantic interest in later years. All London watched him pass in and out : and he laid hold of the public imagination : and men saw in him the whole story of the long years up-gathered and embodied. There he goes, with his white hair—the man who had seen Byron's funeral pass through Nottingham to Newark : who remembered the fly-sheets telling of the battle of Navarino : who had rowed out in a boat to meet the first steamer coming back over the Atlantic from America. How often he had ridden up by coach from Liverpool to London ! And, then, he had heard Newman's last sermon in Littlemore on the Parting of Friends, and remembered the loud sobbing of Pusey and Tom Morris, while the voice of the preacher went on unmoved, until, in silence, he took off his hood and left it on the rail, as he stepped down from the pulpit.

So he could recall : and, then, had he not for forty years and more been the strong stay of St. Paul's, seeing it through out of its piteous shame and

neglect into its present crowded glory ? Was it not
he who had given himself night and day to the work
of liberating it, and cleansing it, and clearing it, and
decorating it, and filling it full with the splendour
of worship ? Everyone who helped him had passed
away : but still he is there, faithful to his charge,
part of the very building itself, punctual at its prayers,
clinging to his place in the choir, following the Lessons
with absorbed expectant attention as if he could not
guess what was coming, untiring in his devotion to
the interests of the great Church, resolutely lying on
his right side in bed (in spite of warnings against the
risk by the doctors) that he might better hear at
night the Clock and Bells of St. Paul's.

So he gained a unique hold over the heart of
London : until, at his death, there almost seemed a
danger of the world forgetting the others who had
shared his task. Liddon and Church were mentioned
as if they were merely accidental contributors to the
good result. No one would have repudiated such a
claim to pre-eminence more earnestly and vehemently
than the late Dean himself. He knew, with perfectly
honest and straightforward intelligence, what he could
do, and what he had to leave to others. And he was
ready always to trust others to do their own part,
which was not his. Thus there were departments of
the Cathedral life which he was delighted to see fulfilled by those who were specially fitted for them.
Liddon's wonderful gifts he thoroughly appreciated.
And not only did Liddon, by his preaching, fill dome
and transept and choir, but, also, in the reorganization

of the Worship, and of the use to which the Cathedral was put, his skill and knowledge and enthusiasm were invaluable. He set the key in which things were to be done. He determined the tone and quality and order of all the Liturgical development. He fixed the limits of what could be attempted. He imagined the general scheme. He brought to the Cathedral the sense of beauty, passion, and romance. He made it a place of fascination, and gave it a spiritual ideal.

Again, it was Liddon who brought up Stainer from Oxford, to whom St. Paul's owes the entire setting of its worship in the spiritual key and temper which is its great inheritance to-day. He built up the choir itself, and the voluntary organizations that undertakes the Evening and Special Services. Liddon, again, planted Barff at the Choir School, by whose steady resolution the School became the nursery of the pure and high tradition which is the inner secret of all the beauty of Worship offered at the central Shrine.

And, then, behind, at the centre, was the fine and masterful presence of Dean Church. He it was who gave to the Cathedral intellectual distinction and value. The world of men could not think cheaply of us, so long as he was our Chief. There was not a man of worth in English Society and Literature who did not appreciate Richard Church. He was recognized as the "finest flower of the Anglican tradition." He stood in the first rank. He won, for all this revival of ours, the respect in which it was held. He was a pledge of its worth to the people who count. And more and more he became the secret central spiritual authority which men sought in hours of doubt. He sat as a moral arbiter: his verdict became our common law: he set the standard: he determined values. We were felt to possess, at our heart, a power of wisdom, of courage, of unworldly intuition, of counsel and ghostly strength. Nothing could be done in St. Paul's that had not in view the fine and delicate scales in which the Dean would put it to test. And, at anxious hours of emergency, we were trusted and tolerated because of the honour of our Dean. I do not think it is possible to exaggerate the significance of his personal presence, as our Head, even though its influence was often felt rather than heard, and though its actual working was as much in secret as was possible. He was a vital asset through all the years of revival, which steadily grew in importance and in effect. We had a conscience in our midst which we were compelled to regard. No one could afford to live in the company of Richard Church, and not be careful how to answer for his conduct. No one could be near him without being aware of a heightened worth in living. So through love, and through the fear that belongs to love, he made St. Paul's what it was. He was unique. There was no one like him.

The dear old man who has since gone from the scene of his labours would wish all this to be recalled. He himself, by his strenuous activity, made their action possible. From the first hour in which the Minor Canon who died but a few months before him had said, " I suppose you intend to reform St. Paul's. You can't. It is an Augean stable," he had set to work to see how it could be done. He had seen that the whole possibility rested on Finance, and that the first necessity of all lay in a bargain with the Ecclesiastical Commissioners. He had contrived his financial scheme, and had whirled Dean Mansel into incompetent activity, before Church or Liddon had appeared on the scene. Everything that they did reposed on this financial basis which was Gregory's special contribution. And, then, under the pressure of this financial reform, he laid his hand on every department of the staff, every corner of the fabric. He reorganized every bit of the mechanism. Gradually the Chapter got everything in hand, except where a knob or two of historic vested interests repelled all treatment.

So Gregory was effectively instrumental in providing the opportunities which others could use : and in securing the resources which were available for others to apply. His driving powers were immense, in this way. It was never better seen than in the work of decorating the Cathedral. There was a pleasant irony, which he himself enjoyed, in the fact that he should have been called to supervise a matter so entirely outside his natural bent and skill. It was a foreign subject to him. It was great fun to see his wonder why we could not make up our minds the moment that the artist's proposals were plainly put before us. " Now, then," he would cry impatiently, " I suppose you are ready to vote : what shall it be ? "

We, poor things, were struggling to estimate those tentative, elusive, intangible impressions, which a work of art evokes. We wanted to go aside for half an hour alone, to collect our dim, inarticulate, hesitating judgment: to suffer the impressions to sink. Voting on the spot was horrible to us. But, after all, he was right. We were hopelessly inadequate, for all our pains. And the best thing that we could do was to do what he did, i.e. trust our chosen artist, and go ahead. So it was done: and he got it along. We made many mistakes, but not more than we should have made anyhow. And there is a great power in a total outsider, who sees what has got to be done and does it. William Richmond liked him better than he liked any of us: and would prefer him greatly to any of us who made faint claims to be heard on artistic matters.

The old Dean was very proud indeed of the decorations: and thoroughly satisfied. It was certainly a wonderful thing to have been allowed to bring about the decoration of the entire Choir and Aisles with all their appointments. It was to him, too, that the Cathedral owed the electric lighting, which was given through the generosity of his personal friend, Mr. Pierpont Morgan. No wonder that he loved to the last to wander in and out of the Cathedral, which bore the impress of his devotion to it from floor to ceiling. His work looked back at him and spoke to him, as he saw the crowds pour in and out, and heard the organ-music thunder round the walls, and knew that the great Church was now made for ever a house for the

worship and the glory of God. And as he wandered
in and out, with his work behind him, a strange
gentleness stole over his old vehement energy: and a
quiet fell upon him, and a passive calm, such as we
had never seen in the rough strenuous days of labour.
Very gently he resigned his task to others. He h d
been Treasurer throughout: and loved it: and
revelled in its figures and books. When I succeeded
to the office, I thought that he would never be able
to keep his hands off the old job—especially as he had
a most kindly contempt, I felt sure, for my financial
capacities. Yet never once did he try to put in a
finger: never once did he touch it again: and all
that I did was accepted with cordial acquiescence,
and with ready joy in things going right.

It was an immense surprise to us—this power of
total surrender in one who could not, in younger days,
set limits to his urgent activities. So old age brought
to him new gifts. He was changed and mellowed.
Peace and tenderness and resignation did their quiet
and beautiful work upon him, until the long day ended.
He had done: he could go home. " Shall we read
the whole Service ? " his daughter asked just at the
end. " No: not the first lesson. It's Proverbs: and
I shall not want Proverbs any more," was his answer.
The discipline of life had been attained. After that,
he was absorbed in the interest of the unseen world.
He would not attend to those who talked to him.
" I am very interested," he explained, while he seemed
to be speaking to old friends, and said " Quite so !
Quite so !" several times. Even then, the strong body

almost refused to die.   Only, after a long unconscious-
ness, it consented to the death that had been so often
postponed.

He left a memory which gathered in force and
richness to the very end.   The Cathedral that he
served so faithfully will never forget him.

X

SAMUEL BARNETT AND THE GROWTH OF SETTLEMENTS

IT was given to Samuel Barnett to see, as few have ever seen, the policy which he had created and advocated not only adopted and fulfilled, but permanently established as part of the normal programme of social reform in the great cities of England and America. He had the good fortune to win a most favourable opportunity in which to bring out his scheme; but no one but he could have used it as he did. It found him prepared and equipped, clear-headed and resolute. It came about through one of those spasms of pity and remorse which now and again lay hold of the imagination of the nation, only to pass away in idle emotion. This time it was not permitted so to do. It was a little book called "The Bitter Cry of East London" which had evoked it, and the pathos of it touched Oxford at a remarkable moment. The University had for some time been drawing towards the social problems of the great cities. T. H. Green had taught us the obligations which bound the Universities to the larger life outside. Various little attempts had been made already to put out efforts to help in slum parishes. School and College Missions were beginning to be started; the University life was no longer enclosed in itself. And then into

the midst of this temper there shot the radiant and
beautiful figure of Arnold Toynbee. He was like
nobody else. His face itself could never be forgotten,
and he had a nobility and purity of tone which
fascinated. He gave himself from the political
economy of the schools to the democracy of the
streets. He went out to meet it, and to help it, and
to teach it ; and in doing this he broke his heart and
lost his life. Something must be done that should
prevent such a memory from dying, so his friends
felt, and Samuel Barnett was the man who saw what
could be done. He had had close and intimate experience of the city life and all its needs, and he saw
specially where the need was sorest.

The disaster of the cities lay in the fact that the
parish system, which is the fundamental assumption
on which our English life rests, had wholly broken
down. The parish supposes that in each locality
there are the materials for a small but complete
community. There would be men and women of
various grades, out of whose exchange of services and
functions the organic life of the body would be
realised. There would be the play and counter-play
of balanced capacities within a single organism.
There would be people found at each spot who have
leisure and education enough to carry through the
administration of civil affairs and to contribute light
and learning to the welfare of the society. But in
our great cities, especially in London, this ideal had
ceased to be possible. As a fact, there was no variety
of conditions within the lines of the usual parish.

Each parish had been specialized down until in a given area all the people were on the same level ; and this meant that in the poorer areas everybody was poor. All who had any other and better position in the world had fled to other districts. There was nothing left behind but a residue of powerless poverty. There were no people on the spot who had leisure enough to take up ordinary civic duties. There were no people of education enough to be able to put the resources of civilization into action. A wholly unnatural condition therefore had been produced ; and the first necessity of all was to bring back into any such stricken district the type of men and women who were normally expected to be there and without whom the civic life could not proceed.

This does not mean an artificial importation of alien elements into conditions to which they do not belong and in which they have no natural office. It is simply the restoration of the natural conditions which our whole public life assumes. It gives back the very people who alone can functionize on behalf of the body. It restores the right relation of people to one another. It re-establishes a graded variation of conditions which will allow for the interchange of services. Residents in Settlement do not go there to patronize or to lecture. They go there to become the normal organs without which human life is unable to exist. They take up the service and duties which must be undertaken by someone if ever the forces which civilization creates are to find channels and instruments through which they can reach those for whom they are designed and who have the right to their beneficial activity. Such was Barnett's idea of a Settlement, and this was the idea which took shape in the Toynbee Hall. From that Hall, through the residents in it, he hoped to build up all the true, and proper, and full, and rich functions of a civic body ; and this the Hall has done consistently and resolutely ever since it began, and with ever-growing skill and experience. This gospel Barnett came down and preached in our College Halls, and the whole University laid hold of it and understood. He came as a prophet just when it was wanted, and men saw in it exactly the opportunity which their gathering interest in the problems of poverty demanded for its exercise and fulfilment. He surprised us by his quiet common-sense. He had nothing about him that excited us. He sometimes spoke with awe and bated breath of things which seemed to us commonplace enough. Once, for instance, in Balliol Hall, he had described to breathless undergraduates all that might be possible for them if they came to work for the poor in London, and then he mentioned, as a culmination of their dreams and aspirations, that possibly they might at last become Poor Law Guardians ! There was rather a sudden fall in the excitement for the moment at this vision of the end ; but we saw gradually that to him this meant that you would have got to the very heart of things in a way that really touches the life and needs of the poor. He was very quiet, but he had a sort of enthusiastic common-sense, and a tenacious wisdom, and a convincing experience, which made people absolutely believe that he knew what he was at and had got hold of the real thing.

At once those undergraduates in Oxford who more especially belonged to the Church of England, required that we should supply them with a like opportunity for service, and the result was that the Oxford House in Bethnal Green rose together with Toynbee Hall, and we held common meetings to plead for both. Henceforward Settlements multiplied everywhere, and Barnett had indeed seen of the fruit of the travail of his soul before he died. He had sown the seed, others had raised the flower. It was true that before him there had been a man of singular nobility of soul called Edward Denison, who, impelled by the inspiration of F. D. Maurice, and charged with pity for the poor, had settled alone in London, and had seen that what was wanted was just that which Barnett's Settlement had completed. But he died young, and his memory is kept alive in Christ's Cathedral by a window at the West end of the South Aisle, noticeable for Burne-Jones's early work. But Barnett was the prophet who had seen the whole thing, and who was ever seeing more, and whom everybody accepted as their master in this matter.

Settlements have long ago passed the prophetic stage, and they have now fallen under criticism ; and there are those who would suggest that they have their limits. Of course they have, and we know what their limits are now. But if what we have said is true, they do not embody any passing mood, but are permanent necessities ; for the conditions which first created them, far from passing away, are rather being aggravated. The dispersion of classes is becoming yet more intense; the desertion of the poorest districts by those who are qualified to organize their administration is more complete than ever. The Settlements, therefore, bringing into action people who otherwise would not be on the spot, and whose presence is absolutely essential to the continuance of civic life, are as vitally needed as ever. People may be less excited about them than they were, but this is through their success, not through their failure. They have become part of the established order of things; and all established orders of things have a certain flatness about them. There may be less flag-waving; but the resolute determination that they should go on and be supplied with men qualified to do the work for which they were intended has become part and parcel of our sense of social obligations. Canon Barnett has done a work which is not going to die. His reputation for organizing practical work hid a little from the public eye his strong spiritual bias. But if we asked him to preach a C.S.U. Sermon for us, at one of our gatherings, he would earnestly and pathetically plead that we should not, as Priests, suffer the serving of tables to choke out that inner life of the spirit which it was our first duty to feed and nourish. He had something of the Quakers' craving for the soul's rest in secret peace.

XI

FATHER STANTON

THERE are few moments more dramatic in our Religious History than the recovery in the Slums by the Oxford Movement of what it had lost in the University. How final that loss looked in Oxford itself can only be realized by those who have heard people like Edward King, of Lincoln, or Oakley, Dean of Manchester, tell of the dark days, when nothing remained of the Movement but the faint flickering flame on the altar at St. Mary's which the loyalty of Charles Marriot still sustained in life. Pusey had been silenced. Newman had gone : and, in his going, had swept the place clean. The Heads of Colleges and the Dean were busy in stamping out the last embers, by refusing Tutorships to known Tractarians, and by bullying the few Catholic Undergraduates who clung to Charles Marriot at St. Mary's. They saw their triumph come. The Provost of Oriel, the President of St. John's, the four Tutors, went about at large seeking whom they should devour. The Cause was lost. So it seemed. When lo ! it suddenly took on an entirely fresh lease of life. It made a new departure. It was to be heard of in all sorts of unexpected places. It wore unanticipated shapes, and spoke a different language. It had ceased to be Academic. It had become popular. It offered itself to every kind of novel opportunity and risk. It plunged into the dark places of our awful cities. It spent itself, with sacrificial ardour, in the service of the Poor. It shirked nothing: it feared nothing. It took blows and insults with a smile. It went ahead, in spite of menace and persecution. It spoke home to sinning souls and broken hearts, fast bound in misery and iron. It invaded the strongholds of Sin. It itself wore poverty as a cloak, and lived the life of the suffering and the destitute. It was irresistible in its élan, in its pluck, in its thoroughness, in its buoyancy, in its self-abandonment, in its laughter, in its devotion. Nothing could hold it. It won, in spite of all that could be done by Authorities in High Places, or by rabid Protestant Mobs, to drive it under.

The Old Leaders still left, Pusey and Keble, found themselves justified, more than they had ever dreamed possible, in their gallant belief that the Church was alive, and was spiritual, and could become, indeed, the Mother of the broken and the poor. It was a magnificent rally of a Cause expelled from its own native home only to win a larger victory elsewhere. And, of this new stage of the Movement, Arthur Stanton was the very star and crown. Other names there are that belong to the heroic hour—Lowder, Linklater, the Pollocks, and their like. At a later date, came along the wonder of Dolling. And, then, there was that splendid band of Missioners—Twells, Bodington, Body, and Knox Little—memorable names. But, amid the crowd who gave to the Movement this second-birth of energy, there is no one quite so typical of its best spirit as Stanton. He gathered up all its

most effective characteristics—all the splendid heroism
of its temper. He gave it its most vivid expression,
through the power of a fascinating personality. And,
then, he lasted it out to its very end. Those flashing
eyes of his retained their fires undimmed. That
beautiful face was alive to the last with all its dramatic
charm and infinite vitality. His heart was as warm
as ever to the young: and as tender as ever to the
outcast and the down-trodden. The Gospel that he
preached held in it all the evangelical ardour of faith
which had been its note from the first. The Bible
still spoke with a live tongue through him. Never
was his spiritual sway over listening souls more potent
than in these very latest years of ministry in the one
spot to which he had dedicated his whole active
Priesthood. The " world " never touched that un-
caged spirit of his. His humour, his spontaneity, his
delightful freshness were still brilliant and abounding,
so that he never appeared to fall under the shadow of
old age. He passed away, at the very summit of his
powers, unflagging, unbeaten, and loved with a quite
peculiar love, by all who owed to him the secret of
their salvation. He was singularly sane, and perfectly human, in all his treatment of souls. He hated
the pettiness into which priestcraft so easily lapses.
He loved independence: health of mind: strength
of judgment: and the open air of nature. He enabled
men to trust themselves, in the light of God's Pardon.
All his healthy scorn went out against convention.
This is why the " Establishment " so sorely tried him
with its intolerable pomposities, and dignities, and

H

proprieties—its stuffiness, its stiffness, its ridiculous posing. He had suffered greatly at the hands of Authority. And St. Alban's bore always the marks of the old prolonged struggle. Its Clergy had been forced to be traditional rebels. They had had to fight with their backs to the wall. They were driven into a sort of isolation which kept them back from mingling with the general life of the Church, even after the struggle was over. Now, there has come about a new period and a new peril. The "Movement" has long ago become a favoured fact. Its dangers are those which come from popularity, from success. It has waxed fat. It has the world with it. It is very easy now to be on its side. It has lost some of that sacrificial fire which belongs to the day of conflict and adventure. All men speak well of it, Bishops and everybody else. That is why a whole generation seemed to close with the death of Arthur Stanton. He was the finest symbol and sample of the men who saved the day for the Cause, when it flung itself out upon its splendid venture in the streets of our stricken Cities. All our hearts go out to Edward Russell who, since 1867, has been as a brother to him, in that incomparable brotherhood at St. Alban's which the years could not break: and who is, to us, the purest and fairest evidence of the beauty of perfect Priesthood. He has all our prayers.

XII

SAMUEL ROLLES DRIVER

THE first result of Dr. Driver's death was to throw back our memory to that day, now so far away, when we trooped to Oxford for that great rally of the old Tractarian movement—the burial of Dr. Pusey. What a passing away it was! In and out of that doorway in the South-west corner of Tom Quad, the wonderful chief had gone ever since 1826. Nobody living could recall the time when he had not been there. And all the amazing days had come and gone: and still the same presence belonged to the same spot. Still, that invincible faithfulness of his persevered, and preserved, and prayed, and toiled, and loved. Still, the grey eyes lifted, now and again, from their lowered bent, and let the prophetic light come through. Still, now and again the burdened face was illuminated by that sudden and incomparable smile which Stanley so vividly remembered. Still, he held the fort, and never swerved or shook. Still he spoke, and wrote, and studied, and counselled. It was as if the whole Past was made present to us, as we watched him pass to and fro. And, at last, the end, so long delayed as to have become almost incredible, had come. The old man was dead. And up from every corner of the country came creeping the old men still left to whom his name had been a watchword and an inspiration. It seemed the last act of the historic Movement. Everything that was left from out of the momentous memories must be there. We younger men watched the long procession of men whose names had been familiar, but whom we had never before seen in the flesh. Here they were—bowed, grey, tottering, making their final effort, delivering their witness to the end. On and on they filed, round and round the quadrangle, bearing the old hero home to his rest, laying his body by the side of the wife whom he had so absorbingly mourned. As they turned away from the grave, they knew that they would never meet again in such a company, on this earth. They too were, now, to pass away with him whose name and presence had meant so much to them. And what would follow ? New issues were beginning to shape themselves inside the old. New problems were knocking at the door. There were fresh questionings : and there must be a fresh response in answer. Change passes over all. Something had ceased which once had moved. The thoughts, the phrases, the watchwords, which had quickened men's souls were not indeed lost, but were taking on a new colour, were accepting a new emphasis and proportion, were assimilating new materials. How far would this process go ? What was to be the extent and the limit of the change ? Who would guide and control the assimilation ? What would, ultimately, be corrected, and what retained ? All this lay in the unknown future. The anxious questions, so varied, affected with peculiar force the very subjects with which the dead chief had dealt. He had hardly touched them himself. His greatness as Professor lay in another direction. He had an intimate and massive knowledge of the old Hebrew Testament which was unrivalled. He was possessed of immense stores of learning. He had unflinching industry: and a wonderful insight into the spirit of the Book. But he had not exercised the historic sense which is sensitive, above all things, to differences of time and place. His mind had been formed, before the formulæ of Evolution and Development had become the normal determinants of all our thinking. His thought did not work in that particular fashion. But it was a big thought, for all that: and could open out to the new Science with surprising freedom of range, when it turned that way. Still, its own method and standards were not those which that critical spirit has now made so familiar. And, therefore, it could not be for him to give us the clue into the new world, nor to equip us for the great adventure of estimating the Old Testament in the light of all that the historical treatment of Comparative Religion had brought to bear upon it. He had other and splendid work to do, which he had nobly achieved: this particular task was still awaiting its master. So we buried him: and, with him, we buried a whole generation, which could never quite recur. As we turned from the grave, we passed into another atmosphere with another perspective. We had left an epoch behind us.

And the man, who could play this particular part, stepped in at once. There were whole domains of spiritual experience in which Dr. Pusey had been master, and which he would leave untouched. But the one thing that Dr. Pusey could never have done for us, he did : and that, at the precise moment of his arrival, was the one thing that, above all others, wanted doing. He was the very man who could best answer the particular question which so urgently besieged us. That old Book ! How did it stand ? What was its purport, its authority, its significance ? By what scales were we to take its measure ? In what terms were we to describe its early stories ? How much did it actually claim to reveal ? And how far was it dependent on exactly the same resources as any other record of man's first religious broodings ? What had it in common with other sacred Books, and in what did it prove itself absolutely unique and distinctive ? Every year a neat incisive French book was pushed across the counter to us. Every other month a cumbrous German tumbled out his loaded wares upon the floor. Now and again a giant like Wellhausen came along and swept us off our feet. Where were we to go, and when to stop ? And, slowly, we found that Driver could give us the answer. He took everything in : but he retained his own judgment : and an admirable judgment it was. He was openminded : level-headed : self-possessed. He never surrendered his own English sanity. He never lost his balance. He could be trusted down to the ground. He was bold where boldness was in place : and he was singularly lucid in saying what he meant. No obscurities disguised his clear decisions. He showed you

why he said what he did : and how his conclusions
were reached. His steadiness of temper never failed
him. He was obviously fair, and straightforward,
and reasonable. He had nothing to conceal : he was
not playing a hand. He simply faced the facts, and
delivered a plain verdict. And all this, with unqualified loyalty to the truth as he found it : and
with unshaken sincerity of intention. As we followed
him, we dropped our fears and our suspicions. We
could not but put confidence in so sure and quiet a
guide. He saw no cause for alarm. He believed in
the friendliness of the light. He could afford to
follow up what was true. And, still, he did not shock,
or disturb, or offend the simplicities of Faith. He
never provoked needless trouble. He never let a
word escape him, which would wound traditional
sentiment. He never jarred or hurt. The sheer
wisdom of the good heart put everything right and
straight. He just said the right thing in the right
way. He just put things in their proper places. And
we became aware how good a workman in these matters
an Englishman can be. It was such a comfort to be
free from the sense of that elderly childishness which
besets German criticism. It labours away with infinite
industry : but it is so uncertain in the handling of its
material, so innocent of proportion and perspective,
so ignorant of the vital values of human experience.
Is it his political training that gives the Englishman
his surer touch on life, his saner estimate of facts ?
Certainly, Driver showed those particular qualities at
their very best, which form our racial and national

contribution to the work of intellectual research. He never failed in the exercise of these qualities. He never flagged in his zeal for study. He never slackened in his patient industry. Always, he kept abreast of the work to be done. Always, he held his knowledge at the disposal of any student, who applied to him for help and guidance. Right to the last he was at it. His last thoughts were concentrated on his study of the Book of Job at which he had begun to work. So he saved the day. So he reassured us. So he taught us how to retain and read the Old Testament with sincerity of heart and faith, gaining, and not losing, by all that the new Criticism had to tell us of its origin and its sources, its history, and its growth. To him more than to any other man we owe it that we were carried over safely from out of one period of thought into another. He devoted himself utterly to the one main purpose of his life. Outside that, he did not attempt to act. He was shy : inarticulate : reserved. He could not freely range beyond his proper tether. But he was felt at once by everyone who came near him to be singularly simple-hearted, guileless, self-less, without the ghost of a personal ambition, without the suspicion of a by-motive. And, then, behind all this, he gave his whole heart away to his wife and to his home. Here, for him, lay all his treasure. He possessed there the response that his soul craved. He died in the simple and pure faith of a little child.

XIII

JOSEPH CHAMBERLAIN

In that solemn hour, when we sat waiting in Westminster Abbey for the coming of Mr. Gladstone's funeral, shrouded in a national sorrow, I found myself looking straight at Mr. Chamberlain during the long silence. And I set myself to the task of finding the signs in that face of the high qualities which the character behind it assuredly possessed. Neither face nor character had succeeded in attracting me. And I felt guilty of some refusal to acknowledge their greatness. And I proposed to acquit myself of that guilt. But, I must own, I was baffled still. I could not make it out. The face, somehow, fenced me off. It refused to disclose its secret. Force, of course, there was, plain enough. No one could mistake the masterfulness, the directness of purpose, the hard energy. But there I stopped. The compact outline had no suggestiveness in it. There seemed no inviting problems to be worked out : no vague impressions : no attractive obscurities : no ins and outs : no minglings : no fancies : no dreams. You left off at the face. You never got deeper. The clear clean surface repelled all inquiry. It prompted no curiosities. It simply asked you to take it or leave it, just as you liked. It was quite indifferent to influence from outside. It remained, fixed and unelastic,

betraying nothing of what was passing before or
behind it. After all my very best endeavour to be
interested, I left off exactly where I had begun.
Now this shows some lack of sympathy on my side,
I have no doubt. Nor do I doubt for a moment that
there were infinite worlds of personal interest which
the face, in silence, only masked. He was, certainly,
capable of kindling intense and enthusiastic affection.
He was a most companionable man, and very delightful
in his companionship. He had personal charm of a
marked character. His own friends, as everybody
knows, were devoted to him like lovers. Birmingham
lived in him. Colleagues in the Cabinet had a quite
peculiar affection for him : and it was particularly
noticeable how he drew into the intimacies of
a cordial friendship a man so far apart from him
in every conceivable quality as Mr. Balfour. He
had a certain magnetism which the stiffness and
coldness of his outward bearing totally failed to
suggest.

Mr. Asquith, in his funeral speech, fastened on the
cardinal significance of Mr. Chamberlain's career. In
him, a new type of Statesman arrived in England. We
had got outside those governing classes which had
historically supplied the country, for years, with the
men it required for its service. These men were
always to be had : with a great tradition behind them :
and a recognized standard of statesmanship. On them,
we had always drawn : and we had known what we
were getting. Outside them, it had been left to the
Law to bring in the new blood that was so necessary.

Through the Law, doors were always open by which new men could step in, by sheer force of ability. And, in spite of the deep-seated distrust of the legal mind in Politics, there were always, in each generation, two or three who survived the imputation of being Lawyers, and were recognized as leading and independent Statesmen. But the men of commerce, though they had filled the Party Ranks, and had done a great deal of useful Parliamentary work, had not yet imposed their own type on the Political world. They had adapted themselves to the established tradition. They had not shown the special characteristics of a new brand. But Chamberlain carried with him into his Politics the mind and form which had been proved under the conditions of Industrialism, in the service of a Commercial Municipality. He had grown up with this background, within these perspectives. And to that which they had helped to make him he gave expression in Parliament with extraordinary vitality and vigour. He applied to Politics the full force of that particular character which an industrial community breeds. He saw facts, and how to work them. He drove, hard and strong, in the direction in which he wanted things to move. He had ideals: and he stuck to them: but they were ideals which struck him swiftly, and immediately, without much thinking. They laid hold of him straight away: and he flung his whole energy into making them effective: and he never looked back. He never reviewed his grounds critically. They passed into his imagination, and all that he had to do was to run them for all that they were worth, with unhesitating sincerity of conviction, with a logical and uncritical whole-heartedness. They were ideals that commended themselves to the plain man. They could be presented in their working habit. They belonged to a flesh-and-blood world, and met its direct and present needs. And he could do battle for them with an incomparable verve that knew and felt no misgivings, and had, at its command, a splendid gift of fighting language. In carrying them through, he was singularly free of party conventions, and traditional watchwords. He relied, as industry had taught him to rely, on his own naked force and his own individual impact. He did not try to link them in with historical associations. He simply went for them bald-headed. That was why it was so easy a matter for him to pass from one side of the House to the other. He had no deep-seated tradition to offend. When once he was clear what he wanted to do, his whole mind was set on getting it done: and it did not so much matter by what Party it was to be carried through. Whatever it was, it had his whole powers at its command. And here it was that he rose to his full height. He was a debater of the first order. In nothing else did he quite attain to the front rank. But, in debate, in pressing his own case, in beating down opposition, in turning aside attack, in retort, in controversy, in vindicating the honour and righteousness of his cause, in all the swift art of rhetorical argument, he was amazingly effective. I should have thought it difficult to imagine a more dangerous adversary on a stormy night in the House of Commons. He could give blows that resounded. He could put his argument into sharp stinging bullets of speech. He caught up cries, and turned them to his own purpose. He was master of himself: and of the situation. Without any positive eloquence, he made language a magnificent weapon, which he wielded with extraordinary alertness. Everything that he said told. It went home. It was rare good business: and the more strained the situation, the better he rose to it. Few could surpass him in the fence and thrust of Parliamentary warfare. And there was no mistaking the honesty of conviction which brought out the whole man into the heat of the fray.

There are three moments in his career which await complete explanation. There is, first, the strange recoil from backing Home Rule under Mr. Gladstone's Leadership. Morley's Life leaves it uninterpreted. The personal equation certainly played a large part in the split. On both sides, there was a lack of personal sympathy and understanding. It was a queer and unfortunate blunder that finally held the two men apart. Then there is the Jameson Raid: and that hurried visit to the G.P.O. at night: and the closing of the inquiry, with the consent of Sir H. Campbell-Bannerman, and Sir W. Harcourt, and Labouchere. What did it all mean? It was a remarkable instance of the command of the tongue that can be exercised by a whole company of people in public life. Not a soul blabbed. What did it mean? Had

Mr. Chamberlain been beguiled innocently by subtler schemers into a position which he had never intended, and could not defend ? No one knows. Anyhow, rival Statesmen proved themselves capable of a very honourable reticence. Then—there is the unhappy handling of the circumstances that led to the Boer War. A book like Sir William Butler's autobiography is disastrous reading. It leaves an indelible mark on the memory. Its direct challenges have been met by a conspiracy of silence. They have never been answered. The tragedy is that if only we could have taken another view of the interpretation of Suzerainty, the thing would have passed under Lord Salisbury and the Foreign Office instead of Mr. Chamberlain at the Colonial Office. And it is morally certain that, if Lord Salisbury had handled the negotiations with President Kruger, there would have been no war. Mr. Chamberlain's methods were far too rough and crude for diplomacy : and his presuppositions far too fixed. He thought war inevitable : and that is a presupposition which would ruin all the chances of Diplomacy. But, whatever judgment may historically be passed on these three episodes, no one will ever doubt Mr. Chamberlain's own absolute sincerity of purpose. He had no intricacies and no subtleties that confused his moral judgment. His intellectual capacity did not work in that way. It was narrowed down to its immediate outlook ; and spent all its force in the one direction in which it was moving. It was shut off from all side issues by the very momentum with which it drove ahead. Thus he was not really tempted by the perplexities that beset those whose range is wider. No doubts disturbed him. No cross-currents confused him. Straight ahead he went: and so retained perfect honesty of conviction.

XIV

CARDINAL NEWMAN

Mr. Wilfrid Ward's "Life of Newman"[1] is a splendid piece of work. It brings us back under the old spell, in spite of all the years that have come between; and it brings home to a generation that lacks personal knowledge what it was to have felt the living touch of John Henry Newman. Once again we feel there was nobody like him; he occupies the entire scene, wherever he is, and we are drawn along by the witchery of an incomparable personality. It is the man himself who enthrals, and the personal equation is never quite absent from anything that he says or does. This no doubt gives to his words and acts that absorbing fascination of which we have spoken. Through every phase of his writing you feel the touch of the man's nature, and the look of his face, and the light of his eyes, and the magic of his voice. You can't get away from him. Every word seems to have in it a human gesture. And therefore it is that something of what poor Kingsley so crudely tried to say, retains a germ of truth. These words and sayings of Dr. Newman's can never detach themselves quite from the particular mood in which he is writing, and the particular situation in which he is involved. They never quite

---

[1] "The Life of Cardinal Newman." By Wilfrid Ward. 2 Vols. Longmans.

acquire a simple, direct, objective value of their own. You have to know why this or that was written just then, and what was the motive at work which made Dr. Newman so write ; and that motive will be found so often, not in the actual thing that has got to be said so much as in some accidental occasion on which he has chosen to say it, or in some indirect effect which he has calculated on producing.

It was true in the old days, as Kingsley clumsily felt, that each sermon in St. Mary's was preached by a preacher whose convictions were themselves in movement and undergoing change ; and this or that sermon would only represent the state of mind that he had reached, just at the moment when he preached it, a state of mind perhaps that he was already leaving behind. The sermons were often signals thrown up of the direction in which he was travelling, and of the immediate anxieties which lay upon his soul. And this did involve the difficulty that they could only be interpreted aright by knowing exactly each passing crisis in relation to which they had been produced. We learn from Dr. Newman that, after all, Kingsley's attack was the occasion for which he had been waiting, so to speak. It supplied him with just that opportunity for justifying himself which he had long felt to be urgent, and all the vehemence and passion of the counter attack are to be understood as necessary for the purpose in view, rather than as spontaneous emotions provoked by Kingsley himself.

Or, again, there is the letter to the Duke of Norfolk. He does not write it because he wants particularly to

I

repel Mr. Gladstone's attack; he would not have written it if that were all. But he writes because the occasion enables him to say what he has to say about his foes in his own House. He is really delivering his mind on Manning and Ward and the " insolent and aggressive faction "; and he can do this without offence under the form of a retort to Mr. Gladstone. All through the difficulties of " The Rambler," and " The Home and Foreign Review," you feel the same complication. He can write strongly against " The Rambler," but the strength that he puts into the repudiation comes from his anger at the way in which " The Rambler " had hurt its own cause by the bad temper in which it has advocated it, while he himself agrees generally with the line on which they are writing. Altogether there is the difficulty of placing, exactly, the man who is so sensitive to his own idiosyncrasies and specialities that he can never quite fall in with anybody else. He is not at one with Döllinger, nor with Simpson and Acton, nor, again, with Dupanloup and Montalembert; so that always explanations are wanted, as to why he is at once with them, and yet not with them; and always there is a little aloofness preserved; and you feel at last that Dr. Newman must be Dr. Newman; he cannot commit himself quite to anything entirely outside his own intimate personality. And yet his loyalty to the Body is complete, and his desire to serve is passionately sincere, and his real humility is most touching. It is simply a sort of spiritual fastidiousness, that makes him conscious always of the personal element itself, to a degree that weakens action. And yet again, we see it is just this personal element which draws our very souls to him, as we feel the depth of the significance that he put into his own chosen motto " *Cor ad cor loquitur.*"

And as we once more revive our love for the man, how tragic is the treatment that this heart of his, with which he spoke, received; the wounds that he had in the house of his friends! There is Rome, the incredible, impossible, intolerable Rome, with its Italian Cardinals, who have not the faculties by which to understand the language that Newman is speaking, or the anxieties that he feels. They have not a notion what England is, or the English, or why the Catholic Laity feel themselves ousted from all true citizenship, and unable to take their place with their fellows. All Newman's soul beats up in vain against blind walls; they have not a notion what he is talking about. What can Cardinal Barnabo make of it? England, in Newman's sense, is to him an unknown land. There are few passages more brilliantly funny than Newman's own précis of his conversation with Cardinal Nina. Poor Cardinal Nina! He came to him as a friend, meaning to be so kind, and to say all the nice things; and little knew the biting irony with which they were being recorded.

And then the Pope. Newman goes with his whole heart surrendered and submitted, just to lay his life at the feet of the successor of the Apostles. And imagine what it was to find at Rome, between him and the Holy Father, a jolly, bluff, ignorant Irishman, in the person of Monsignor Talbot! He cannot get past this man and his influence. It is Talbot who has the Holy Father's ear; it is Talbot upon whom his prospects of conciliation depend. If we want to know how this galled, we have only to read the bitter little note in which Newman declines the kindly offer of the Monsignor that he should preach to a really educated Protestant audience in his Church at Rome. This is too much for Dr. Newman. "However," he says, "even Birmingham people have souls," and "I have neither taste nor talent for the sort of work which the Monsignor would cut out for me." He begs to decline his offer.

And there is the Holy Father himself, most lovable of men, but absolutely ignorant what the problem is which his own infallibility is required to solve; utterly ignorant of all the intellectual anxieties which are sweeping over the minds of the laity as Newman knows them; utterly unaware that there are such anxieties; utterly out of touch with the very situation which cries aloud for his infallible authority to act. He smiles and jokes his way along, and carries the Council with him to declare his infallibility, by sheer delight in his good-humoured puns. And yet you love him all the time, and are amused to find that in the end he has passed the definition of his own Infallibility in the contrary sense to the one which he himself intended. For certainly it has come out that the Infallibility proclaimed is to be understood, not in the sense of the party who carried it, but in the sense of those minimizers whom they decried; so that instead of Mr. W. G. Ward's vision of a Papal Bull arriving every morning for your breakfast with "The Times" and toast, there has not been really one single infallible utterance in the forty years that have followed the proclamation.

The hopeless incapacity of Rome to understand and use Dr. Newman gave him those thirty-five miserable years which the piteous photographs in Mr. Ward's book make visible. The only thing I regret is the publication of that pitiful picture of Dr. Newman seated on a chair with Father Ambrose St. John. It is too depressing, and serves to explain the overwhelming pathos of that sight at Littlemore, in 1868, recorded by Canon Irvine, who saw, leaning over the Lych Gate, sobbing as in deep trouble, the worn, broken figure of a poorly dressed old man, with the collar of his old grey coat pulled up to hide his face, and the flaps of his hat pulled down, so that Canon Irvine could not persuade himself that it was really Dr. Newman, there by the wall. Thank God the sun came at last, and gave him the peace in which he died. He had said piteously before, that the power of ever believing in and trusting his superiors had ceased to exist for him, and no wonder that he said it, after all those wretched years of disappointment, when time after time the support that had been promised him from headquarters would die away from under him, without his knowing why, or how, only made aware that things had turned against him by the silent suction which withdrew from him all on which he had been led to count. It is the silence with which the thing is done which is so appalling. Nobody speaks, but it all happens, and the thing that he has set his heart to do is not to be done, and he cannot tell why.

But with the Cardinalate came the return of confidence, and the one man who had understood, Leo XIII.; and it is just like Newman to be touched almost to excess, and beyond bounds, by finding himself at last personally trusted. He is like a child in the delight with which he gives himself to the sunshine, and the favour. Every quick instinct in him revives, and he is keen to put his new position to use, now that no one can block the way for a live Cardinal, who can speak for himself to the Holy Father, and can make his own opinions felt and prevail. He is full of his old task, that of giving to the Catholic youth some chance of intellectual hold upon their traditional Creed. He still foresees that terrible torrent of infidelity that is coming, under the storm of which all Faith will go down which cannot ground itself in rational convictions. He will be at it; he will bring out all his old weapons, now finely polished, and perfectly equipped. But, indeed, old age was upon him, and he had not time now to do what might have been done in the lost years behind him. He pours out his heart now, as ever, to those elect friends of the Anglican days who had always understood him, and had never failed him through the darkest hours. There is always a touch of sunlight comes to him whenever he takes up his pen to write to Frederick Rogers, or R. W. Church; and always for them he is light and airy, and brisk and humorous, and natural, and absolutely charming. There is nothing stands between him and them, and he knows that he may say everything to the friends who know, and so satisfy that personal craving for sympathy and understanding which from first to last is the note of the man.

There are some quaint revelations about his private devotions. Is he at play here, or is it irony? Certainly, he lets his fancy go. He is most familiar with his beloved St. Philip, whose boots he would be delighted to black in heaven if only St. Philip wears boots there. He asks him for many things, and constantly detects his helping hand. On the other hand, he really has to scold him for allowing him to get into such messes as he does, and he rather wishes that Our Lady would speak a word or two to St. Philip, to make him more careful and more attentive. There is a most amusing correspondence with a Holy Mother, who wishes to put her special image to full use on Dr. Newman's behalf in the crisis of the Achilli trial. But Newman thinks that this might be putting too much of a strain on Our Lady: he would not like to get her into difficulties. "However," he writes, "I am a disbelieving old beast," and the confession may be taken for what it is worth. His reasons for believing in the miracle of Loretto are amazing, and call forth a little warning note from Mr. Wilfrid Ward. Evidently, Dr. Newman liked to indulge in this vein of childishness, and seemed to find relief in it, as well as some amusement.

" Lead, kindly Light." Time after time, through the two volumes, these words of the immortal hymn seem to rise in one's heart as the one perfect expression of the life that is being lived before our eyes. Time after time Mr. Ward himself finds them the only words that befit the occasion. Did Dr. Newman use them, himself, of himself, as the long days dragged on ? Certainly they are charged with just the temper that carries him through ; and always there seems vibrating in his voice and lingering about his strangely plaintive face the feeling of one who is wistfully seeking the home that he never finds and who only waits to see again the vision of the angel-faces that he has lost awhile. " Lead, kindly Light ! " The words have passed into the imagination and literature of England ; and, always, they will bind the heart of the entire people to the memory of a man who once read out, in bitter experience, under the " encircling gloom," the full force of their pathetic secret.

XV

HENRY SIDGWICK

HE sat patching up the poor little tent that he had managed to set up, within which he hoped to house the philosophy of common-sense. So he pictures his intellectual career. How uninviting, and uninspiring the task sounds! Could anything be duller and dismaller than that? What place can be found for heroism or hope? Yet it was impossible for Henry Sidgwick not to interest and to attract everyone with whom he came in touch. He could not be dull or dismal if he tried. He was invariably charged with delightful and stimulating energy. There was nothing human from which he stood aloof; no department of life from which he shut himself off. Always, he carried with him an alert and kindly hopefulness: he woke up all that had the capacity to wake: he was alive with quick and ready sympathies. Nor did he fail to bring something into play which had vital inspiration in it, and the light of an heroic purpose. This is what makes it so difficult to speak of him without conveying a wrong impression. If you try to describe his speculative position, or his spiritual attitude, or his political and economic outlook, it is bound to wear the air of something a little ineffectual and uncertain. He hovers: he distinguishes: he waits: he cannot arrive: he is in suspense. He sees this: and that: and more: and less: and steers a dubious way, at last, that is eclectic and individual: and can build no school nor leave a definite mark on philosophic thinking.

Yet he himself was singularly effective: he told at once, and decisively, on those who came under him. He was spontaneous: and fertile, and eminently ready. He had his resources in hand, and brought them into play with ease and rapidity. Everybody felt his importance: his authority: his readiness: his insight: his weight. He counted for much. He was a most valuable and effectual intellectual asset. There was no hanging-back: no indecision: no vague and doubtful handling. The entire man was at your service, equipped and complete.

So, again, reading his Life,[1] you might easily imagine him to be cursed with the malady of introspection. He is greatly engaged in self-analysis: his self-criticism is alarmingly acute, and searching, and busy. He lies, throughout life, under the necessity of questioning his final convictions, and of determining the conditions of his doubts. Something ineffectual, here too, you might suppose: something morbid, and anxious. Yet no one could see or know Henry Sidgwick for a moment, and even tolerate the thought of his being overstrained or morbid. That is just what his whole being denied. He was transparently simple, direct, forthcoming: he seemed utterly unself-occupied: he had no anxious preoccupations: he

[1] "Henry Sidgwick."   A Memoir.   By A. S. and E. M. S. Macmillan.

gave himself to his company with singular and most charming freedom : he was obviously possessed of the true spirit of inward cheerfulness, which enlightened his countenance, and gladdened all his speech. Never, surely, was there anyone who brought fewer shadows with him : who was so quick to lend himself out to any interest that was moving ; who could so lightly and joyfully enter into almost any companionship that opened to admit him. Never was there a temper more genial in its co-operation with others : more keenly sensitive to all that gives enjoyment to human intercourse : more selfless in the give and take of talk. He was a prince of good companions. And, always, with his kindly gaiety, he made everyone aware how wise, and sane, and good was his outlook : how fair his judgment : how humane his experience. His typical manner in company made everybody happy : and had in it a freshness, like keen and sweet air. The effect is admirably told by his nephew, A. C. Benson :

" The actual manner of his talk was indescribably attractive ; his gentle voice, his wise and kindly air, as he balanced arguments and statements, the gestures of his delicate hands, his lazy and contented laugh, the backward poise of his head, his updrawn eyebrows, all made it a pleasure to watch him. Yet his expression as a rule tended to be melancholy, and even wistful.

" I remember once a supreme instance of his conversational powers. It was at a small dinner-party ; he took in a lady whose social equipment was not great, and who was obviously ill at ease. I wondered what subject he would select. He began at once on the subject of the education of children, in the simplest way, as though he only desired information.

The lady, who had a young family, became at once communicative and blithe ; and what might have been a dreary business was turned into a delightful occasion."

To this sympathetic temperament nothing human came amiss : he was never moody, or unequal, or uncertain, or cold, or preoccupied, or out of touch. Yet we can see, in this memoir, how much there was to depress his buoyancy, and to cloud his sunshine. He felt so sorely what he had missed. He doubted his own capacities. He looked out wistfully at heroism and enthusiasm that was denied him. He belonged to the Mid-Victorian days, where men still were miserable over the wreck of their faith. It was still a solemn and an awful thing, to have doubts. To Roden Noel, or Myers, or H. G. Dakyns he writes pathetically about himself ; for example :—

To H. G. Dakyns, Feb., 1873.

" As for me, I cannot write easily ; I have been for some time in one of my moods of disquieting self-contempt, which cannot be made to vanish by the mere imagination of a friend.

" This I wrote days ago. The truth is that the ' Weltschmerz ' really weighs on me for the first time in my life ; mingled with egoistic humiliation. I am a curious mixture of the *megalopsychos* and *micropsychos ;* I cannot really care for anything little ; and yet I do not feel myself worthy of—or ever hope to attain—anything worthy of attainment.

" Ethics is losing its interest for me rather, as the insolubility of its fundamental problem is impressed on me. I think the contribution to the *formal* clearness and coherence of our ethical thought which I have to offer is just worth giving : for a few speculatively minded persons—very few. And as for

all practical questions of interest, I feel as if I had now to
begin at the beginning and learn the A B C.

" Why this letter has been so long in writing I do not quite
know. Perhaps it is owing to a peculiar hallucination under
which I labour that I shall suddenly find my ideas cleared up
—say the day after to-morrow—on the subjects over which I
brood heavily. Take this as a psychological phenomenon. I
am now working at a review of Herbert Spencer, which, I
think, adds to my general despair."

Again to Myers, July 6th, 1873 :—

" I have had spiritual reasons enough to write to you for a
long time, but they have all been outweighed by the sort of
lethargy of spirit in which I still linger, feeling that my little
stream of life, with its mingled current half speculative, half
transcendental-human, has run itself into a sort of sandy
desert, where it is temporarily spreading and drying up and
flowing underground andaltogether behavingin an unaccountable manner. . . ."

Or again to the same on August 1st :—

" My only merit (if it be a merit) is that I have never
swerved from following the ideal

'Evermore unseen
And fixt upon the far sea line,'

but I have a double sorrow, first, that I cannot come to know
the relation of the ideal to the actual ; and, secondly, that I
myself show so mean and uncomely to my own vision. Further
as to you, I have another sadness in feeling that during the
years in which we have exchanged thoughts I have unwillingly
done you more harm than good by the cold corrosive scepticism
which somehow, in my own mind, is powerless to affect my
'idealism,' but which I see in more than one case acting

otherwise upon others. Still your friendship is one of the best delights of my life, and no difference of ethical opinion between us can affect this, though it may increase my despondency as to things in general. . . ."

Such introspection is sad enough, and the question is still—how did he succeed in so conquering this interior self that it had no effect at all upon the impression he produced on others ? The answer is plain enough. In spite of all his intellectual hesitation over the deepest problems of life and conduct, he possessed in himself absolute soundness and sweetness of moral character. It was this that shone through his whole being. It was impossible not to trust, with absolute confidence, in a nature so genial, so kindly, and so sane. Men felt certain that they could lean on him with perfect security, and man after man turned to this philosopher who could discover no intellectual basis for ethics, for the surest and deepest counsels that they could obtain in a moral crisis. They felt with him as Glaucon or Adeimantus feel at the opening of the second book of the Republic, when Socrates has left no convictions standing and the moral world lies round them in ruins under his merciless dialectic, and who yet turn to the very man whose criticism has been so destructive as to the one man in all the world whom they can still trust to re-erect the ethical world and restore their moral confidence. Perhaps Sidgwick may be unconsciously sketching himself as he writes to F. Myers in April, 1872 :—

" My difficulty is that I cannot give to principles of conduct either the formal certainty that comes from exact science or the practical certainty that comes from a real Consensus of Experts. And I feel that your peculiar phase of the ' Maladie ' is due to the fact that you demand certainty with special peremptoriness—certainty established either emotionally or intellectually. I sometimes feel with somewhat of a profound hope and enthusiasm, that the function of the English mind with its uncompromising matter-of-factness, will be to put the final question to the Universe with a solid, passionate determination to be answered which *must* come to something."

Such soundness of moral heart as this must come to something ; and is it not obvious why Clough had such an intense personal fascination for him ? For in Clough we have the same spiritual phenomenon : (1) A delicate, sensitive self-analysis which acts as a paralysis on certainty of conviction, and yet (2) a fresh and genial soundness of disposition, peculiarly English and sturdy in its moral health, and forcing on one the assurance that he knows and will come through and find himself at last. Sidgwick's finest expression of this temper is given in the famous letter on the effect of Tennyson's " In Memoriam " on the men of his generation :

" Well, the years pass, the struggle with what Carlyle used to call ' Hebrew old clothes ' is over, Freedom is won, and what does Freedom bring us to ? It brings us face to face with atheistic science : the faith in God and Immortality, which we have been struggling to clear from superstition, suddenly seems to be *in the air ;* and in seeking for a firm basis for this faith we find ourselves in the midst of the ' fight with death ' which *In Memoriam* so powerfully presents.

" What *In Memoriam* did for us, for me at least, in this struggle, was to impress on us the ineffaceable and ineradicable conviction that *humanity* will not and cannot acquiesce in a godless world ; the ' man in men ' will not do this, whatever individual men may do, whatever they may temporarily feel themselves driven to do, by following methods which they cannot abandon to the conclusions to which these methods at present seem to lead.

" The force with which it impressed this conviction was not due to the *mere intensity* of its expression of the feelings which atheism outrages and agnosticism ignores ; but rather to its expression of them along with a reverent docility to the lessons of science which also belongs to the essence of the thought of our age.

" I always feel this strongly in reading the memorable lines [cxxiv.] :—

> If e'er when faith had fallen asleep
> I heard a voice, ' Believe no more,'
> And heard an ever-breaking shore
> That tumbled in the Godless deep ;
>
> A warmth within the breast would melt
> The freezing reason's colder part,
> And like a man in wrath the heart
> Stood up and answered, ' I have felt.'

" At this point, if the stanzas had stopped here, we should have shaken our heads and said, ' Feeling must not usurp the function of Reason. Feeling is not knowing. It is the duty of a rational being to follow truth wherever it leads.'

" But the poet's instinct knows this ; he knows that this usurpation by feeling of the function of Reason is too bold and confident ; accordingly in the next stanza he gives the turn to humility in the protest of Feeling which is required

(I think) to win the assent of the ' man in men ' at this stage of human thought :

> No, like a child in doubt and fear :
>   But that blind clamour made me wise ;
>   Then was I as a child that cries,
> But, crying, knows his father near ;
>
> And what I am beheld again
>   What is, and no man understands ;
>   And out of darkness came the hands
> That reach through nature, moulding men.

" These lines I can never read without tears. I feel in them the indestructible and inalienable minimum of faith which humanity cannot give up because it is necessary for life ; and which I know that I, at least so far as the man in me is deeper than the methodical thinker, cannot give up."

All through his life Sidgwick seems to have felt that if Theism is to be retained by the mass of men, it will only be through the heart that can be thrown into it in its Christian form. But this was always crossed by the doubt whether the support of religion to Theistic morals, which had hitherto shown itself to be vital and necessary, might not turn out to be a stage only towards the time when men would find sufficient to ground their morals on a social instinct. Yet again this very doubt was itself traversed by fresh speculations as to how Christianity might yet show itself able to meet modern intellectual needs. Dr. Gore notes especially how eager and keen was his interest, to the very last, in the hopes that might yet make everything new to him.

K

Throughout his life he counted as a force that ever made for all that was fair and honourable in men's lives. He taught us all what sincerity of purpose ought to mean, and what it is to retain spiritual veracity as the moving and dominant principle of life. He was a born friend and won affection from every side. He became the very embodiment of conscience to those with whom he was in touch, and few men can have passed away so utterly unbesmirched by the world. The secret of it all is given in the words with which Dr. Gore takes his farewell of him:

" One could not know him without thinking that neither the world, the flesh, nor the devil had any place in him or about him. There was in him an extraordinary simplicity and goodness. When I came away from the last interview with him—after the operation from which reprieve was hoped, but which in the event proved to be not much more than the prelude to the end—after that last interview, when he had talked with his habitual grace and vigour and cheerfulness, and with a most moving courage in the face of death, there was only one thought which came to my mind, in which I seemed in the least degree able to sum up and express the impression which was left upon me, and it was that most sacred of all promises—' Blessed are the pure in heart; for they shall see God.' "

I saw him on that evening recorded in the memoir, when he took the chair at the Synthetic Society, immediately after the fatal sentence had been delivered by the physician. He betrayed it by no sign at all. He spoke on Prayer: on its broad, genuine justification: on its limitations in regard to particular

requests. In all, he retained his sweet serenity, his
unclouded lucidity, his sanity of purpose. Looking
back, afterwards, in the light of what we then knew,
I could just recall a keener glitter in the eyes than
was usual with him, and a slightly heightened tone of
intensity. That was all. Remembering the goodness
and the beauty of his character, it is impossible not
to think of all that had got to be given to it, of richer
development. Here, on earth, to the very last, it was
still in suspense, waiting for the moment in which it
might surrender itself wholly to the great venture of
faith. Still, the thought held back; still, the brain
was hampered in its effort to arrive: still it was forbidden to him to fling his whole manhood forward
under the compulsion of assured convictions. There
was still, therefore, a lack of élan: of total freedom:
of vital and unhesitating release. This was the
consummation for which he tarried. He was far too
sincere to force it: yet, until it came, the whole
fullness of his life had yet to be revealed. The long
discipline of delay here, in its thoroughness, in its
sincerity, will, surely, find its interpretation elsewhere,
when the travail of the soul has been completed.
Reading the life through, with its wistful and delicate
charm, one could be sure that it was not in vain that
he passed away, still eager in pursuit of the truth in
Christ, towards which every spiritual tendency in
him had ever pressed.

XVI

JOSEPH HENRY SHORTHOUSE

THE sight of the Life and Letters of J. H. Shorthouse,[1] by his wife, awakes the old thrill that shook our blood thirty-five years ago. How wonderful it was to feel the advent of a really new book—to recognize a moment that would be memorable! No doubt, we lost our heads a little. We used very big language. We exceeded. Things have recovered themselves since then: and a certain balance and perspective have been reached. And there has been the natural reaction that followed the slow discovery that Shorthouse had shot his bolt: and that nothing more would come from him on that level. Once again, we found that we were in face of a writer who could put his whole message into a single output: and it is always difficult to credit, and to finally estimate, a " single speech Hamilton " and a single poem Wolfe, and a single book Shorthouse. Yet the thing can be done: and the actual product must be taken at its own proper value. It is an ideal that ought to be sustained for the encouragement of men who find themselves possessed of a very distinct gift, which, nevertheless, cannot bulk large and suggests a limited store of energy. Why should not men of this type succeed through concentration ? Their chance of working for posterity

[1] "J. H. Shorthouse's Life and Letters." By his wife. Macmillan.

is to produce some one thing of their very best, into
which a life's effort is crowded, and on which a whole
world of pains has been bestowed.

So this or that man has come and gone, leaving
behind him the one lyric that will haunt the memory
of man as long as hearts are young : the one hymn,
that will be sung year after year, with a sob in the
voice and a tightening of the throat, while mourners
stand to watch a coffin sink into an open grave. Such
triumphs have been won by men of the second rank,
whose vital force is not sufficient to hold out for more,
but who can yet leave behind them just one little
memory, which the world will not willingly let die.
" John Inglesant " may yet prove that this can be
done. We read, in the Life, how complete and how
deep was the absorption that went to its making.
Shorthouse was writing it for himself : and into it he
put himself : and he thought of no public, but only of
the delight of saying what he felt, and of embodying
all that could give this earth a meaning and a sanctity
for him. Ten years he brooded : and, bit by bit,
he wrote : and over it he hung ; and round about it
his imagination clung, and his reason pondered : and
he watered it with his anxieties : and he fed it with
his hopes : and he nursed it in his dreams : and he
fused it with the fires of his spiritual ardour. He
spent himself in giving it its perfect form and finish :
he feasted himself on the delight of searching out the
most delicate and exquisite expression. So there, at
last, it emerged, with all this intensity of personal
existence to quicken and ensoul it. And it found its

response at once. Men knew the touch. The thing was alive. It was a strange, eerie, moonlit, ecstatic life : but life it was, with the soul of a man in it. And we all went mad : and Mr. Gladstone enheartened us in our faith by giving us the utmost sanction, in that, as he solemnly assured us, not only did *he* rank the book so highly : that, of course, would be of little weight : but there was more than that to be said, for " Arthur Godley agreed with him."

And, indeed, looking back at it now, there is a special note of charm and distinction in the book which ought to be sufficient to preserve it, in a permanent siding of its own, amid the general deposit of transmitted Literature. There are certain dramatic moments in it which, in their own way, stand alone ; such as that in which all that is chivalrous and heroic in Inglesant goes into the utterance of the famous lie, by which he saves the King's honour ; or, again, the hardening of the man in him, as he faces the hostile howl of the mob, hungry for his blood as a spy ; or, again, the magical hour at Little Gidding ; and yet again, in the mountain shrine, where he offers his vow, on that fair Umbrian morning, which breathes peace and forgiveness.

There is an atmosphere, delicate and subtle, admirably sustained throughout. There is a real beauty of style : and a certain vague dreaminess of outlook, which holds us as in a trance ; and the scene is suffused as in the mystic glamour of a mellow Autumn morn : and there is a spiritual finesse, which, however lacking in robust force, has yet a winning wistfulness about it, such as marks the true pilgrim wandering between two eternities. We may have been slightly bribed into undue delight by the surprise of finding our familiar Anglicanism lifted up into the throne of the mystical and poetical ideal. That unhappy air of being a Via Media, a half-way house, was gone: it was transfigured into the fine and delicate poise of the free soul, moving, entranced along a secret path, known only to the elect, amid the perilous ambushes that might ensnare it on the right hand or the left, if it ever wavered or swerved. We had the same feeling as we read, which, according to Dr. Newman, swept over the Bishops and Clergy as they bewilder-ingly recognized themselves in the high imagery of the Christian Year. Only, we were pleased and flattered. It is so seldom that the poets and the artists notice us: or make anything of us. We are the prey, generally, of "Punch," and of screaming farces, and of the shocking sketches of our performances in the Illustrated Papers. The literary imagination but rarely recognizes their opportunity in us. It fastens on the rough and ready lines that are always at its hand, in Papist or Puritan. So we suffer in silence under this cold neglect: until, at last, our confidence in our own picturesque and imaginative possi-bilities dwindles, and we half doubt whether our Anglican position permits of artistic treatment. We despair of ever getting beyond the stage and level of "the Private Secretary." That, we sorrowfully suppose, will be our highest appearance in the Litera-ture of the Imagination. Even a Surrey melodrama, with an heroic Curate in spotless collar and cuffs, and a magnificent muscular development, hardly suffices for our consolation. And it was, therefore, with a bound of relief, that we found at last some one who could do us justice. Yes! And who could drape our particular attitude in a mystic haze of wonder and glory, of which we, in our wildest moments, had hardly felt ourselves capable.

On the other hand, gracious and imaginative as was the story of John Inglesant's spiritual pilgrimage, it wore the air of being only adapted for the elect. It was too subtle, and too rare, for the common ruck of men. It showed us a faith which haunted secret shrines, aloof and special. Our pilgrim picked his way along, with the deft and careful singularity of a cat along a wet garden path, stopping at intervals to wash its face with its paws, and to take a watchful look round against the peril of a possible dog.

Something too much there was of this. The soul was too afraid of besmirching itself : it was strangely individual, in its subjective demand to move on along its own separate career, on the lines that it sifted curiously out for its own peculiar direction. The big world is only there as a maze through which it has to find the best clue for its own safe arrival. Men and women play upon it : but they are of significance only so far as their influence tells on it. They come and go : it uses them : and passes on, working out its own spiritual fate. This solitary eclecticism gave an unearthly charm to the moving figure, but it left it, also, rather thin, and glamorous, and moonlit. It

lacked breadth: and solidity: and force. And all
the more, when it was liable to strange trances in
which it yielded itself to hypnotic pressure, whether
in the body, or out of the body, we can hardly tell.
The burly world of flesh and blood seemed very far
away from this elect visionary. This temper was
intensified in the later work of Mr. Shorthouse: and,
gradually, the magical little stories, with their delicate
embroidery of spiritual sentiment, became such stuff
as dreams are made of. Still, they had the fine charm
of the style: and they convey a pathetic sense of the
passion of this pure soul, in its Birmingham Office,
for all the rich fragrance of high old-world society,
slowly stepping along its marbled terraces in forgotten
gardens where silent statues brood over shining
waters, and no breath of the common air ruffles the
courteous dignity of unhurried days. It was the
recoil from Birmingham, and Vitriol, and Mr. George
Dixon, that spoke in all this. And that gave it dramatic
significance. At last, in the Preface to George Herbert,
the eclecticism went beyond our patience: and
pleaded for a religion that should be a perquisite
of the refined. This brought us to a stop. He wrote
but little more.

He was delightful to meet. In the first excitement,
we eagerly invited him over to Oxford, and he came
and talked metaphysics and religion with our " gang."
He was disappointing in appearance: rather thick
and short: with nothing notable about the face. And
he had one of those terrific stammers, which keep
you in an agony of suspense lest something should

give way : and he had the true stammerer's courage which fights its way through to the word it wants, and resolutely declines the hopelessly inadequate phrase offered it by pitying outsiders. But he never let this hinder his talk : and never showed any self-consciousness over it. He spoke freely : and earnestly : and was most winning. I recall a discussion in which he took an out-and-out mystical-platonic line : and implored us to abandon all outworks of every kind that embodied the Christian Ideal, and to fall back, for defence of the Creed, upon him and his chosen knights who alone would stand in the great day of Armageddon. But as he frankly confessed that a knight of the true Order only occurred about once in a century, we dimly felt that our fighting line would be rather thin, when we called up our last reserves. But no such fear troubled him. He was dauntless. One saw how dearly he loved the few, the elect : and how aloof he was from the pressure of facts in his glamorous and fascinating garden of romance.

Yet, after all, was it not this very aloofness, this very rarity, which gave to him his distinction, and to us the delight of surprise ?

Out of Birmingham it had come to us — this adoration of the delicate and the rare ! Out of Birmingham, this breathless awe at the mystery of things —this fine Platonic touch—this dream of the unseen —this vapour of romance ; out of the heart of the black Midlands ! Out of Philistia, this vision ! Out of the carcase of the dead lion this exquisite honey ! That was the secret of our rapture. Once again the

immortal victory had been won. Once again the dull
dunder-headed stolidities of Commercialism had shat-
tered into fragments under the uprush of the
imagination. Once again the Horn of Roland had
been blown in the cleft of Roncesvalles ; and all the
Fontarabian echoes were awake. The spell of Italy
had found its way into the little back office with its
stools and desk : and had drawn a soul out into the
light with all its ancient efficacy. The touch of
mystic romance can win its victories amid the Hard-
ware House as surely as on Umbrian Hills. Wonderful!
The undying miracle repeats itself. That is what
thrilled us : and above all when the miracle led us
home to our own English shrines, and found its rest
in the tender delicacies of English lawns round grey-
toned minsters.

How this wonder came about ; how it grew into
life at Birmingham ; is told in his wife's book. There
we are admitted into the spiritual beauty of a Quaker
home : and we learn that not all our Midland middle-
class were of the type that filled Mr. Matthew Arnold
with such incurable anguish. No doubt, provincial
Philistinism was, in those far-off days, unspeakable :
but Quakerism is of another kidney. It has always
kept itself sensitive and fine and gracious : and it added
to this, in Shorthouse's case, the keen play of wit,
and gay debate, and happy intimacies. Here is a
happy picture :

"It was in 1850 that he first accompanied our party on a
journey. We went into Yorkshire, to Settle, Malham Cove,
and Gordale Scar ; into Wharfedale, to Bolton Bridge, the

Strid, and Barden; to Fountains and Rievaulx Abbeys; thence into Teesdale and to Scarborough and Whitby. Though he was only sixteen, there were the same characteristics which form so marked a personality now. He was a dreamer—one whose imagination acted the part to himself of ' guide, philosopher, and friend.' This was the great interpreter of nature, art, life, and of everything else. He was a poet born, idealizing everything, and it must be this power that has made him an historian. Certain historical events took complete possession of him at this time, and, though he appeared desultory and to dislike patient study, he had a faculty by which he appropriated every fact, however small, which illustrated the event.

" Thus there was built up in his mind a picture, ideal but true, of the past, and he had a wonderful power of putting this ideal picture into language. He was even then a brilliant conversationalist, very vigorous in argument, and anything but dreamy when stirred up by opposition.

" He responded to the moods of Nature with a sensitiveness that was natural to him, but it was her quiet aspects which most affected him. He was a native of ' the land where it is always afternoon.' There were certain scenes on these walks which appealed to the poetic faculty within him, and deeply moved him—the bridge at Eskdale Mill in the August heat, Wastdale Head by moonlight, the valley of the Duddon under a low sun on a hazy afternoon, and the old church at Seathwaite, with its everlasting dream of peace."

Mr. Hunter Smith, who writes a short introduction, gives an admirable picture of the bewilderment of Birmingham at this citizen:

" The average Birmingham citizen ' was somewhat in the position of a Weaver Bottom, who, through a troubled dream, is dimly conscious of a world of mystery and glamour, which he could in no way realize.'

" There was something monstrous to the imagination of

the practical common-sense man that he should meet on
'Change a man whose favourite word was ' mystic,' who
seemed no less shrewd in that place than other men, yet
seemed to be in some quaint way an onlooker in the game,
sometimes seemed to be indulging in quaint soliloquies, and
had a Chaucerian twinkle in his eye and a smile on his face
which might be kindly or might be sarcastic.

" So that neither in politics, nor religion, nor greatly in his
habits of life, was the author of ' John Inglesant ' much in
harmony with the majority of his fellow-citizens. The
assertion of individual religion they could understand, the
opposition to certain phases of other people's religion they
could understand; but the blend of freedom of thought with
scrupulous attention to religious observances, which was the
chief note to outward observers of Shorthouse's character—
that was a thing they could not ' reckon up.' A man who
could not be labelled Low Church or High Church, and was
neither a Unitarian nor a Ritualist, was to the average Birmingham citizen in those days an unknown quantity."

And then he gives his own estimate of Shorthouse,
with singular success:

" Is it displaying an exaggerated partiality for my friend's
memory to say of him, with due modification, as Dean Church
says of Spenser, that few of his time approached him in
' feeling the presence of that commanding and mysterious
idea, compounded of so many things, yet of which the true
secret escapes us still, to which we give the name of beauty ?
A beautiful scene, a beautiful person, a mind and character
with that combination of charms which, for want of another
word, we call by that half-spiritual, half-material word
" beautiful," at once set his mind at work to respond to and
reflect it.' And this also is true of all the work of Shorthouse :
' Face to face with the Epicurean idea of beauty and pleasure
is the counter-charm of purity, truth, and duty.' "

The book gives at length an appeal for the agnostic at Communion, which Shorthouse wrote to the " Spectator," and which had in it much of his mind. I remember well discussions over it with him, and how we thought he was perhaps pressing his point to the verge of intellectual insincerity. We were prepared to set no barriers that would hinder the approach of a wistful and inarticulate agnosticism. We pleaded, I think, that the case became difficult where there was a formulated counter-creed, which desired not so much to arrive some day at the Faith of the Church, as to bring the Church's Faith over to its own formula. However, whatever the little differences we had about this, he had got true and strong possession of the real heart of sacramentalism, and he saw clearly how far wider were the possibilities of reconciliation that lay in taking an Action as the symbol of union rather than a Creed. An act allows for every variety of approach and of interpretation, and yet is itself positive and concrete and solid. Thus it is that a sacrament may bind together into vital cohesion those who can find hardly any other mode of expressing their unity of belief. And the Church's bond of union is, after all, a sacrament, of which the creed is but the authorized interpretation. This cannot be better expressed than in Shorthouse's own words in a letter written to Dr. Talbot, Bishop of Winchester :

" Of course I know that there are differences between us, but we agreed upon this, at least, that in all the world's story

there is no form of comfort and consolation to the masses
of the people, suffering and sinning, like that of Jesus of
Nazareth ; that no revelation of the Divine has ever spoken
with any force beside this revelation ; and that in the sacrament
the nearest approach is given us to this unique Consoler, apart
from all the mistakes and misrenderings, and misapprehensions
which, some of us think, have darkened His mission from the
moment He left the earth. I do not think that it is a wild idea
that the sacrament may yet be a basis of reconcilement between
the Agnostic and ourselves. The power that won the world
must still have some force."

XVII

HUGH PRICE HUGHES

How vividly I remember parting with Hugh Price Hughes, within two hours of his death! We had all been down to a lecture by M. Sabatier on St. Francis, in the Hall at Sion College. There our gifted Chairman had opened an admirable speech intended to introduce the hero of the occasion, but which slowly disclosed to a perplexed audience that he had got hold of a wrong M. Sabatier, who had died some years before. He had just landed him in a Professorship, at Strasbourg, " the open door," as he said, " through which German criticism had passed into France," when the Dean of Ripon rose in an agony and whispered loud and long in his ear. He appeared to be convinced with difficulty of his error, and by a bold sweep pulled matters straight by saying abruptly, " Well, anyhow, M. Sabatier went to Paris, and here he is." After this, all went well. I sat next to Price Hughes on the platform and parted with him at the end, after shaking hands, and asking after his health. It was with a strange start that I opened my paper in the morning to see " Sudden death of Mr. Hugh Price Hughes." I had left him at five and he died at seven.

The slight languor of apparent convalescence that hung about him did little to conceal the keenness, the swiftness and the buoyancy which were habitual with him. There was the quick look and the alert speech, and the vigour of movement which are felt throughout the record of his life, written by his daughter.[1]

The especial interest in reading it lies in watching just those forces which were in action upon ourselves, in their work upon one whose environment was so different. Everything that told upon the generation of Churchmen who grew up in Oxford in the Sixties told upon him also. And this is all the more accentuated since he, by being placed at Oxford for his Pastoral work, came into living touch with the man whose influence passed so deeply into the religious thought of that day—Thomas H. Green, of Balliol. He it was who shook us all free from the bondage of cramping philosophies, and sent us out once again on the high pilgrimage towards Ideal Truth. It was his profound Evangelical heart which made all that he taught us intellectually become spiritual and religious in its effect. The mysteries began to stir again about us, and reason received anew the sense of sacred vocation. And again it was Green who identified the interests of this ideal imagination with the common affairs of living men and women; who charged us with the democratic ardour which made him always the active champion of the poor and the preacher of the obligations of citizenship. He showed us the philosopher at work as a king, at least so far as kingliness could find its scope in the narrow municipality of

[1] "The Life of Hugh Price Hughes." By his daughter. Hodder and Stoughton.

L

Oxford. He broke down the academic bars, and gave of his very best to the town life about him. So he moved us, so he moved Price Hughes. For us all he wore something of the prophetic air, and his too early death gave power to his prophecy.

So, again, upon him as upon us, at a pregnant moment, there smote in the agonized cry that broke from out of the soul of Josephine Butler; and in that cry he, too, found a prophecy and an inspiration of strange power to hold and to exalt, so that life could never be the same again.

Then, again, all the recoil from individualism which had carried us into the full current of the Tractarian Movement, and had widened our eyes to the larger horizons of the Kingdom, did the same work for Price Hughes. More and more he repudiated the individualism of the old Evangelicals, and began to dream the great dream of a Church which should gather up and reconcile opposing tendencies and intellectual characters, and should blend them into one complex and varied body. He laid fast hold of the primal principles of Catholicity, and saw how vital it was that the whole sum of spiritual experiences in the past should be stored and transmitted as a continuous heritage of power, into which the individual soul found itself taken up merely as a moment in a vast activity. There must be continuity in the story of Redemption; that which had belonged to it at any period must not perish in its brief day, but must make its contribution to the ever-growing enrichment of man's salvation.

" Dr. Berry and my father were convinced that the Federation must recognize itself to be a conscious branch of the visible Catholic Church, with the dignity and spirituality pertaining to such full membership. Nonconformists were not entering the New Jerusalem through side gates as certain contended they were, and as some of them had almost come to believe, but through one of the great accredited gates which St. John saw in that vision which Dr. Berry liked to preach about.[1] Those who enter a city by a historic gate along a well-worn road should, if they are wise and devout pilgrims, my father thought, reflect on those who have gone before, and on certain habits and beliefs and observances which were essential to their progress, and which could not altogether be lightly laid aside. No wisdom of the race but has its meanings for all time, its part in the great whole. As citizenship and all that citizenship involves is but entering into a heritage, so, my father thought, was Christian Churchmanship, in which certain new-comers possessed of full civic claims have the richest, because the largest, heritage, if they will only enter into it— not disdain and overlook portions of it, because of the short-comings of previous generations and the slowness of the working of God's purposes. My father claimed, that is to say, as did Dr. Berry, that certain Nonconformist bodies were an accredited portion of the visible Catholic Church, just as many contemporaries claimed the same for Anglicanism."

He flung into this Ideal, not only the full energy of his faith, but also all the practical force by which he could hope to make it actual. And it was in the heat of this great hope that he came to the doing of his two most characteristic achievements—the formation of the Council of the Free Churches, and the production of their Catechism. He saw plainly enough that a

[1] See the " Life," chap. xv., " Holidays at Grindelwald."

formal Catechism is the immediate consequence of a
Church Ideal. If men are to unite in fellowship, the
impulse that draws them into unity must become
articulate. The body must be conscious of what it
is that constitutes it a body. Watchwords must be
found which the Brotherhood can pass round; they
must be in possession of a language through which
they can rehearse and realize the community of souls
in which they propose to live. If you once say that
Christ intended and formed a Society, you have said
also that he intended and created a Creed. Price
Hughes was indignant with old negations; he desired
to see Protestantism come forward into action as a
positive and coherent power, which could tell upon
human affairs, and make itself felt in the drama of
History, because it was in possession of a positive and
coherent confession of Faith. It was a bold move;
it went directly counter to every tradition of the
Congregational Churches; it broke with the ordinary
Liberalism of the day, which had been steadily working
away from what it only knew as " the bondage of
formularies." Yet here were the very Bodies which
stood for freedom of conscience and the democratic
spirit, making it their first act to impose upon themselves a formal Confession. Nor did that Confession
flinch from the dogmatic definiteness which it knew
to be essential to its main purpose. Greatly through
the influence of Price Hughes, the Unitarians were
excluded from the new formation. Both Council
and Catechism were to base themselves thoroughly
and confidently on the Redemption worked by Jesus

Christ, and on that alone. Personal experience of this salvation through the Cross was, for Price Hughes, the sole qualification for Church membership which he could afford to recognize. In both endeavours he, with his friends, was successful. The trained skill of Dr. Oswald Dykes gave the Catechism a sure and delicate certainty of touch : and it remains one of the most remarkable confessions produced outside the action of Church Councils. It surely marks an epoch in the story of Protestantism—just as the Council of Free Churches signalizes the amazing return of all the forces that made the Reformation, towards the lost ideal of Christian unity. To show the thoroughness with which he and his colleagues had faced the revolution in Protestantism which they were working, read Price Hughes's comments on the Question in the Catechism : " What is the Holy Catholic Church ? " and its Answer—

" Question : ' What is the Holy Catholic Church ? '

" Answer : ' It is that holy society of believers in Christ Jesus which He founded, of which He is the only Head, and in which He dwells by His Spirit ; so that, though made up of many communions, organized in various modes, and scattered throughout the world, it is yet one in Him.'

" It will be noted that this definition makes no reference whatever to the metaphysical abstraction entitled the ' Invisible Church,' which was invented in the sixteenth century. Of course we all believe in the ' Invisible Church ' in the sense that the Church Triumphant in heaven is a part of the true Church not visible on earth. As we often sing :

'One family we dwell in Him,
    One Church above, beneath,
  Though now divided by the stream,
    The narrow stream of death.'

"But in Protestant controversy the 'Invisible Church' is used in a totally different sense, to describe some Church of which every believer in Christ is a member, even when he totally neglects all the duties and obligations of practical fellowship with his fellow-Christians. London swarms with ecclesiastical vagrants, who flatter themselves that because they believe in Christ, and are therefore, according to their own notions, members of the 'Invisible Church,' they suffer no loss by holding entirely aloof from the organized fellowship of every Christian communion, and by refusing to bear any of the burdens or discharge any of the duties of the Christian sanctuary. Anything more entirely opposed to the original purpose of Christ or the best interests both of the individual and of human society, I cannot imagine. I am deeply thankful that the Catechism Committee, without attempting to define or to discuss any 'invisible' entity, have limited themselves to defining that real, practical, visible organization which exists on earth, and does the work of Christ on earth. If we had nothing in existence here except the so-called 'Invisible Church,' which is so dear to well-meaning, obstinate, and self-assertive Christians who resent the discipline of co-operation with their fellow-Christians, the powers of evil would not have much to fear. We frankly accept the Church which was organized by Christ and His apostles as a visible, audible, and tangible society; and at the same time, without in any way destroying the existing ecclesiastical organizations which are required by the varieties of the human mind, we proclaim the true bond of ecclesiastical unity. The Church is one neither in the Pope nor in the Sovereign, but in Christ Jesus, its Divine Head and Lord. The great movement which has

produced this Catechism is itself an illustration of that ancient
catholic truth. We are obviously one, not only in external
co-operation for defence or attack, but in doctrinal conviction
and spiritual aspiration. And it is well to remember here
that we are a majority of those inhabitants of England and
Wales who make any profession of religion. In the English-
speaking world we are an overwhelming majority, representing
at least two-thirds of all who speak the English tongue and
profess the Christian religion. Under these circumstances,
thoughtful persons will estimate the significance of our recently
discovered unity. The visibility of the Church is expressly
reaffirmed in the next question and answer.

" Question : ' For what ends did our Lord found His
Church ? '

" Answer : ' He united His people into this visible brotherhood for the worship of God and the ministry of the Word
and the Sacraments ; for mutual edification, and administration of discipline, and the advancement of His kingdom.' "

Our hearts cannot but leap out to greet principles
which are our own, and ideals to which we have
sworn allegiance. But it is impossible not to wonder
a little how the old bottles can stand the strain of the
new wine. What is there that the Free Churches
can bring forward to which this high and splendid
language of a Catholic Church can attach itself ?
What is there that can be constructed by Committee
in the Memorial Hall, Farringdon Street, which can
lend itself to such august imaginations ? We cannot
but recall the bewilderment that used to overspread
us as we read the splendid language of Dr. Dale,
portraying the ideal of the sacramental Church.
Then too, the question would obtrude itself, to what

exactly in Congregational organization can all this apply ? In recognizing the continuity of a society founded by the Lord and existent as His Body—a society, audible, visible, tangible, and that holds together and transmits the spiritual experiences of the past as an organic inheritance for believers through all time—we have come upon something mystical and majestic, which holds hidden in the abyss the secret of its open manifestations here below. This is what clothes with mystery the human instrumentalities through which it operates. This is what lends the hush of awe to the Buildings, and fills the Shrines with the cloud of Adoration : " the Lord is seated between the Cherubims, and the doorposts of the house shake, and all the house is filled with the smoke of His glory." Is this the sort of language that can be lightly and easily transferred to institutions of our own making ? And, surely, when once the word continuity has been introduced into the conception of the Society which our Lord founded, then that continuity must have found some expression for itself : the organism must have that in its construction which testifies to the continuity of its life. It may be quite an accident or an open question whether this involves an Episcopal system. Anyhow, the continuity of the life involves something that would insure it ; and the question then begins, what that was. And this makes it extremely difficult to see how an entirely modern mode of organization can enter into the task of transmitting the organic continuity.

Then, again, gallant as the effort was to mass the

Protestant bodies, it was actually determined in its formal outlines by limitations that were particularly British ; and it limited the sense of Catholicity again by confining it within the lines within which Churches that had no relation to States happened to exist. This had the misfortune of excluding the great Kirk of Scotland ; and, however excellent a principle in itself, it ought obviously not to have claimed to curtail the full conception of Catholicity.

But why go on girding, in our stupid English way, at a man who combined the fervid imagination of the Celt with the invincible optimism of the Semite ? The joy and the charm of his life lie in the exuberance of his hopefulness. He brings into play everything that delights us in the Celt, and this carries him past all Saxon criticism. He does us good by being what he is. Enough for us that he dreams his brave dreams, and follows the gleam, and burns with fiery indignation of sin, and spends himself in building Jerusalem in England's pleasant fields.

His daughter delights in bringing out all that belongs to this side of the man, and she seems to think that there is nothing that does a Celt so much good as spending his life in hammering Saxons. In the vehemence of this process he arrives at his perfection. For at last something of the toughness of the fibre, of the stolidity, of the patience, which makes his stupid foes so hard to conquer, passes into him and adds force to all his other natural gifts. Certainly the interest of Hugh Price Hughes' life lies in watching how a man of such a temperament could still work his way

along when wadded into the solid bulk of a Methodism
that was Saxon to the core. Against the weight that
encumbered him, he beat up with a heart that never
lost its chivalry or its ardour. He shocked, he shook,
he startled, he provoked ; and at times the relationship
was strained almost to breaking. But he held on in
devoted loyalty, and won wisdom without losing heat,
until he had really won the hearts of those who had
learnt to thank him for the energy of his rousing
clamour. He broke through the barriers which
comfortable congregations had set up, and compelled
the pews to remember the poor. He showed what
enthusiasm and zeal could do under the banner of
Methodism by passionate work in the open, in his
West End Mission. For this Mission, he had the
courage to attempt his famous enterprise of a Sister-
hood :

" My husband and I had long been struck with the way in
which the Roman Catholic and Anglican Churches, and also
the Salvation Army, utilized the services of its most devoted
and capable women. We felt that in Methodism there were
many women equally devoted and capable, who would render
untold service to their Church, and to suffering and outcast
humanity, if some opportunity were afforded them of definitely
organized work, to which they could devote their lives. Without any thought of disparagement for the services rendered
by humble women in the past as Bible-women, city missionaries,
etc., we felt the time was come when women who had received
the inestimable privileges of education and culture, were
called to devote these great gifts to the service of the Church,
and that they would be able to do a kind of work impossible to
others.

"We wanted a band of large-hearted, sensible, capable Christian women to be a centre of service and help in the great whirlpool of West London life—not to look down upon miserable and distracted humanity from a superior height, but to place themselves by the side of the sinful and the sad. We wanted them to be ' the Sisters of the People '—the name which was afterwards adopted."

He sent the vitalizing breath of Democracy pouring through the stuffy chambers which had been closed to the new arriving force. He drew the souls of the young towards a Faith which could prove its power to vitalize social conditions. He threw himself heart and soul into the municipal work of London. At a great moral crisis in national affairs, he showed what could be done in determining a national verdict by the sway of the Nonconformist conscience. It was he who made the phrase his own. His daughter tells admirably the tale of that tragic hour, when, white with the stress of conflict, he paced up and down his room and found the phrase on his lips at last, " Parnell must go." He had risked his reputation in his own society for the cause of Home Rule ; he had committed himself to the cause with all his habitual self-abandonment ; it was a matter to him of life and death. It is not hard to measure, therefore, the strain that was involved, when on the following Sunday he faced the indignant Irishmen whom he loved and told them that they must surrender their chief for the sake of the Great Hope.

He was carried through hours like this by the soul of chivalry that was in him. But he had also strong

practical instincts and was always fixed on what could
be done at the moment, and had a hearty contempt
for dreams that could not be brought to book and
turned into the real stuff of life. He showed his
capacity in speech, more especially, by the way in
which he carried things through, and could persuade
men to come to a definite resolution. It was largely
this practical judgment that determined the Im-
perialism of his later days. He was vividly impressed with what England was doing and could do in
the world. He admired the scale on which big results
could be effected by her. He felt the power of the
facts before him ; and then, so feeling them, he
brought into play upon them his chivalrous imagination. He pictured the Empire under the guise of
a Knight-errant, riding abroad, redressing human
wrongs over all the face of the earth. We all know
this picture ; we have had it worked for all it is worth
for a good many years ; and it has its truth. Only,
if we profess Knight-errantry as our motive, we must
nourish a very pure heart and show ourselves un-
stained by any taint or greed of gold. We can recognize
our office as Knight-errants, and we can use high
language of a mission from God ; but we must be
very careful how we use it, and must be tremblingly
aware of the standard by which claims of this character
are judged at the great judgment bar. Hughes's
language is a little too cheery and light-hearted over
this aspect of things. But, indeed, there was always a
great simplicity in the man, and a certain impulsive
boyishness of character, which kept him young in type

to the very last, and gives great attraction to the memory here recorded. Full of affection and revelling in all that home could give him, he had an immense store of happiness on which to draw; and the spirit of his boyish conversion, so simple and so touching, abides with him as an unfailing spring of energy and joy, until he passed at a stroke into the silent places.

XVIII

FREDERICK TEMPLE

How honourable the records of our great Churchmen have been of late ! We seem to have escaped out of the miasma ; we have got far away from the period when we read the lives of Cardinal Manning and Archbishop Magee. There are no skeletons now lurking in cupboards, and no uncomfortable reflections to make, and no queer corners to turn, and no odd revelations of temper and tone. As we work through the days of Edward Benson, Brooke Foss Westcott, Mandell Creighton, and Frederick Temple, we go straight along from end to end without a jolt. We are hardly ever called upon to apologize or excuse. As we close the books we have a longing to rush off to the bitterest adversaries of the Church with the books in our hands and say " Do read this. We should wish you to know what our best men are like. Are they not good and worthy folk ? Is it not good to hear about them ? "

Perhaps the Life of Frederick Temple,[1] above all, leaves this kind of impression. It is, as everybody might have expected, so extremely straightforward. There are limitations about the man of which we will speak later on. But the career is intensely in-

[1] " Memoirs of Archbishop Temple." By Seven Friends. Macmillan.

telligible and justifiable : all is honest and transparent :
you can follow the growth and recognize how natural
it is. When he gets into tight places you understand
exactly how it has happened, how true he was to
himself and how well he came through. It is a wonderfully coherent whole, and perhaps this comes out all
the more remarkably through the efforts of seven
different men to describe him. They can but reiterate
the same impression, and whatever they may do, it
is the same man in front of you all the time, standing
solid and four-square.

But you will say, We knew all this before about
Temple ; we knew that he was this strong, honest,
simple, God-fearing man. What new light has the
book thrown on a character with which the whole
world was familiar ? Well, I think the intense
boyishness of the character throughout is a surprise.
He is delightful as a boy himself at the start.

" The boys laugh at me very much because of my trousers,
which they say are too big, but I don't care much about them."

" I got your letter yesterday in the midst of a battle with a
boy called Elton. He was able to hit me very hard blows on the
face, while I could not touch him there at all. The cause of
the battle was this ; he coming up gave me a blow, in fun, but
being rather cross I did not like it, and I told him so, upon
which he gave me another and I returned it, and so it began."

He is just as much a boy as ever when, far on in life,
he is writing to his own boy at the age of six. " I have
not found any boys to amuse me. I wonder where
they are all gone ? Are they all eaten up ? "

> " The plague of boys
> With all their noise
> Is better than being without them.
> Tell mother to write
> At once to-night
> And tell me all about them."

" How often am I to tell you," he writes to the same boy, whom he accuses of impudence, " that your father, when he was a boy, had all the impudence that would be needed for at least three generations ? "

There is in him a delight in chaff and fun of a very boyish kind—a love of frolic and of rollicking home-talk which lasts him right to the end, and gives one an extraordinary sense of the buoyant vitality of the man and the inherent youthfulness of his spirits. Children always saw behind the apparent grimness which took in the grown-ups, and recognized in him a comrade who would know what the fun of a romp was. To this boyishness belongs what is noted by friend after friend in the Oxford and early Rugby days—his almost boisterous cheerfulness. He was so joyous, they keep saying. The joyousness was irrepressible. Old J. C. Shairp, recalling the Balliol days, could never get the sound of the great laugh out of his ears, and the bounding freedom of his motions.

> " Among the young green leaves and grass, his laugh the loudest rung,
> Beyond the rest his bound flew far and fleet."

The austere lines of the face in later days hid so much of the joyous boy from us. But it was there brimming over in full view for all who saw him then.

And can it be that the austerity only impressed itself
on the face as years went on, and that the roughness
and burliness which became so characteristic were not
there at all to start with ? There is a strangely smooth
handsomeness in the picture of him as the young
Headmaster of Rugby, without a line in the countenance. There are some incomprehensible statements
made about him at that time. " I never remember,"
says one of his friends, " associating him with any
idea of roughness all those years." And again, " the
Rugby boys knew that they had a kind Headmaster,
and now learnt that they had also a strong one." This
is recorded as the result of the first time he said " No "
to a request. Now is not that a surprising statement ?
If it had been put the other way up everybody would
have understood. From the first moment that he
took the floor, so to speak, there would not be a boy
in the room who would not know that the Headmaster
was a strong one, one would think. Afterwards they
would learn that he was also a kind one. That is the
way we should have put it. But obviously the men
who knew him in those days find the other order most
expressive. There is a good deal that tallies with this
in the book. Apart from the famous story of the
" just beast," it is striking that nearly all the well-
known tales of his abrupt utterance seem to belong
to his Episcopate. We should like to hear more about
this. For surely Arthur Butler is speaking of Rugby
days when he tells of one who was just what we knew
him to be.

M

> " Hard on himself, to others bluff and cold,
>   The great dear master that we loved of old !
>   Now with a gesture strong, and massive phrase,
>   Like to a boulder of primæval days,
>   Unpolished, rude, the ponderous sentence rolls,
>   To lie unmoved, a landmark in our souls,
>   Low in the valley, telling whence it came,
>   The winter's ravage on the rocks of flame."

Then again it was unknown to us of later days how deeply metaphysics had absorbed him, and how profoundly he had been affected by the imaginative and mystical thought of S. T. Coleridge. It would almost appear as if this bent of his nature had been deliberately repressed. Jowett speaks of it as " renounced " out of regard to the necessities of practical work in the world. Archdeacon Sandford seems to argue that there was much of this in the early manhood which had to go under. There is a striking passage of his own in a letter to a son who was reviving for him his old metaphysical memories : " I swam out to sea myself once in this way of yours without arriving anywhere, till a ship that was passing by picked me up." A note suggests that the ship was the Gospel of St. John.

With this revelation of his more mystical broodings we learn also how far more deep was the influence on him of the Oxford Movement than we had quite suspected. Letter after letter to his mother records the effect of Ward, and Newman, and Pusey. His intimacy with Ward was very close, and Ward, as usual, poured everything into him that he had to say. Temple's recoil at the news of Ward's engagement and honeymoon, in the very crisis of the Homeric battle round " the Ideal," reveals how far he had gone in sympathy with Ward's teaching. There is a curious memory of Newman at St. Mary's. " He is an exceedingly ugly man, his features are the hardest I ever saw. His face looks as if it were made of board, and he has the appearance of very great austerity." That was only the first impression, and he gets more and more affected by the unworldly beauty of Newman. But he is still irritated at the way in which his followers imitate every motion that he makes. " Mr. Newman must be a very wonderful man to have such an immense power over all that come into contact with him. All his acquaintance imitate his manner and peculiarities. The reason is that in their minds his manner is so connected with every good feeling that mere association leads them to imitate him. It is, however, very absurd to see them all hold their heads slightly on one side, all speak in very soft voices, all speak quick and make long pauses between their sentences, and all, on reaching their seats, fall on their knees exactly as if their legs were knocked from under them."

But it is Pusey who moves the very depths of his being. His moral earnestness, his spiritual austerities, his depth of unworldliness found their response in this brooding mystical boy. " Last Sunday Dr. Pusey preached before the University at the Cathedral. I do not think I ever heard a more beautiful Sermon. It lasted nearly two hours, but I could have listened more than an hour longer I am sure." He is rather distressed to find that his Tutor, Tait, is so much against Puseyites. " The Pusey party," he writes to his sister, " are the quietest and most unobtrusive set you can imagine. They have been much misrepresented, and that of course helps rather than injures them. They are exceedingly clever men, and decidedly they embody the chief part of the religious portion of Oxford." While writing that he still thinks their doctrine dangerous, but slowly gets drawn nearer and nearer to it, while he is losing fast his reverence for the Reformers, and writes to the same sister at the time of the Martyrs' Memorial : " For my own part, I find that the more I read their history, and still more their own letters, the worse impression I have of their characters." However, in spite of the profound fascination the Movement exercised over him, he preserved still the attitude of a critic and a spectator, as of one watching with absorbing interest, yet from some standing ground of his own. The Archdeacon has a fine passage summing up the permanent effect upon his life of what then influenced him. " There were legacies of the school which he never lost—an awe and reverence about his religion and worship which all could see, and the sense of a supernatural presence which inspired them—an elevation of aim in daily life which lifted him above conventional standards, while nevertheless he remained absolutely simple, and lived his life in common things—a belief that the Church (though he gave no narrow interpretation of the term) was no convenient institution framed by man, but the creation of Christ Himself—

a hold on things unseen which made the world beyond the grave and the communion of saints perpetual realities to him—above all, a belief in the objectivity of the Christian faith, with the Cross and the Resurrection and the Divine Sonship of Christ as the Centre and the Head. ' Our Lord is the crown, nay, the very substance of all revelation. . . .' ' If He cannot convince the soul, no other can. The believer stakes all faith in His truth ; all hope in His power.' "

The full force of what he so learnt at Oxford came out in the great Sermon at the opening of Truro Cathedral Choir—the greatest Sermon on the Church which has been preached in our generation.

Yet it is true that he remained outside the Movement, independent and self-contained, and this is the note of his life. In spite of lying freely open to the influences that played upon him ; in spite of his warm and keen camaraderie ; in spite of his intense home intimacies and impulsive affections, there is always a certain aloofness and aloneness in the man himself. He is still looking on at life, and noting it, and working and thinking ; but he remains somewhat detached. Nothing quite assimilates him. He makes his own way, and men admire and love him—but still as men who look on at a splendid spectacle of heroic energy. They do not follow him as a school ; they do not take up watchwords from him ; they do not exactly find themselves swept into his currents. He gives them a superb example of what work means, and roused by that example they work, too ; but on their own lines while he works on his.

This, I think, is what we felt in London. Perhaps
at Rugby it may have been true that his masters
assimilated his mind and intention more than we did,
and felt a closer companionship of thought. To us,
I think, he always appeared like a great ship, furrowing
its way alone through the seas. I never could understand why, for he had a great deal to say that might
well have carried people along. He was a deep and
strong thinker, and delivered himself of many mighty
utterances on great truths. Yet he never built up a
body of thought which counted ; it never seemed to
pass into the common stock ; you could not trace its
influence in the intellectual world. The Bampton
Lectures passed curiously out of sight and notice,
yet they were a powerful contribution to the problem
of the day, and were the result of long pondering and
close reading. What was it that held it all back somehow ? Why did people not take more account of
such an intellectual force as he embodied ? Something isolated, something detached, something aloof
was in it and withheld it. It was the thinking of a
lonely man. There is an interesting letter of his own
to Dr. Scott, while at Kneller Hall, in which he seems
conscious of this : " I am quite aware that my defect
in writing consists in my inability to enter readily
into other men's views of the thing of which I am
thinking. I do not readily conceive how it will look
from their side." And again he writes to Dr. Scott,
from Rugby, in 1860 : " You need not encourage me
to be obstinate in my own convictions—I am already
tempted enough in that way."

Archdeacon Sandford tells us how real was the discipline to which he set himself when he was made a Bishop, to learn to be all things to all men. All through his life he was trying to master this lesson, and " to Temple, strong, self-reliant and unworldly, this perpetual need of having to think of others was a salutary check."

Still the aloofness remained to the end. It gave immense strength to his sturdy individuality, and it did not hinder his beautiful simplicity and humility. But at certain crises of his life it did close up the avenues by which a situation could make itself felt, and caused him to blunder a bit, in ignorance of what was expected of him. It was a touch of this that made him break away from the Dock strike just at the crisis. He did not quite take the measure of the difficulties that he had imposed upon the leaders of the strike. He had come up hurriedly, summoned from Wales by our urgent entreaties. Canon Mason's letter in the Life recalls vividly that anxious night when the little knot of us met and decided he must come back. It was getting late in the evening, and we could only discover vaguely that he was in Wales. Cyril Bickersteth was determined to rush off to the nearest town to Wales and wait there till we wired to him as to where the Bishop might be found. We were all holding him back by his coat-tails from this impossible adventure, when there came a rap at the door and a wire from Fulham, to say Dolgelly. Bickersteth flew from our hands, only to find that he had got no money at all, and to turn back to implore us to lend him the needful. We poured out what we could from our pockets and he vanished into the night towards Euston. But before I was awake in the morning, there was a telegraph boy at my doors with a wire from Bickersteth, at Shrewsbury, asking, " What am I to say to him ? What is he to do ? " So unequipped was our ambassador. But he was equipped in other ways, for his personal appeal was irresistible, and up came the Bishop. He settled down at once to the work and met John Burns straight away. I always remember the decision with which he gripped the meaning of the strike proposals. The higher wage meant fewer men employed, less casual jobs. Was Mr. Burns aware of that ? Perfectly, said John Burns. " You daren't tell your men so," said the Bishop. " I'll say it to them to-morrow, on Tower Hill," said Burns, and he did. The Bishop glued himself to the business, and it was while he was at the work that the employers made the concession which ended the strike. But there intervened the failure of the leaders to carry through with the men that which they had agreed to with the Lord Mayor and Bishop. It was this failure which broke the Bishop's confidence in them, and he went back to Wales. It was just the sort of weakness on their part which his innate sense of justice would condemn. But he might have gone a little beyond justice, and have made allowance for the awful strain that the conciliating proposals had made upon the leaders. It was a failure to see it from their side. Again, at the famous judgments delivered as Primate on Incense and Reservation, he misjudged, surely, the temper at which we had all arrived and the kind of action that was expected from him. The whole world was ready for him to come out frankly as a Father in God, the highest living authority in the Church, and so to find for us all a way of escape from the technicalities of Law and the dead weight of obsolete Acts of Parliament. "It was not a court," as he said himself, that we wanted, but a living voice. Yet somehow or other he missed the spirit of the opportunity, and we found to our amazement that we were back within the worst fetters that a dead past had put upon us.

I remember feeling this note in him of aloofness in his great speech at the Guildhall, in which he took leave of London. He stood in the dignity of his own conscience, declaring, in his blunt and truthful manner, that he had done what he thought was right while he was with us, and we knew that he had, and that he had a perfect right to say so. Only I longed for something that would show one that he recognized the limitations that belong to any individual conscience, however lofty and upright, and I wanted to hear him say, "I may have been wrong where I thought I was right." He looked within and was sure of himself. But one wanted to be sure that he would also receive from without that which the outer life could bring him. It was not that there was the least touch of pride in all this, nor was there any suspicion of his own humility. It was a moment for self-revelation, and self-revelation was rare with him, and one was touched all the more by the fact that he opened his heart so freely. Only it intensified the sense that one was watching the man in his solitariness, and was wondering whether he ought to be quite so detached.

For the rest, the whole impression of the man sums itself up in the words " moral weight." It was a personality of astonishing force and vitality. It bulked so large. It filled the place wherever he was. There seemed no room for anybody else. Only in Mr. Gladstone have I felt the same personal energy, dominating all by its presence. It seemed to flatten everything down that it told upon. Very often, in sermons and speeches of the plainest possible language and of the simplest truths, the enormous moral energy of the man himself, breaking out through every obstacle, in a voice that was hardly a voice so much as a sound, would shake the soul of his hearers with a violence and a passion which were unlike anything else in the whole wide world. The whole heart of religion was in him. His soul was given to his Lord and Master with all the complete self-surrender of a child. And the effect of this told on us, who listened, as with the power of a prophet of God : and we found the tears in our eyes that start from out of sheer spiritual emotion—tears of relief and joy that rose in response to the cry from the living heart of one to whom, for all his ruggedness, tears were always near. It was at moments like these that we knew how we loved him.

XIX

H. G. WELLS'S " NEW WORLDS FOR OLD "

" Undiluted atheism, theft, and immorality. . . . I know of no language sufficiently potent to express fully my absolute detestation of what I believe to be the most poisonous doctrine ever put forward."
HIS GRACE THE DUKE OF RUTLAND.

HIS Grace, if ever he reads the book which Mr. Wells offered as a response to this utterance,[1] ought certainly to feel as if a flat iron had gone quietly over him and just wiped him out. Even the Duke himself, if, after shutting the Castle window through which he had uttered his shriek over Socialist Nottingham, he were to retire to his comfortable study and read the book, would, as he closed it, murmur softly to himself, " Well ! I never ! So it is Belvoir, which, after all, is the product of an industrial system worked by non-moral forces : it is Belvoir which is the result of economic motives which are certainly godless : it is Belvoir which is worth so very much more than I ever have earned the right to possess, or than my service to society can ever be worth. So it is I who stand for atheism, theft, and immorality ! How very odd ! Talk of glass-houses ! I will never throw just these particular stones again ! "

From the first moment in which Mr. Wells has started to express his idea of Socialism, we find that

---

[1] " New Worlds for Old." By H. G. Wells. Constable and Co.

we have our feet set on the ways of righteousness with almost startling decision. For his Socialism begins in the assertion of rational principle as the governing force of social life. The Duke's castle stands as the product and symbol of a society which has left itself to the government of chance. It is extraordinary that the protest against Socialism should be made in the name of law and morality. For it is law and morality for which Socialism clamours. That is what Mr. Wells has to say. Socialism is the outcome of our horror at the helpless welter of our present disorder: at the immorality of our hugger-mugger muddling. What men see before their eyes is an Industrial Society, which cannot be brought under moral standards: and which wrecks the stability of organic human life. That is the trouble. And, when the Industrial Society, under the panic of attack, takes on its lips the sacred names of home, of marriage, of childhood, and sallies out to champion these high causes, Socialism meets it with the paralysing inquiry " Where are your homes ? You are destroying them, wholesale, for the money-gain of married women's work at the factories. What about the children ? The babies are dying in their thousands, because there are no mothers to feed and tend them. What is this marriage you make so much fuss of, when you crowd these huge populations into stifling tenements, where the sanctity of marriage and of motherhood is a far-off tale of little meaning ? "

" One hears," writes Mr. Wells, " at times of the austere, virtuous, kindly, poor Scotch home, one has a vision of the ' Cottar's Saturday Night.' ' Perish all other dreams,' one cries, 'rather than that such goodness and simplicity should end.' But now let us look at the average poor Scotch home, and compare it with our dream.

"Here is the reality.

"These entries come from the recently published Edinburgh Charity Organization Society's report upon the homes of about fourteen hundred school children, that is to say about eight hundred Scotch homes. Remember they are *sample homes*. They are, as I have already suggested by quoting authorities for London and York—and as any district visitor will recognize—little worse and little better than the bulk of poor people's homes in Scotland and England at the present time. I am just going to copy down—not a selection, mind— but a series of consecutive entries taken haphazard from this implacable list."

Then comes the hideous intolerable tale. We just give two specimens.

"191. A widow and child lodging with a married son. Three grown-up people and three children occupy one room and bed-closet. The widow leads a wandering life and is intemperate. The house is thoroughly bad and insanitary. The child is pallid and delicate-looking, and receives little attention, for the mother is usually out working. He plays in the streets. Five children are dead. Boy has glands and is fleabitten. Evidence from Police, School Officer and Employer."

"192. A miserable home. Father dead. Mother and eldest son careless and indifferent. Of the five children, the two eldest are grown up. The elder girl is working, and she is of a better type and might do well under better circumstances; she looks overworked. The mother is supposed to char; she gets parish relief, and one child earns out of school hours. Four children are dead. The children at school are dirty and ragged. The mother could get work if she did not drink. The children at school get free dinners and clothing, and the family is favourably reported on by the Church. The second child impetigo ; neck glands ; body dirty. The third, glands ; dirty and fleabitten. Housing : six in two small rooms. Evidence from Parish Sister, Parish Council, School Charity, Police, Teacher, Children's Employment and School Officer."

He then gathers up the whole case in the following passage.

" Consider, for instance, the circumstances of parentage among the large section of the working classes whose girls and women engage in factory labour. In many cases the earnings of the woman are vitally necessary to the solvency of the family budget, the father's wages do not nearly cover the common expenditure. In some cases the women are unmarried, or the man is an invalid, or out of work. Consider such a woman on the verge of motherhood. Either she must work in a factory right up to the birth of her child—and so damage its health through her strain and fatigue, or she must give up her work, lose money, and go short of food and necessities, and *so* damage the coming citizen. Moreover, after the child is born, either she must feed it artificially and return to work (and prosperity) soon, with a very great risk indeed that the child will die, or she must stay at home to nourish and tend it—until her land-lord sells her furniture and turns her out !

" Now it does not need that you should be a Socialist to see how cruel and ridiculous it is to have mothers in such a dilemma. But while people who are not Socialists have no remedy to suggest, or only immediate and partial remedies, such, for example, as the forbidding of factory work to women who are about to be or have recently been mothers—an expedient which is bound to produce a plentiful crop of ' concealment of birth ' and infanticide convictions—the Socialist does proffer a general principle to guide the community in dealing not only with this particular hardship, but with all the kindred hardships which form a system with it. He declares that we are here in the presence of an unsound and harmful way of regarding parentage ; that we treat it as *a private affair*, that we are still disposed to assume that people's children are almost as much their private concern as their cats, and as little entitled to public protection and assistance. The right view, he maintains, is altogether opposed to this ; parentage is a public service and a public duty ; a good mother is the most precious type of common individual a community can have, and to let a woman on the one hand earn a living as we do, by sewing tennis-balls or making cardboard boxes or calico, and on the other, not simply not to pay her, but to impoverish her because she bears and makes sacrifices to rear children, is the most irrational aspect of all the evolved and chancy ideas and institutions that make up the modern State. It is as if we believed our civilization existed to make cheap cotton and tennis-balls instead of fine human lives."

Now, we may detect difficulties in all this : we may fasten on it with needful criticism : we may discuss and dispute methods and modes. But there is one thing that we may never do, so long as we profess to have the use of our reason. We can never suppose that such Socialism as this is an attack on marriage, parentage, and the home. Why, these are its fundamental values. These give to it its perspective : its standard : its motive. It is because it believes these to be undervalued that it exists. It would make motherhood the highest social act. It would see, in children, the primary social asset. It would set itself to rescue, redeem, secure these elemental vitalities. Its bitter complaint against our existent system is that it rides roughshod over these sanctities. It allows the home-life of England to go under in ruins : and, so, poisons the wells on which all its health depends. This is the cardinal note of our Socialism : it consecrates motherhood. And let us always remember that if, from Plato's Republic down to our own day, Socialist dreamers have vexed their souls over the irritating obstruction which so often results from the selfish interests of individual homes, and have been inclined to deal roughly with the particular parentage, it has been, not out of too little regard for the beauty of home, but out of the excess of their passionate desire to see that beauty secured and extended to all. To them, home and fatherhood and motherhood are so priceless a heritage, so precious a possession, that they cannot endure to leave them to the dreadful accident of chance, or to the cruel freaks of individualism. They, in their brave impatience, would sweep them up too hastily into the national organization, for fear lest their holy virtues should be recklessly lost. They value them so highly, that no cost seems to them too great for their preservation. That is why, at times, they have been tempted to run the risk of damaging parental responsibility. It is out of the excess of their esteem for it : out of the extremity of their indignation at its misuse.

Certainly, this Socialism is on the track of the higher civilization in that it stands for the freedom and exaltation of womanhood. And, again, far from being a greedy grab to satisfy present hunger, it dedicates the present to the future. It asks of the living generation to find its primal inspiration, its dominant impulse, in the desire to secure to those born from it their full opportunity for health, growth, and joy. Each generation is to consecrate itself to the good of its children. In this, Socialism puts itself in line with all the higher-evolution in nature, which exhibits, in dramatic vividness, the survival of those races in the struggle for existence, which surrender themselves most entirely, in altruistic devotion, to the cause of their young : and to the solidarity of the whole community.

Socialism, again, has this special ethical significance —that it counts on evoking out of the heart of man a moral motive of sufficient force to carry the weight of the world's industry. It is, itself, the vehement protest against the moral cowardice which despairs of them : and which declares that men will never work except on a motive of self-interest which conscience and religion alike condemn. Modern industry deliberately gives itself over to the devil, by refusing to trust itself to any motive-force but selfishness. In doing this, it goes dead against its own experience. For even now, under these ungodly professions, the industrial system would not last an hour if it were not for the effort thrown into its resource by those who work out of generous love of others, or out of delight in the excellence of work in itself. There is absolutely no good work done of a high order, in any department, that is not done under some better impulse than self-interest. And, of course, the entire world of art would cease to exist, if it was not inspired from

N

end to end, with the sheer joy in excellence of crafts-manship.

Mr. Wells is triumphant in his confidence here.

" I will confess I find it hard to write with any patience and civility of this argument that humanity will not work except for greed or need of money, and only in proportion to the getting. It is so patently absurd."

" For all who really make, who really do, the imperative of gain is the inconvenience, the enemy. Every artist, every scientific investigator, every organizer, every good workman, knows that. Every good architect knows that this is so, and can tell of time after time when he has sacrificed manifest profit and taken a loss to get a thing done as he wanted it done, right and well ; every good doctor, too, has turned from profit and high fees to the moving and interesting case, to the demands of knowledge and the public health ; every teacher worth his or her salt can witness to the perpetual struggle between business advantage and right teaching ; every writer has faced the alternative of his æsthetic duty and the search for beauty on one hand and the ' saleable ' on the other. All this is as true of ordinary making as of special creative work. Every plumber capable of his business hates to have to paint his leadwork ; every carpenter knows the disgust of turning out unfinished ' cheap ' work, however well it pays him ; every tolerable cook can feel shame for an unsatisfying dish, and none the less shame because by making it materials are saved and economies achieved."

And, again, Mr. Wells's Socialism is ethical in its treatment of private property. It does not destroy it : at least according to its modern formularization. It proposes to regulate it by desert : to make it the signal of efficiency. It will be allotted where it has been earned. There will be a reason for it, whenever it exists. It will not be left to grow by hazard: by luck: by greed: by exaggeration: by interest. This proposal is drastic, no doubt: but its base is moral.

And Socialism has an ethical End in view. It regards Society as existing for the sake of the living men and women who are its product. Its justification lies in the excellence of the type of citizens, who result from it. All its organization, its wealth, its methods, are to be tried by this test of living character, as the right issue. That is the best State which provides the fullest opportunity for the growth and the freedom of living human beings.

Socialism, then, in the form advocated by its latter-day representatives such as Mr. Wells, is ethical in its elemental impulses on behalf of motherhood and childhood. It is ethical in the basic economic motive which it assumes and demands. It is ethical in its application to private property. It is ethical in its altruistic ideal. It is ethical in its exaltation of women. It is ethical in its ultimate standard and aim. We must shut, once and for all, then, that lattice window at Belvoir Castle through which His Grace found vent for his voice.

But, now, comes the cardinal point. Socialism proposes to work out this ethical programme by deliberate and conscious reason. It embodies, in itself, the appeal for a scientific treatment of human life. It expresses our abhorrence of the haphazard chaos of our existent societies. It parades before our eyes the silly confusion, the barbarous excesses, the stupid mess, that comes from leaving blind industrial forces to work out their own irrational conclusion. It points to Park Lane, and the Slum at its back: to the demoralization of a glut of millionaires: to the roaring trade, and the starving unemployed. Could anything be more irrational: more futile: more perverse: more insane ? The cure obviously lies in Society entering into intelligent possession of itself. It must organize: and organize itself with a purpose: and bring reason into full command: and control its own destiny, and its own resources, and its own methods, according to its own intelligible principles that can justify themselves to reason and conscience. Socialism is the attempt to bring social life under organic order and control.

Now, all valid criticism of Socialism turns on this possibility. Obviously, as an arraignment of our present disorder, Socialism is unanswerable. Civilization represents man's effort at self-control, at rational development of himself and of his resources. It is absurd of us to have supposed that Civilization would result by abandoning self-control, by declining to direct it, by omitting the pressure of deliberate purpose. So to decline, so to omit, is to lapse upon irrational barbarism. *Laissez faire* is barbarism. It is the savage's own hall-mark. No organic Civilization can result if we omit all its primal elements. Civilization has got to undertake its proper responsibilities: and to set itself to recover control over its own welfare, by deliberate science. So, only, can it redeem itself from disease.

But this recovery and extension can only be gradual

and tentative. It must steadily press its work forward from the region already brought under cultivation over the backwoods or jungles that have yet to be won. And the area to be covered is incalculable and immense. Human nature is full of secrets and surprises. Our present science is but a little way beyond the frontiers. Untold explanations lie before it. Socialism, under this aspect, cannot be a completed scheme. It must be a growth: an evolution. Otherwise, if it attempts to handle the whole body of human life by the light of its present science, it will clap human nature into a strait-waistcoat. It will arrest it: imprison it: stifle it.

Here is our problem. And Mr. Wells is admirably aware of it. He appreciates all the difficulties that limit its advance. He shows, with excellent lucidity, how impotent was the dream of a mystic democracy, that was to establish Socialism by divine instinct when once the Marxian catastrophe had won the opportunity and cleared the ground. He tells, with a sympathy now strange to him, of the influence of the Fabian Society, in recognizing the necessity for securing a vast body of congenial and socialized administrators, if the actual administration of Socialism was ever to be a reality. He argues, with keen interest, for the need of a new nation, with a new soul and mind, framing new and adequate institutions in which to house its soul, if the administration is ever to be, not a bare bureaucracy, but a vital expression of the democratic spirit. He knows how long this will take : and how delicate and deep is the task : and how many are the perplexities that it presents. And, perhaps, he is, too often, inclined to rebut these perplexities by turning round on Society as it is : and retorting on it its own defects. " Who are you," he cries, " to talk of homes wrecked : of parental responsibility endangered : of personal independence undermined : of the curtailment of individual freedom ? Do you give individuality its freedom ? Do you never damage parental responsibility ? Do you breed strong independent individualities ? " This is wholly successful, as a retort. But it is no more.

Nevertheless, Mr. Wells is most fortifying. He wins by his very moderation, and his frank confessions. He convincingly exhibits the force of the ethical ideal in Socialism. Everything that is morally sound : everything that is obviously and necessarily corrective of our existing troubles : draws one way : and makes towards the ideals that Socialism presents to us. Our immediate task lies, surely, in that direction.

But fresh questions swarm. How far will this high Socialism, sketched by Mr. Wells, prove itself constructively capable of occupying all the ground, of covering the entire field of human nature ? Has it allowed enough for the elasticity, and variety, and growth, and surprises, and heights, and depths, and infinities, and incalculabilities, and transcendences, that lie hidden in man ? This has got to be shown. We shall only know by degrees : by trying what may be done : by pressing forward possibilities. And all this tentative process is determined at every step by the amount of moral force at our disposal : by the degree to which individual consciences can be socialized by the amount of social soul on which we can draw.

There is no book that can help us better to understand this than " New Worlds for Old." There is not one syllable from cover to cover that gives the reader a moral jar. The tone and temper are perfect throughout. Personally, I regret that Mr. Wells should repeat the picture against which I have already ventured to protest—the picture in " Boots " which appears to suggest that it is hard lines, when we want a pair of boots, not to be able to catch the nearest cow and cut a pair, there and then, out of her hide, without a stupid private proprietor turning up with his absurd " I beg your pardon: but that cow is mine." Most certainly, the public proprietor, the Social State, would be, at least, as rigid and instantaneous in its intervention with " Pardon us ! That happens to be *our* Cow "—to the immense relief, let us note, of the cow !

I have another little quarrel with Mr. Wells on minor points. He agrees with Tolstoy and others in the vision of a " Higher Anarchy "—in an Ideal, that is, in which all external law ceases for those who are perfect. In this, he has the authority with him, no doubt, of many high Christian Saints : and, among these, I see, from an excellent Fabian Essay, that I must class Dr. Dearmer. Yet I would lodge my protest against it—in the name of Richard Hooker who, on his death-bed, mused on the orders and ranks of the Angels. Heaven is social : so we believe. And, if social, then, it needs to be realized in law : it looks for outward manifestation: it finds its joy in organic co-operation. Form will always be essential to perfection: the spirit will always need a letter: the heart must have its speech. Behind the City of men that we build with slow labour, we must be aware of the City of God—a city four-square—with streets and walls: measured by an angels' reed. Creighton's epigram " Socialism is impossible until all men are perfect: and when they are perfect, it will not be wanted " breaks down in that second alternative. Perfection will cry out for formal realization. It will delight in finding for itself adequate expression. When we are all perfect, we shall declare it to be a fact by building the fabric of a State which corresponds, in actuality, to our ideal. Man lives by the Word: and the Word releases the thought: and enacts the will: and satisfies the imagination: and gives glory to the spirit. We are for ever advancing according to the measure with which we can express ourselves: and the consummation of our gradual advance will not reverse the law by which it has been attained. We do not merely frame a City for the necessities of earth and time. We look for a City still, not made with hands, eternal in the heavens.

XX

THE CONFESSIONS OF MONSIEUR RETTE

St. Augustine has a great deal to answer for. He has justified the publication of Confessions. "Confessions are always interesting," as the late Lord Salisbury said in the last debate on Home Rule in which he took part—whether they be the Confessions of St. Augustine or the Confessions of Jean Jacques Rousseau: or the Confessions of—"Lord Ribblesdale." Would he have said so if he had read the Confessions of Monsieur Rette? They would, probably, plead that they were but following in the wake of St. Augustine. But they, most certainly, reveal how great is the genius by which St. Augustine redeems the risky business of exhibiting in public the innermost experiences and most private emotions of the soul. Only Byron can afford to carry across Europe the pageant of a bleeding heart: and even he had but a temporary and suspicious success, in spite of his superb and unflagging power. We all regret it now: and wish that he could have found other poetic material than his own domestic affairs. Those of us who are tempted to repeat St. Augustine's experiment had better, first, recall St. Paul's own verdict on the necessity which drove him to the like painful self-exposure—"I speak as a fool."

The book which has provoked these reflections tells

the story of a mental passage from atheistic Socialism to the Catholic Church—from the Devil to God.[1] And there is no doubt that we start from the Devil We have seldom felt ourselves so close to him. The picture of " the sin in the house " is horrible. The man and woman live with one another in the temper of tigers, with tigerish growls, and tigerish caresses. They are like wild beasts in a cage. And, for the public and literary life, there are curdling blasphemies, and ghastly hates, and hideous devilries, and mean jealousies, and degrading ambitions, and hollow hypocrisies. What a world ! No language of ours can rival the curses and denunciations that the writer himself flings back at it, as he escapes out of it. He simply swears volubly at it in modern French slang of extraordinary force, out of which we could but faintly extract a lucid meaning. The scene is filled with a crowd of lecturers, politicians, speakers, teachers—all vile, disgusting, immoral, insincere, blasphemous. Can such a world be possible outside hell ? The picture asks too much of us. We recoil into disbelief. We cannot accept such a railing accusation. It is too vehement : too unqualified : too obviously exaggerated : too blatant.

And this sense of excess, extravagance, follows us into the tale of the Conversion. That first condition of sin haunts and impregnates the whole story. The demoralization of the old life hurts and spoils the new. The conversion is as feverish, as over-balanced, as

---

[1] " Du Diable à Dieu."

hysterical, as the sin. It is, always, too much. The sentiment is overpowering. The passion is violent. The emotionalism is extravagant. Again, we recoil. It cannot carry conviction—this flaming rhetoric, this swooning fantasy of tears. It compels us into reaction. Where so much is doubtful, we begin to doubt all. The whole spiritual portraiture begins to wane and break. Distrust overcomes us. What can we rely on, in this vaporous mist ? What bed-rock is there, beneath this quagmire ?

Yet this wholesale distrust is quite unjust. The man is telling a true tale, as he experienced it. And that which repels us was obviously real enough to him. Only, it would seem that the pig-life, which had preceded, had made a sweet and sane judgment impossible. Nerves were distraught: tissue was degraded: reason was out of gear : imagination was perverted. There could be no discipline : no moral equipment : no spiritual training. He had known absolutely nothing of what Christianity meant. When he tried to pray, in the agony of a spiritual crisis, he could only recall two of the sentences of the Lord's Prayer : and that doubtfully. He had to be taught how to cross himself, like a child. Therefore it is that, out of this wild hurly-burly of sin, he emerges totally unfit for rational and disciplined concern with spiritual things. He has a very long way to go, before he can hope to acquire the Christian temper, which is for him, not a recovered possession that had been lost, but an utterly unknown wonder that has got to be discovered. We can pray God that he may yet win this for his own. But, unfortunately, he tells the story of the conversion long before he has succeeded in stripping himself of the temper bred under the evil past: and the result is that the heated and feverish nerves give to the new found faith the same repellent excess which is characteristic of the dreadful beginning.

And the effect is disastrous. Very simple uneducated men can succeed in preserving their simplicity, as they shout aloud at street corners the sinful experiences out of which they have been drawn. They are not self-conscious: and their desire to save others, by exposing the issue of their own shame, is so simple-hearted and sincere, that it carries the whole disagreeable thing through. But you must be rather ignorant to do this. When once the literary, self-conscious artist attempts it, he is in dire peril. Only an Augustine or a Dante can manage to steer their bark safely through the shoals. Men of a lower spiritual and intellectual stamp than these had better keep silent until years of slowly recovered health have restored to them the right mental equilibrium by which alone such delicate secrets of the naked soul can be handled. The Prodigal ought to have left the memory and the moral result of the swine in the far country a long long way behind him, before he ventures to write a record of his journey home. There is much yet to be done by him and for him, when the feast and the song and the music of his blessed return have died away, and he sets himself to the serious business of winning back the sweet temper of that home which he had outraged.

We wish that M. Rette had had the patience to wait. The Devil is gone out of him : but the expulsion has left him half dead : and the book has terribly suffered from being written in this unhealthy condition. Only one scene remains on my mind that is, in the least, striking and effective : and that is, the moment when the earnest Socialist carpenter asks him to tell him and his friends how science explains the origin of things : and he suddenly and promptly realizes that he has nothing to tell them. This is told vividly : and naturally : and it hits.

It is strange how slight and superficial is the intellectual quality of the work done by these distinguished literary converts in France. Even the tender little book of François Coppée attempted nothing here. Rette's reasoning is of the cheapest and poorest. He appeals, in his Christian Apologetic, to the bankruptcy of science, the sterility of philosophy, the worthlessness of life. As if the pillars of the House of Faith could ever find sure foundation in a bog. We must believe in man, if we would believe in God. An Apology that takes its start from arrant scepticism will never help to create the spirit of belief.

XXI

A RADICAL PARSON

MR. TUCKWELL'S Reminiscences[1] are the record of a Stalwart, racy, strenuous and confident. They have a buoyancy, as of bounding waters. They move with a resistless swing : they never hesitate or falter. There are no backwaters : no recoils of energy. True, there is the confession of a vast disappointment. We are carried back to the burning hopes that fed the cause of rural Enfranchisement. We are back in the days of Victorian liberation when there was, still, no limit to the vision of what sheer freedom would bring with it. The effort of Reform was spent in breaking down the obstacles that thwarted and withheld. If only the power could be set free, it would, of its own inherent force, make for its own supremacy of achievement. So all Liberators believed. Win the vote for the down-trodden ; and the thing is done. They will work out their own salvation.

We are long past that hour of splendid heart. We know, now, how hard and slow is the toil of construction, long after the liberty to act freely has been secured. The task of evolution is more complex than the task of liberation. It will not lend itself to such

[1] " Reminiscences of a Radical Parson." By Rev. W. Tuckwell. Cassell and Co.

simplicities of expression. It cannot concentrate itself into such downright and incisive war cries. It sprawls vaguely over immense areas : it has to go on in a hundred different directions at once. It has to blunder through a long tentative period of experiments, before it finds its true lines and channels. Misdirections and perversions blur its outlines. Unlooked-for qualifications have to come into play. Social Reconstruction is a huge and many-sided business. Everything has to go on at once. The van has to wait for the rear to come up. The entire body has to move altogether, if it moves at all.

Therefore the after-work that has followed the era of Liberation, has shown itself so depressing : so disappointing. It has lost the radiance : the glow : the glory : of the days which are so vividly brought before us by Mr. Tuckwell, when the issue was so clear, and the fight so Homeric in its simplicity, and the day of victory so triumphantly near at hand. Mr. Tuckwell finds the cause of the great disappointment that followed the County Franchise Bill in the cross-lead given to Liberalism by Mr. Gladstone's sudden championship of Home Rule. To him, it seemed like a betrayal of the Cause of the Labourer. It was the Country vote that had swept Liberalism back to power. And the country was hungry for reform. It had its needs clear and strong : the programme was perfectly plain : allotments : parish councils : etc., etc. Everything was ready. The momentum was tremendous : the steam was up : the engine could hardly hold itself in. When lo ! away we are to go on another tack. We are to learn another language. We are to liberate anybody and everybody except ourselves. We are to enter on a desperate adventure, with no hope of success : and at the cost of shattering all our prospects of united action. England was to fling itself aside.

So it felt. It is impossible not to enter into the despair of the Labourer's friends ; and impossible, too, not to admire, from the bottom of the heart, the loyalty with which Mr. Tuckwell nevertheless threw himself into the Irish Cause, and learned to love his Irish Colleagues, and spoke, and travelled, and worked, for all he was worth, on behalf of that which stood for Liberty. But his own dismay at the turn that things took, has made him a little blind to the situation as it presented itself to Mr. Gladstone. He hardly allows for the urgency of the Irish problem. For years it had been the nightmare of our politics. It had forced itself upon our attention : upon our conscience. We had been compelled to see what it was that England was about. We could not escape from a decision, when once the issue was driven to the front. For years, everything had been arrested by it. Now, with the new franchise, a real and united Ireland spoke : and the demand that it enforced was overwhelming to all who deeply cared for liberty.

And for liberty, Mr. Gladstone was impassioned. He had challenged Ireland to speak : and it had spoken. The choice of England lay, now, inevitably between liberty and deliberate coercion. It was natural enough that this should reveal itself to the

G. O. M. as the supreme political issue at stake in that Great Election.

However, this is all ancient history now. Home Rule was, at any rate, a magnificent offer, made in all the genuine passion for freedom, and with all the splendid self-abandonment, which were the secret of that incomparable sway which Mr. Gladstone wielded over our hearts. It remains, still, the landmark of what England owes to Ireland. But, with it, there came, somehow, that cleavage between Liberalism and Labour which Mr. Tuckwell traces to those dark days, when the English democracy learned to suspect the political move, which, whatever its own merits, served to suspend and postpone all the hopes on which its soul was set. Not for a long time did Liberalism open its doors frankly and freely to the demands of Labour. It tolerated rather than closed with it. It failed altogether to win its confidence. It only went with Labour where it had to : it did not gladly give itself away, as to a cause that called for its supreme endeavour. It will never find its soul until it has done this. That is the true and powerful moral that Mr. Tuckwell would draw for it. For this end, he has laboured gallantly, ever since he saw the opportunity for which he craved so unhappily missed. His own vivid words tell us how he got to work again : in the chapter on English misery. He had borne his share in the Home Rule fight. He had shown how Irish Coercion involved the annihilation of all those elements of freedom for which in our own country men had struggled through centuries successfully. But his

o

intimacy with English Proletarianism had deepened with every month that passed : and the misery that he encountered haunted him with a sense of guilt:

" Thus by degrees I left Ireland untouched—it had no lack of champions—and I confined my platform talk to English grievances. My friend Dr. Henderson, now Dean of Carlisle, had one day told me of a lively old lady in his neighbourhood who was ill, and likely, as it seemed, to die. The clergyman came to prepare her for her end, and talked to her with professional eloquence of the joys of heaven. But she was not so ill as they supposed, nor so receptive of spiritual expectation as he was prone to offer it ; and she answered, ' Sir, what you say may be very true, and heaven may be a very delightful place ; but—Old England for me ! ' So I defined my politics to mean the happiness of Old England ; such an administration of her land, her laws, her education, commerce, and finance, that every class, and every member of every class, might not only be beyond the reach of grinding want and habitual poverty, but might have leisure for recreation and improvement ; that science, art, literature, might not be a monopoly of the few, but the universal heritage of the many ; that every man who was not a criminal—and crime is the offspring of neglect and want ; every man who was not a sot—and drunkenness is the refuge of domestic misery ; might have, first of all, food, clothes, shelter, in sufficiency, and then access to those higher enjoyments—mental, moral, spiritual—which alone place man above the beast. Was this, I asked, the heritage of Old England now ? Had her wealth, increasing fabulously within the century, increased in equitable proportions ? Had the golden shower, condensing from the steam of our engines through the vaunted industrial period, fallen upon a fair majority of our people ?

" In answering the question I spoke that which I knew, and testified that which I had seen. I had crossed the deep gulf,

oceanum dissociabilem, dividing our separated classes; had
invaded the squalid hovel, which touches, naked but not
ashamed, the seclusive paling of the rich man's park;
penetrated the Jago tucked away behind the aristocratic streets
and squares. I had traversed, not once nor twice, the foul,
dark courts of the London city slums; had questioned the
hapless inmates as to their work and means of livelihood; had
seen in one room the girl working at trouser-finishing sixteen
hours daily, and receiving five shillings in wages at the week's
end; in another, the man and his wife making postmen's
coats for twelve hours in the day, and when the week's work
was taken home remunerated by twelve shillings, out of which
three had to be paid in rent for the filthy hole they called their
home.

> ' There amid the glooming alleys Progress halts on palsied feet,
> Crime and hunger cast our maidens by the hundred on the street,
> There the master crimps his haggard sempstress of her daily bread,
> And a single sordid attic holds the living and the dead.
> There the smouldering fire of fever creeps across the rotting floor,
> And the crowded couch of incest in the warrens of the poor.' "

In that indictment he has said all that made him the
fervid fighter that he was. On and on he told the
terrible tale. On and on he preached the essential
remedy. He was, heart and soul, with Henry George,
in identifying social redemption with the recovery by
the community of the soil. He still looks to see the
happy day when the entire wealth of the land,
heightened immeasurably from its present beggarly
level through the fertilizing action of free men in
secure possession of their own holdings, shall all lend
itself to public and national well-being. And how,
indeed, can there be any other end than this for our

desperate ills, by whatever process of gradual change it is to be brought about ? Only, it cannot be done as an isolated policy. The public demand made upon rent must tally with the rise in demands made on all forms of private wealth for national ends.

Nor, indeed, does Mr. Tuckwell follow Mr. Henry George in confining his programme to one issue. Very large, very wide, very deep, is the body of Reform that he calls for. He asks for Partnership between Labour and Capital: for the recovery of ancient Educational Endowments for the use of the poor: for the nationalization, or disestablishment, of the Church of England : for a Parliament in which

" Interests will be no longer paramount ; in which the great landowner, or the great shipowner, or brewer, or banker, or railway king shall not pull strings and engineer machinery, to defeat or embarrass measures which are vital to the community, but inconvenient to himself ; a Parliament strangely unlike the present Parliament, first, in that it will be, in all its parts, expert, well-mannered, conscientious, patriotic ; and secondly, as having been chosen by and sent to legislate on behalf of the enfranchised millions of Englishmen and women."

And, as he contemplates this new Parliament, and all that it might do, a vision rises, which well discloses the prophetic heart of the man :

" As I think of the power they possess, which their combination can make absolute, the England of the future rises before me as their grandsons, perhaps, may see it. It is an England in which the horrors I have described will be the forgotten nightmare of an old, bad dream ; an England whose artisans and labourers will be prosperous, independent, self-respecting, recompensed by work which shall yield profit to themselves, and not to their so-called masters. Education, and resource, and the joy of intellectual development, shall be the common heritage of all. Fewer palaces shall adorn the land, but fewer gaols and workhouses shall cumber it. The large-acred square will be a rarity, but the penniless vagrant will be extinct. Men will not point with pride to the great duke, his fourteen country houses and his £200,000 a year; but neither will they hear with shame of the despairing pauper in his pigstye cottage with his nine shillings a week. 'For behold,' said a great, inspired Radical twenty-five centuries ago—and it is for us to achieve the promise which his countrymen were too feeble to fulfil—'For behold, I create a new heaven and a new earth, and the former heaven and the former earth are passed away. The voice of weeping shall not be heard in them, nor the voice of crying. They shall build houses—*and inhabit them;* they shall plant vineyards—*and eat the fruit thereof.* They shall not build, and another inhabit; they shall not plant, and another eat; but they shall obtain joy and gladness, and sorrow and sighing shall flee away.' "

It was in view of the obvious criticism which such a vision would invoke from those who would see in it but " wild and whirling words " that he tells carefully and in detail the story of his own practical experiment, by which he has become so well known to all who have hopes that we may yet get back to the land. This chapter is sure to be read : and will form an admirable text book for all who desire to make experiment. Every Parson with a Glebe in his own hands ought to read every word of it : and, then, ask himself " Why not ? Why not I ? "

There is a notable convergence of authority and experience, all in the direction of justifying Small Holdings. We have got the secret. We know how they can be made to work. And, if so, then England might be saved through the Parsons' Glebes, if the Parson has but the courage and the faith to begin.

Mr. Tuckwell tells us how his fighting life closed:

" To all active combatants there arrives a time when breaking health or creeping septuagintiasis, or both, cry ' Halt ! ' They have fought their fight, and must make way for younger men. It came to me about the middle of the 'Nineties ; and I hung up my sword with less regret, because the battlefield on which I could have wielded it was deserted. The helplessness of our leaders had begotten apathy in our ranks ; already, before the Liberal defeat, I saw all Israel scattered on the mountains."

Certainly, he had fought his own fight most gallantly : and might well withdraw to repose. He speaks to us out of days when a simpler and more naïve self-confidence was possible than now, when the enormous bulk of the problem has humbled, where it has not crushed, us. No one goes forward now with such flying banners, and with all the trumpets blowing. The situation prohibits it. The long dull grind has begun. We lie weighted under the complex burdens. It is all going to be so slow : and the future depends on the tenacity, rather than on the heat, of our faith in Social Progress. That is, perhaps, what we sadly feel, as the book drops from our hands. Yet it is good discipline for us to be swept into the glow and the rush, which carried the fight forward in the generation that is beginning to pass. Here is the spirit in which it was done. Here is the hope through which alone victory can be won. The book is dedicated to his daughter. Mr. Tuckwell may well be proud to recognize his own message, as it is given, with such singular beauty and force, through her lips, to those very workers whose toil he lived to lighten.

XXII

MARY E. COLERIDGE

No one can take up Mary E. Coleridge's poems[1] without feeling, at once, that he has come upon a prize. He will find himself inevitably retaining it in his hand: turning over the leaves: dropping on poem after poem which entices him to search for more. He will either grow more and more absorbed: or he will call aloud to those about him to listen while he reads this or that which has charmed him. And this will happen because there is such a touch of felicity in the diction, and such a note of distinction in the imagination of the writer. The verses are written as they must have been written. The lines fall instinctively into the exact form needed. Each poem is singularly compact and decisive. It produces a direct impression, with absolute security of aim. Yet this is done without any hardness of outline: without any forceful insistence. Each impression is left in its true poetic essence, suggestive, subtle, and undefined. There is never too much said. The thought is delicate: wistful: pathetic: refined: intense. The words used are, often, the simplest possible: and especially, in concluding lines of short poems, where they seem to drop into pre-determined places with a certitude that carries complete conviction.

[1] "Poems by Mary E. Coleridge." Elkin Mathews.

The absence of effort shows how entirely natural it must have been to the author, to throw her emotion into verse. It was her normal outlet, to herself, in secret, whenever she was moved. She had written stories which created much stir. Everyone knows the " King with Two Faces." She had printed a small volume of verse, which won the high approval of Robert Bridges, who wrote, after her death, to express strongly his admiration of her work. These poems were largely found in her note-books, written down for her own relief, unread, often, by any, and unknown. Not even those who were nearest to her seem to have been aware how much there was, until after her sad death through a sudden operation. Some were sent to friends, as her greeting, whether in their troubles or their joys. So they sprung into being, out of spontaneity of feeling. And their happy perfection of wording is the witness both of their sincerity and of their instantaneous promptitude of production. It is a very rare gift that can give to a short quatrain the fullness of epigramatic satisfaction :—

> " The sum of loss I have not reckoned yet,
>   I cannot tell.
> For ever it was morning when we met,
>   Night when we bid farewell."

There ! Everything has been said. Nothing more is wanted. The words are in their place : it is simple as daylight : yet the note struck is deep and rich. The workmanship is perfect. It recalls Landor

at his best. Or, again, there is strange meaning easily
and lightly touched in the following six lines :—

> "NEW YEAR'S EVE.
>
> " Speak to the Wind and bid him stay,
>   Lest that within find out a way.
>
> " Call to the Sea to hush his wail,
>   That is failing which must not fail.
>
> " Cry to Time as he goes by,
>   That is dying which cannot die."

And—again—here is the swift felicitous movement of
a fleeting feeling :—

> " NEWS.
>
> " Ask me not how it came,
>   If I sought it !
>   My very thoughts are flame
>   Since first I thought it.
>
> " I saw it not with eyes.
>   It was not spoken.
>   These mysteries
>   Have neither sign nor token.
>
> " Ah ! say not, ' Is it true ? '
>   In faith uphold me !
>   I know not how I knew.
>   My heart told me."

She has a subject peculiar to herself which recurs.
Perhaps its best expression is in the following poem :—

> " Ah, I have striven, I have striven,
>   That it might vanish as the smoke ;
> Angels remember it in heaven.
> In vain I have striven, I have striven
>   To forget the word that I spoke.

" See, I am fighting, I am fighting
        That I may bring it to nought.
    It is written in fiery writing,
    In vain I am fighting, I am fighting
        To forget the thought that I thought."

There is a most delicate little poem, sent to a friend
who was mourning a lost child :—

" THE SINGING OF THE CHILDREN FOR THEO.

    " Little Theo's gone away,
            Gone away.
        We shall never see her play,
            See her play,
        Here and there, the livelong day.

    " God in Heaven loves us all,
            Loves us all.
        Little Theo heard Him call,
            Heard Him call ;
        And she let her playthings fall.

    " God in heaven loved her so,
            Loved her so.
        ' Little Theo, will you go ?
            Will you go ? '
        And she left us here below.

    " Very gently let us sing,
            Let us sing.
        Theo now remembering,
            Remembering,
        Loving more than anything ! "

Here is another tender plaint for the dead, telling
of an experience that we all know but too well :—

" Only a little shall we speak of thee,
  And not the thoughts we think ;
There, where thou art—and art not—words would be
  As stones that sink.

" We shall not see each other for thy face,
  Nor know the silly things we talk upon.
Only the heart says, ' She was in this place,
  And she is gone.' "

I have quoted these short and rapid flights of song, because they are wonderfully difficult to achieve with this ease and distinction: and they are especially characteristic of her delicate quality of tone. There are stronger things to be found in the volume: and they can be read there by those who treasure fine work, done from the soul. But it is the quick, and flying breaths of song, filled with pathetic music, which will haunt the imagination of those who read. They will, surely, find a haven within those Anthologies which, by happy instinct, secure out of the wreck of time those precious things which we cannot willingly see die.

XXIII

EDMOND ROSTAND'S "CHANTECLER"

HAVE you made it out ? Because it is well worth it.

It has been rather unfortunate in its introduction. First the Press boomed us into immense expectancy ; then flamed with notices of the first performance ; then became aware that it all sounded rather fantastic, and possibly that it showed itself incapable of being acted, in spite of the splendid efforts of the actors ; and then dropped it dead. Yet, whatever its merit as a play, and however impossibly fantastic it may appear as described, it remains certainly true that it is a magnificent piece of literature. It is charged with high ideals ; it strikes a very high note ; and it utters itself in incomparable French.

Of course, there are whole scenes which to the poor Anglo-Saxon outsider are absolutely unintelligible. They embody acute and rollicking chaff of the latest literary excesses in Paris ; they are full of jokes and puns and repartees ; and at intervals the punning becomes perfectly reckless. English words are scattered at haphazard up and down the text ; and at times it approaches pure farce. Still, even an humble Englishman can appreciate the general fun of the guinea-hens' five-o'clock tea. It is so fast and furious that it carries you off your legs, however baffled you

are about details; and if, indeed, modern French
literature is as precious and artificial and outlandish
as the remarks put into the mouth of the peacock in
the play imply, then anyone can understand the
protest on behalf of nature, and love, and nightingales,
and roses, and all the simple elements of poetic emotion
which is put into the mouth of Chantecler as he
climbs up a ladder out of the hothouse air of the
" five-o'clock tea " and delights in recognizing that out
there, in the open world, grass is still growing, and
there is a calf getting milk from its mother, which, he
thanks God ! has not got two heads.

However, all this funning can be rapidly passed
through ; and I am bound to confess that at hardly
any point in the play do I understand any one remark
made by the cynical blackbird. His points are always
too delicate, too remote for an ignoramus to make
out ; and yet I have no doubt that he plays a most
effective part in the actual drama. But what remains
on the soul is the splendour of the phrases in which
Chantecler tells his secret, and the thrilling moral
triumph with which he vanquishes his own discom-
fiture. How this nobility can possibly be given on
the stage through people tied up as pheasants and
cocks it is impossible to conceive ; and even the fifteen
hundred pounds paid for the golden pheasant's dress
hardly explains it. I should have thought that the
spiritual temper was far too great to be compatible
with the conditions of a pantomime. However,
acting in France is on such a high level that they may
be able to get through even this. In the meantime,

there are three moments in the play which everybody ought to master.

About the first I will say least, because it is the one moment that the critics did lay hold of. It is the beautiful song to the sun uttered by Chantecler at his first appearance, after his first crow. He offers his adoration to the sun because of the glory it sheds on the little and the obscure; it dries the tears of the tiniest grasses; it makes a living butterfly of a dead flower; it blesses every forehead and makes the honey ripen; entering into each flower and into each cottage; and still, as it divides itself to each, remains entire, like a mother's love. He sings to the sun, and offers himself as its priest, just because it chooses so often, when it is on the eve of setting, the humble window of a cottage to fill with its last glow of bene-diction. It turns into glory every little jug and basin, and sheds gold on every little shining weather-cock. Glory to it, then, in the meadows, and glory to it in the vines! Blessings on it as it shines in the blades of grass, and in the eyes of lizards, and the wings of swans! It makes the grand lines of life, and also the tiny details. He adores it because it brings the scent of roses into the air, and gives flame to the springs, and is as God in each burning bush. He sings praises to this sun of gold, without which things would only be what they are.

That is the great song which gives the note to Chantecler's devotion all the way through.

But the great moment arrives when the golden

pheasant, the splendid embodiment of free life in the open woods, has fled from the guns of men, and taken refuge in the domestic farmyard, where the hens all go up ladders to bed, to her infinite amazement and scorn. Chantecler offers her a home, and she sleeps as well as she can in the dog's kennel, stifled though she be to find a roof above her head. He is astonished to see how dowdy his hens look, now that this fascinating creature has appeared among them, and learns from her something of the life of the open road. The dramatic play turns now altogether round her desire to show him that the love of a heart to a heart is worth far more than his ideal of duty to the Universe. While he is only anxious to make love feed the passion with which he fulfils his task to the world at large, she is determined to win from him his secret; and at last he tells it her. " I know I am going to say it, and I know I shall be wrong," he says. But will she be worthy after all to hear it ? He will risk it.

He tells her first that his very shape is the sacrament of his mission. He is curved like a trumpet or a shell, so that he may become with his entire body a pure organ of musical sound. That is the beginning of the mystery. Then next, impatient and proud, he scratches the turf with his claws as if looking for something there in the soil.

" It is seeds you are looking for, I suppose ? " suggests the pheasant.

" Never ! " he says, " I never look for them. I find them now and then ; and, if I do, then, in disdain, I offer them to my hens."

" What is it then," she asks, " for which you search, as you scratch so vehemently ? "

" I am seeking," he says, " to plant myself in the earth. I must get rid of grass and stones until my eight claws are down in the soft, black soil ; and then, once in touch with the good earth, I sing. And in this, lady pheasant, lies half the secret of my song. It is not a song that you sing by looking for it, but a song that springs up out of its native soil like sap ; and the hour when the sap rises in me, the hour, in fact, when I feel the touch of genius, is the hour when the dawn just hesitates at the edge of the obscure heaven. Then, filled with a shuddering ardour that discharges itself through my whole being, I feel myself necessary ; and, curved and strung, I yield myself to the earth, which speaks in me as through a shell ; and I cease to be a bird and become rather the channel through which the cry of the earth escapes into the sky."

" Chantecler ! " cries the lady pheasant, almost swept away by his rapture.

" And this cry that rises out of the earth,—it is a cry of love for the light, it is a cry of passionate and vehement love for that golden thing they call the day, which all want to see again—the pine trees with their bark, and the little mosses, and the tiniest pebbles ; it is the cry of all that craves colour and flame, the suppliant cry with which the wet meadow asks for a little rainbow to glorify every tiny blade of grass, and the forest clamours for a fire to burn at the end of every alley. This cry which passes through me into the azure heaven is the cry of all that feels itself dis-

P

graced to be lost in a vague abyss and deprived of the
sun without knowing why. It is the cry of cold, the
cry of fear, the cry of ennui, the cry of the trembling
rose in the night alone, of the hay that desires to be
dried for the mill, of the wet tools that have been
left out of doors ; the cry of the innocent beasts who
do not wish to hide anything that they do ; and of the
brook that wants to be seen to the bottom ; and of
the mud that wants to become dry, wholesome soil
again ; and of the tree with its flowers that wants to
have more flowers ; and of the green grape that would
like to have its side browned ; and of the trembling
bridge that desires to feel, gently shimmering on its
planks, the shadows of the birds and the shadows of
the branches. It is the cry of all that wants to sing
and to get rid of mourning and to revive and do
service again ; the cry of the stone that is happy to be
warm under the hands that rest on it, or the ant that
runs over it ; it is the cry toward the light of all
beauty, and all health, and of all that desires to find
its joy in the sun, and to do its work, and to see the
work that it does, and to be seen doing it ; so that
when this vast appeal for the day rises in me, my soul
grows large ; and I hold in and contract the cry for
a moment, that it may become yet more sonorous,
until at last I am so convinced that I am going to
accomplish an act, I have such a faith that my crowing
will make the night crumble away like the walls of
Jericho that, charged with the coming victory, my
song rings so clear and loud and peremptory, that the
horizon, shaken with rosy trouble, obeys me."

"Chantecler!" exclaims the pheasant again.

"Yes, I sing," he says, "and in vain the night offers me the compromise of twilight; for I sing, and suddenly I recoil, astounded at seeing that I too have become red in the light, and that I, the cock, have made the sunrise!"

"You do it," she says, "you make it all come to pass?"

"Yes, all that opens the flower and the eye of man, and the window, and the soul. Yes, I do it! My voice scatters the light; and when the sky is grey it means that I have sung badly."

"And why then do you sing in the day?"

"Well, I keep myself in practice," he says, "or indeed I swear a great oath to the spade and the rake that I will accomplish my duty in waking everything up."

"And what wakes you up?" asks the pheasant.

"The fear of forgetting," he answers.

"And do you really believe that at the sound of your voice the whole world bathes itself in light?"

"Well," he answers simply, "I do not know very well what the world is; but I sing for my own valley, trusting that in every other valley there is another cock who will do as much."

And then, to verify his words, he proposes to enact the great drama before her eyes. The skies are already going pale; it is going to begin. "Ah, great sun, I feel you there moving," he cries, as he looks towards the far horizon. "I laugh with pride through all my red combs."

And then he crows, Cocorico! and the light falls
here, there, everywhere. A star goes out, and already
the green in the sky turns orange. He crows, Cocorico!
and lo, there is yellow glory about the pines. He
crows, Cocorico! and the grey becomes white. He
crows with a higher and higher enthusiasm; and still
he cries to her that if only she will love him, he will
turn all the soft words that she speaks to him quite
low into glorious sunlight for the world beyond. Let
her but say that she adores him, and he will turn a
mountain into gold.

But still all her love is absorbed by him into the
duty that he fulfils, until at last, as the blue comes on
the river, and the white on the roadway, and all the
cocks are crowing at once in all the far valleys, she
cries " There it is, the sun, the sun ! "

" Yes," he says, " I see it is there, but I must snatch
him up from behind that wood," and at the final
crow it rises, until they are both flooded with the
glory of the light! Cocorico! " There it is; it is
done "; he says, " it is immense." He can sing no
more.

That is his triumph. Then, far on, comes the
disaster out of which he rises to a yet higher victory.
It comes about through the song of the nightingale.
The night has comes and all the little birds sing their
orisons, while the little rabbits sit up in the silence and
listen, and the invisible chorus of birds praises God
for putting air into their bones and the blue of heaven
on their wings, and gives Him thanks for the past
day, that has been so sweet, and for the water from

which they have drunk, and for the little grains that their tiny beaks have pecked open, and for the excellent little eyes that He has given them, and the little horny tools by which they can kill all the little slugs in the garden. They ask forgiveness for any venial fault which has made them eat a gooseberry or two when they ought to have been killing insects. They pray for man, if he has in his injustice at all thrown stones at them though they circled him with songs, and perhaps caught some of them in his net; yet let him be forgiven in memory of the one man, the blessed Francis of Assisi, who spoke of the "birds, my brothers." Let him pray for them, that holy man, that they may find the little seeds of corn that they desire.

"Amen," they say—"Amen," say the rabbits—"Amen," says Chantecler.

But in the night the nightingale sings. For the first time Chantecler feels that he has heard a voice more beautiful than his own. He is quite overcome and apologetic. His voice sounded to him now quite "red" as he calls it, "red and brutal."

"Ah! but mine," says the nightingale, "sometimes appears to me too easy and too blue," and she begs the cock to recognize this sad and yet reassuring fact, that no one, neither the cock of the morning nor the nightingale of the night, can quite sing the song that they dream of singing.

"Oh! but," he says, with a look of passionate desire, "if I could have the song that was as a cradle to men's souls!"

" Ah ! but I," retorts the nightingale, " cannot make duty musical."

" I cannot make people weep," says the cock.

" And I never can wake them up," says the nightingale. " But never mind, one must sing and sing on, though one knows of songs that one prefers to one's own ; sing on until—" an explosion, a flash, a little dead red body falls at the feet of Chantecler— " Killed ! " he cries, " when she's only sung for five minutes."

Chantecler has lost control through sorrow, and does not see that the night is flying fast. He is occupied wholly in calling to the little insects and beetles, the true sacristans who know well that the tomb which is least sad and most holy is the earth that opens at the place where the body dies. So they dig its grave. And now the golden pheasant has her chance to comfort Chantecler. She lays her wing over his head so that he may not see how fast the dawn is coming. Sobbing he lies there.

" You see how tender my wing is," she says, " and my wing is but an open heart, a couch on which to repose, a kiss that becomes a roof." So she holds him seduced by fair words until " You see," she cries, as she bounds back, spreading her wings, " that the day has come without you ! "

He utters a loud and poignant cry of pain.

" Look," she cries, " how the mosses are growing scarlet."

" But no, no," he cries, " not without me ! "

" And the horizon," she says.

" No," he prays.

" Is golden," she answers.

" Oh ! the treason of it ! "

" A heart is better than the horizon," she pleads.

" Yes, it is true," he says in weakness.

" And you see, don't you," she pleads again, " that a heart against your heart is better than the heaven to which you are no longer necessary ? Yes, and that the twilight is better than the day, when in the twilight we are two together."

" Yes, yes," he sobs ; and then, suddenly hurling himself back from her, he draws up and utters one loud impetuous crow. " Cocorico ! "

" Why are you crowing ? "

" To remind myself," he retorts, " that I have three times denied all that I adore."

" And what is that ? "

" My duty," he says.

" Where are you going and what will you do ? "

" My duty."

" What night is there for you to conquer ? " she asks, with fury.

" The night that lies on men's eyes," he answers.

" Oh, you are going to wake the sleepers, are you ? "

" Yes, and St. Peter."

" But you see," she argues, " that the day has risen without your voice."

" My own destiny," he answers, " is more sure to me than the day that I see."

And now there is suddenly another Voice in the tree, the Voice of a new nightingale.

" Is there another, now that one is dead ? " asks the pheasant in fear, looking at the little tomb where the body lies.

" There must always be a nightingale in every forest," says the Voice.

" And in the soul," cries Chantelcer, with exaltation, " there must always be a faith so sure of itself that it comes back as soon as it has been slain."

" But look, the sun mounts ! "

" Well, that is because I sang yesterday. I made the dawn come ; and I will do more."

" What will you do ? " she asks, with a choked voice.

" Why, in all the grey mornings when so many poor beasts, waking without seeing each other, dare not believe in the dawn, the ring of my song shall take the place of the sun. I go that I may sing."

" How," she asks, " can you recover courage when you doubt what work you have to do ? "

" One simply goes to work," he says.

" But if you are not the cock that makes the morning rise ? "

" Then it is because I am the cock of a more distant sun. My cries will pierce the night with those little wounds that they call stars. True, that I shall not see shining on the bell-towers that final heaven made of all the stars that have drawn together in the night ; but if I sing on, exact and sonorous, and if, sonorous and exact as I, long after I am dead, every farm shall have its cock singing in its yard, I believe that at last there will be no more night."

" When will that be ? " she asks.

" Some day," he answers.

" Oh, then go and forget our forest and its happy freedom."

" No, indeed, I shall never forget that noble green forest where first I learned that he who sees his own dream dead must either die himself or rise stronger than before."

So he strides off.

" He is going," she cries in despair. " Ah, to keep these men when they are faithless—if we only had arms, arms, arms ! Alas ! we have only wings ! Take me with you," she cries.

" Will you be content to come after the dawn ? "

" Never ! " she breaks out with bitter recoil.

" Then, good-bye."

" I hate you," she hisses.

" And I adore you," says Chantecler, already passing out through the underwood, " but I should serve ill the work that I take up again if I were near anyone who thought anything greater than my work."

One last short scene shows us the conversion of the golden pheasant. The cock is in danger, the game-keeper has been seen loading his gun, and may shoot the cock if he does not shoot the pheasant.

" He shall never draw on that cock," cries the pheasant. " He will not do it if he sees me."

" What are you going to do ? " says Patou, the dog.

" My duty," says the pheasant.

She flies towards the danger; and as she flies starts a snare, which closes on her.

" She is taken," says Patou the dog.

" Ah! Chantecler is lost!" says the pheasant, from inside the net. "Oh, nightingale, say something," she cries in misery, " if only he might live and not die by that gun! And I would live too in that dull farmyard; and I would allow, Oh Sun! that you should just mark my place by his side as you draw his shadow. All is waking." "Bon jour! Bon jour! Bon jour! Bon jour! Bon jour! Bon jour!" All the birds are singing.

" Oh, let him live," she cries.

" Ha, ha!" says the jay, flying across; and from afar comes the cry of the cuckoo.

" I abdicate!" she cries. "And thou, Light! with whom I dared to dispute him, pardon me; and let there be, oh Morning Rays, the victory now of your golden powder."

A gun is heard.

" Ah!" she cries, " he is killed!"

Far off there comes back to them the crow of Chantecler.

" He is saved!" cry all the little birds, and the rabbits dance and tumble on the grass.

" God of the little birds!" says a voice fresh and clear in the trees.

" It is the morning prayer," say the rabbits, and they are all still.

" They are coming to the net," cries the wood-pecker.

"Amen," says the golden pheasant, shutting her eyes in resignation.

"God through whom we speak!"—begins the Voice in the trees.

"Hush!" says Patou, the dog. "Down with the curtain quick! Here come the Men."

Everybody flies. The pheasant remains alone with open wings and beating throat, waiting for the giant who draws near.

So the Drama passes. Man is on the scene, and the farmyard and the woods drop back into silence, and their transfiguration is over. No doubt the emotion raised by humanizing the yard has overcharged the situation. It goes beyond what the surroundings will bear. No acting imaginable can save it: for the wine has broken the bottles. But, surely, the wine outpoured is superb. The humour of the piece is too deliberate and elaborate not to give an artificial air to the whole play; but through it all the exultant song of the Cock carries everything before it. His very vanities are innocent and winning; and when they die out of him under the disaster that shatters his dream, he is great enough to be transfigured, by the humiliation, into a voice that is prophetic. Will man, who stumbles in with his guns and snares, prove himself as great as Chantecler? He, too, will fill the earth, first, with himself and with his own imaginations; he will make himself its centre, and regard the whole of Nature as a drama that turns round himself as the pivot. That is man's first childish way of gathering the earth about him and finding his home in it. The challenge comes when he is asked to recognize that, though mistaken about his actual significance in the scene, nevertheless, all this imagination of his did but foretell and anticipate a deeper communion between himself and the life about him, which would indeed, in the last resort, make him earth's prophet, through whom alone she finds her voice and discovers her soul.

XXIV

MR. GILBERT MURRAY'S "ELECTRA" OF EURIPIDES

MR. GILBERT MURRAY's genius in transcription enabled us to sit in a tiny stuffy upholstered modern theatre in Sloane Square, and listen to the actual wonder which broke out, through the perfection of human speech, upon a far away incredible Hellenic Democracy, gathered in its crowds upon the ringed circles of marble steps, under the free light and air of Athenian skies, over two thousand years ago. What did it mean ? How was it done ? The people of Athens had this amazing thing for their familiar pleasuring. This is what they enjoyed on a " Bank Holiday." We faintly recall Clacton-on-Sea, or Margate, on the first Monday in August : and shudder : and tremble. The tinkle of a nigger song, the thud of a banjo, the rattle of the bones, sing in our ears— memories of all that has been " butchered to make an English Holiday." We may fall back on the thought of that vast underground slave world which alone enabled the narrowed Athenian Democracy to secure the leisure and the spare energy which made it what it was. It still remains an astounding and humiliating miracle, that the Greek Drama should have been provided to suit their taste in entertainment.

Can language ever go beyond this incomparable style ? Mr. Murray has made it positively sing round us, with a haunting magic, with an inevitable charm, with a delicacy, and a firmness, and an ease, so that it flows like living waters. We are carried along in it. It possesses us. And it rises into passion, and wrath: and dies away into pathos and farewell: and it breaks up into sharp jets of agonized pity, or scorn, or despair. It answers to every demand made upon it: and, always, the imaginative beauty is blended with the strong intellectual inspiration, until we know not whether the thought or the expression be the more excellent thing.

And the dramatic effects are magnificent: and the catastrophe is led up to with incomparable skill: and the weight of tragic horror grows until the close: and ever and always, the grim closed wigwam of a house waits there, under our eyes from first to last, dumb and aware, the death-trap waiting for its prey ; recalling in naked irony, by its wattled doors, the haughty gate through which Agamemnon had passed to his doom under the invitation of the wicked Queen, who now passes in to the peasant hut to shed the expiatory blood ; crying from within, to pitiless children who kill, as he had cried to her pitiless heart as she smote him with the axe.

Tremendous ! Yet what is it which holds us back in this play, and forbids us to yield ourselves to its appeal? The truth is, that the collision between the exquisite modernity of the spirit in the play and the brutal savagery of the story is too violent. The story belongs to the heroics of barbaric passion. We are face to face with the simplicities of elemental man, as we encounter them, say, in the Jewish Psalms of Retaliation and Denunciation. Man is stripped bare: his naked being exhibits the play of every instinct, unqualified and untempered. If he is angry, he kills: if he has a wrong, he fills heaven and earth with it: he is one thing at a time, and one thing only. All subtleties have disappeared. There can be no room for reflections. Single and simple passions possess him wholly. He is primitive: primal: awful: stupendous.

But, then, here is Euripides, flinging into this savage and heroic setting all that comes from delicate and subtle thought playing hither and thither round spiritual problems: the touch of fine emotion: the thrill of sensitive souls: the movement of quivering wonder, and pity, and tenderness: the lissom interchange of antithetical sympathies: the quick questionings of a conscience that is alive to the conflicts of varying motives and appeals. How can all this consort with the scene on which it is to play its part? If we yield to his spell, then, the play becomes horrible, bloody, gross, impossible. We cannot be in this mood, and endure it. When the chorus propose to Electra to join in a dance at the news of the appalling murder of Ægisthus, we shrink back as from savages. As Electra shouts her terrible whispers into her brother's ear, driving him on to the murder of their mother, we cannot away with it. We cannot listen to the poor Queen pleading so effectively her own sad case, and revealing the awful unhappiness that has robbed her of the reward of her crime, and, then, bear to watch her go into that hut, confidingly, as a beast goes into the slaughter-house. We are sickened. It will not do. The splendour of the poet's work has brought us into another world, where such things as these are intolerable and must not happen.

And, perhaps, the very beauty of Miss Wynne Matheson's acting of her part only served to heighten the sense of impossibility. She was perfect. The image of the loveless, childless woman, the unwed wife, robbed of her natural fulfilment, drained of her true affections, imprisoned within the one morbid passion of her hate, was magnificently given. Yet it is not in Miss Matheson to be other than a beautiful, tender, sympathetic woman. Her grace, her refinement, her delicate tones, as they intensified the fascination of her betrayal, yet served to render the action itself of the part yet more incredible than ever.

We cannot be surrendered to the power of the Euripidean mood, and not be revolted by the deeds done. What are the great Gods doing ? To what hideous mêlée of blood are they driving men and women who have trusted them ? In vain does the dignity of Castor and Pollux, in the final moment, attempt to establish moral harmony. Noble as is their utterance, it leaves Phœbus Apollo uninterpreted and unjustified. A cloud lies on us. The horror of a great darkness has suddenly wrapt round brother and sister, who had moved as under the voice of God, to find themselves aware only of a curse that had fallen on them. Where are we ?

So we crept out of our comfortable cushions, to find ourselves among cabs and omnibuses in Sloane Square. Two worlds had got mixed up together: and had refused to blend. The glory of the Greek poet had been shown at its work of shattering the fabric in which it had framed itself. He had put out his power by which he made himself as one of us, charged with our own modern soul; and, in doing it, had demanded a new moral world, a new atmosphere. The new wine had burst the old bottles. There must be new bottles, if the wine is to be kept unspilt.

Q

XXV

PETER PAN

Poor old London, sick with dismal fatigue, has discovered that, after all, it still possesses the immortal secret of childhood. It can fling behind it all the sad wisdom of experience: it can forget what it has painfully learned: it can drop its dreadful task, and ease its shoulder of the burden. It can cease to be desperately earnest, " regarding neither to right, nor left, going passively by, staggering on to her goal." All this disagreeable business can vanish into limbo: for it can go to Peter Pan. Then, the wonderful change begins.

Week after week, month after month, year by year, weary Londoners crowd the Duke of York theatre, to find that they are weary no longer, because they have become children again. They have recovered the true perspective of childhood. They live within its horizons: they see with its eyes: they never travel outside its thoughts. Silly old manhood has slipped off them. Facts are no longer facts. The Higher Criticism is become a toothless Crone mumbling vain wrath, to which no one listens. Whatever ought to happen does happen: and no one is in the least surprised. It is the most natural thing in the world to find a bright and airy gentleman

226

in beautiful red tights, flying up and down your
bedroom at night, looking for his lost shadow. It is
quite obvious that you will fly away with him right
through the window, far away to Never Never Land.
After a few tries, it is really quite easy.

And, out there, in that country where all things are
as they ought to be, you know exactly what to expect.
There will be Red Indians, of course : who will always
be bending their ears to the ground to listen for
impossible noises that they never hear. And there
will be Pirates ; what else could there be ? And a
terrible Captain with a steel hook for a hand : and
bold buccaneers with black chop sailor whiskers, and
the most awful hair over their eyes, and language on
their tongues. And there must be an alligator : and
bears : and a wolf : and a cave underground where
you live : and fights : and capture : and walking the
plank : and a most surprising victory : and all Pirates
drowned : and a pillow-fight before going to bed :
and a splendid tea : and a return home, flying in at
the Nursery window, to find mother in tears, until
she and all her recovered children hug each other with
sobs of joy. And all is well for ever after.

This is childhood's world ; and over this world,
" Mummy " is supreme. Every thing turns round
her. She always knows exactly what is wanted.
And the one thing that everyone wants is to have
a mother. These poor, poor pirates never had
mothers. That is why they are pirates. As for father,
he is helpless and absurd : he cannot even tie his tie
when he is going out to a dinner-party, without

making such a fuss over it that the whole house is
upset : and mother, of course, ties it for him in a
moment. He tries his hand at practical jokes in the
nursery : which only end in greatly shocking the
children, and sending them very unhappy to bed. So
like Papa !

But were there ever Red Indians half so red as
these ? And has the world ever heard of Pirates
so thick with daggers and guns, and so awful in their
blood-curdling threats ? " By Caius and Balbus." So
their dread oath runs ! And their hornpipe is simply
magnificent ! And did anyone ever before meet an
alligator that had swallowed a clock, which ticked on
for years inside it, to give notice of its approach ?

And grave old gentlemen from the West End sit
and drink all this in : and believe it : and are at home
in it : and feel as if the clustering curls were once more
brown on their shining crowns. And Bloods from
Piccadilly go night after night, and feel as if they had
never been so happy as this : and give themselves
away to sweet and healing laughter : and become
aware that this is the only true world where everything is real ; and recall the happy days when daisies
were daisies : and this earth was a home of wonder
and adventure : and their eyes were open : and hearts
were free : and limbs were light : and slumber was
deep : and mother rustled into the room at night, in
her lovely silk gown, and sat by the bed, and said
good-night, and fluttered a kiss down on the white
brow, as her tender hand stroked back the ruffled
hair. Oh, dear ! Oh, dear ! It is all so long ago !

Yet here it is, again, made ours for one brief hour, in its delicious reality, in its undying charm.

All London owes a debt to Sir J. M. Barrie for this perfect gift: and to the actors who have so entirely caught the spirit of the child. It will never forget the gallant grace of Peter: or the awful ferocity of Captain Hook: or the tragedy of Smee and miserable Starkie, solaced by the strains of the concertina: or the motherhood of Wendy: or the laugh of Tootles: or the quivering joy of Michael: or the smile of tiny little Liza, who, in the piping voice of a child of six, announces herself as " the mother of ten, who wishes there were twenty." And always their hearts will be soft to lumpy, ugly old Slightly—who was the one boy who had had his name marked on his linen when he fell out of his pram, and vanished to Never Never Never Land. "Slightly Soiled": that was the mystic inscription: and it gave a clue at once to his identity. It is a beautiful thing to have done—to have made all the world confess that there is no such joy as innocent joy, and no such laughter as the clean laughter of childhood. After all, it is then that we were absolutely ourselves. It is then that we were original. No convention had moulded us to its type. We could surprise. We said wonderful things that no one had ever said before. We had something of genius about us.

> " Shades of the prison house
> Began to close
> Upon the growing boy."

He went to school, that means : and bent his whole mind on being like everybody else : on saying what everybody said : on doing the right thing. Spontaneity was dead. At last, all the vision

"Dies away,
And fades into the light of coming day."

But it cannot have been in vain that once we were what children still are, incredible as it may seem. And it is an unspeakable boon to be allowed to go back to the forgotten days ; and to recover their tone ; and to taste again their fair free air ; and to dance all over with their speechless glee ; and so, for some kindly and blessed moment, to

"Feel through all this earthly dress
Bright shoots of Everlastingness."

XXVI

ROMANCE IN GAITERS

CHRISTIANITY is a Romance, as Mr. G. K. Chesterton continually informs an incredulous world. Christianity is an Heroic Adventure: or it is nothing. So true! Yet how successfully we of the Home Church contrive to disguise it! No wonder that Mr. Chesterton finds so few believers. Romance! We don't look like it. It is, no doubt, our coyness that hinders us from displaying this character of ours with better effect. We hush it all up in gaiters and buttons. We creep about in obscure and ugly disguises. The last epithet that even our best friends would think of applying to those who are known as the dignified Clergy, would be "romantic." No! Stuffy: fusty: fussy: portentous:—all this we are: but not picturesque. We do not wear the air of having often looked out through

> " Magic casements opening on the foam
> Of perilous seas, in faërie lands forlorn."

No one would look for us in that sort of spot: or expect to find us engaged in any such occupation. We are very obvious: very ordinary: very usual: very commonplace: rather heavy and tiresome: a bit slow in the wind: with a touch of wet-blanket somewhere about us. This rather depressing impression is relieved, to a certain degree, by something irre-

trievably comic in our appearance. This endears us
to the theatres: and a whole wilderness of comic
curates have sprung up at bazaars and other light
entertainments, through the genius of Mr. Albert
Chevalier. And, altogether, the Established Church
wins a certain affection from its adherents under the
title of a " dear funny old thing."

It is quite true that this is not a complete or a just
account of us. We have had our heroes in the Slums:
they are there now. If you poke about the " East
Ends " of our big cities, you find wonderful bits of
free Bohemian clerical life, in jolly clergy-houses, where
there is not a scrap left of dreary conventionalism:
and respectability has been thrown to the winds:
and human laughter, and human tears, fling defiance
at an ugly world: and there is risk, and adventure,
and beauty, and carelessness, and glory. We have all
this going on, and in no small quantity. And the
Transpontine Drama makes gallant efforts to work it,
as a theme: and you hardly ever pass the Surrey
Theatre without catching sight of a picture on the
boards of a magnificent Curate, stalwart and sublime,
standing over the crouching villain whom he has just
smitten to the dust by one blow from a muscular
right arm.

Yet all this is not enough to check that proverbial
impression. It does not seem to count, over against
the dead-weight of massive commonplace which
makes itself felt as our normal condition. As a lot,
we Priests are dull. We are flat. We are unsuggestive.
Romance is not our key-note.

And that is why the Pan-Anglican business was so significant. Suddenly, we all rubbed our eyes, to find that something was up of quite another order. Strange things were all about us. Strange beings from strange places swarmed round every corner. Their titles stretched our spelling powers to breaking point. We had long ceased to remember whether these Dioceses, with their outlandish names, are in Australia or California. Is " Oluwole " a name or a place ? Who can say ? Anyhow, there is not one Island in the far seas that one or all these men had not touched at : there is not a river that they had not forded : there is not a veldt so wide and desolate that they had failed to cross it : there is no ocean that they had not sailed : there is no people, black, brown, yellow or green, that they had not intimately greeted. They murmured weird sounds from unknown languages : they clicked : they snorted : they dropped liquid vocables, like rain. They carried about, in their names and in their talk, the fragrance of historic memories that had been to us fabulous, but which they had taken possession of. India, Persia, China, and all the wonders of Pacific Islands, were to them familiar ground. They had been rocked in the bullock-carts : wrecked at sea : half-drowned in floods and fords : all but eaten alive by men and beasts. And here they were : and they were ours : and they made themselves quite at home. There was a Canadian Bishop who relieved the tedium of a Lambeth Conference by dropping in, during lunch-time, at a rifle-range to indulge his favourite tastes, by shooting at tin bears down a tube: and hitting at every shot. Probably, at certain hours in the day, all those gentlemen who were in the habit of taking sliding headers down the shoots in the West-minster Baths were members of the American Episcopal Bench.

Ah! And it was very real, this romance. As we looked at those men among us then, we recalled Archdeacon Johnson, blind and worn in Nyassa: and the body of Chancey Maples under the lake water: and Bishop Hannington, dying under the malarian tyranny: and the white body of Patteson floating out in the lone boat, with the martyr-palms laid by those who killed him, crossed on his breast. And many a lonely grave of those well known to us, hidden away in far corners of African jungles, came back on the imagination. Here was adventure: here was romance. It was all true that Mr. Chesterton says.

And the odd, and the comforting thing is this——that these returning heroes of ours—these, our braves—looked, after all, very like us. You could not tell us apart. These Bishops, who have swum their way across the foaming floods, "in faërie lands forlorn," might any one of them have been sitting in a comfy Palace in a Midland Diocese. When they mixed in Processions, or mingled with Fulham Garden Parties, you had to ask which was which. "Can you tell me if that is the Bishop of London?" "No! That is the Bishop of Natal." "Really! Thank you! I should not have thought it!" That was the way that conversation ran. You found yourself listening to breathless tales from someone who was just as ordinary-looking as you are.

I always remember the shock of a most proper looking parson, straight from Cambridge, a 'Varsity oar, in his long black coat and stiff starched collar, telling us quite simply of the three separate occasions on which he had just escaped being eaten by cannibals in the New Hebrides. We kept wondering—would they have eaten the coat, too, and swallowed the collar ? It was as astonishing to hear them talk as it would be, if the Ancient Mariner, as he held you with his glittering eye, were to wear gaiters and buttons ; or as if a portly gentleman, in a shovel hat and apron, were to appear with a dead albatross slung round his neck.

Now, this was comforting ; because their romance, in this way, began to infect us. If they were so like us, might not we be rather like them ? Why should our gaiters and buttons matter more than theirs ? Might not our own Home Diocesans swim rivers, and shoot bears, and dive ashore through the surf in the Solomon Islands, as well as any ? After all, we have the Bishop of London. He would hold any one of them at scratch.

It is this English Church, snug and smug among the hedgerows, that has done it. That is the astonishing thing. It has thrown feelers out so far and wide. It has overleaped the paddock fence. It has flung out its frontier line. It has set sail with every wind that blows : and planted its feet on every shore that ocean washes. Who would have dreamed it of her ? She

hardly believes it herself. She finds it difficult to
remember as she sits tied up in Elizabethan Red-tape :
and smothered under the convention of Establishment :
and fat with dignities : and very scant of breath. Yet
it is all true. For here were the adventurers whom
she had sent out, trooping home to din the great
story into her dim deaf ears. They spoke freely :
frankly : strongly. They were not hindered : or
afraid. They did not sit in the Lords : nor dine at
the Athenæum. They had rushed home, from their
swims : and were here, to say what they thought.

And their tales were thrilling. And their outlook
was wide. They were in touch with everything that
was going on over all the face of the earth. They were
in the thick of old worlds passing away ; and new
worlds opening into life and light. They felt the
movement of man's immense story : the ebb and flow
of the influences that are to make history : the rise
and fall of peoples and nations : the momentous
mingling of races.

And all of what they said belonged to us at home :
and we, through them, were at the heart of the mystery.
And in them we, too, made our high ventures, and
spoke the great language of romance : and lifted up
our poor tired old head : and gave great thanks.

This far-reaching life, as it floods back home, will
save the day for us. It will blow away our stuffiness.
It will break up our stagnancy. It will shake us out
of the impotence that comes through a gathering
sense of self-contempt. We are not so thin and starved
in ideals as we feared. We are not so cabined and

confined in the fatalities of convention. We are
citizens of no mean city. We breathe large Catholic
airs. So we cheer up.

And all the more, because this wider life has
recognized how near the problems abroad have become
to the problems at home. All over the earth, the
problems are now social. This tremendous Western
industry has contrived to draw all the five Continents
now within its pressure and its anxieties. Africa:
Asia: America: and the Isles: have been sucked
into the stream. One vast commerce pervades them
all. The whole mass of living nations has got to come
to terms with it: from the Chinese Mandarins to
the dimmest Darkies who can be indentured. This
is what is changing the equilibrium of the entire
world. This is what is raising the Racial Problem into
such dreadful pre-eminence. Therefore it is that
both Congress and Conference spent their strength
so largely on the perplexities that beset Society. And
therefore it is that they deemed themselves as
intimately concerned with the condition of our Home
Cities as with the fortunes of their scattered Missions.
It all stands together: whether it be the Sweated
Industries in the East End: or the exclusion of
Kanakas from Sugar Felds in Brisbane: or the introduction of Uganda Natives into Johannesburg Gold
Mines: or the anxious presence of Chinese and
Japanese on the coast of Columbia.

And, again, there is the immense area of intellectual
disturbance to cover and consider. And here, too,
the one problem is widening out, until it embraces

the entire body of the world's thinking, whether it be done in London, or Berlin : in Benares, or Calcutta : in Cairo, or Boston. In everything, the question for Home Church and for Missionary Church is one and the same. For the first time, through the literature put out on behalf of the Pan-Anglican Congress, was this deep truth fully realized. And, as we lifted our heads to rally to the far calls of high adventure : as we grew aware how much romance lent its glamour to glorify our English Church, in spite of all our efforts to disguise her from herself ; we, nevertheless, became profoundly humble, for all our elation, as we recognized through the splendour of the enterprise to which we stood committed, the shallowness of the effort that we had yet made to fulfil the charge. What we found was that we were in face of the most tremendous moment in the evolution of Humanity : and that, while we just touched it everywhere, we were adequate to it nowhere. We spread so far. Something of ours is to be found everywhere. But, everywhere, the problem was and is beyond us. Everywhere, it is far too big for our puny attempts at handling it. Everywhere, our own contribution to the solution is thin : starved : incompetent : often, contemptible. Nowhere is there a strong staff : nowhere is there real efficiency of support : or adequacy of resources. Nowhere are we fully equipped. Nowhere is there any volume of force discharged : or any massive advance : or any completeness of system and service. Everywhere you can find us : and everywhere, the same rather pitiful tale of impoverishment, of lack of men, of loss of opportunity, of hopeless struggle against adverse conditions with the odds desperately against our scanty forces.

This is our humiliation. We have, in the days behind us, made efforts, that had much gallantry in them, to cover the ground. We strove to multiply Dioceses : to get the system of the Church in evidence : to secure that the framework, at least, was to be seen on the spot. This cost us much. And we remember those who did it with faithful gratitude. But, too often, the framework was all. We popped a Bishop down : and gave him nothing to work with. We supplied the shell : but put nothing inside it. Hence, our forlorn impotence to grapple seriously with the situations that have sprung up within our formal outlines. Episcopacy has again and again verified its validity under the strain of this world-wide expansion : but it has one peril, that it tempts us to think that everything has been done when once we have covered the map of the world with a scheme of dioceses with one Bishop in each. We might just as well suppose that the Ritz Hotel had been built as soon as the steel framework stood up in the sky. Of course that is its essential structure, but so long as it is only a thin and empty cage of steel, it is for hotel purposes singularly ineffective.

Our task, now, is to fill in our sketch : to realize our promises : to clothe with flesh and blood our skeletons that rattle their bones in the wind. We have got to staff our Institutions : to feed them : to stiffen them : to endow them : to set them free to do the work for which they were intended. A shrivelled pea, loosely rattling in a hard hollow husk, has no Romance about it. It is not an inspiring symbol. Yet does it not recall to us a good deal with which we are familiar, in our work abroad and at home ?

It is not enough to undertake a big job : you must be sure that you are fit to undertake it. We dare not think that we can wear a Giant's Robe with impunity. There will come a day, when people will tire of the Robe, and will ask " What about the Giant ? "

XXVII

THE TRIPPER'S TRIUMPH

ONCE a year the vast, blind, welded masses that have coagulated into cities, let themselves loose, to swarm out over sea and land, for the brief rapture of a Summer Holiday. The black bunches of human beings, that cling together like bees, are broken and dispersed : and every hill and shore becomes thick with the moving hosts. What a number of us there are, stuck tight together in London ! We see and know, as the hordes disperse. We begin to believe the incredible estimates that we have been told, of the capacity of the human race for packing close. The entire population of England could stand in Hyde Park. The whole population of the world could get into the Isle of Wight. Impossible, you say ! Well ! See what London can disgorge, without so much as noticing it. Her streets seem just as full, though the central stations may have been, for weeks, a wild pandemonium ; and the loaded trains have crawled, like fat worms, bearing their burdens hour after hour away from the city to the sea. Ah ! Those trains ! We encounter them suddenly, on some lightly-planned move that we were making between country house and country house. We find ourselves in face of a crisis. A huge train is drawn up, into which we had hoped to skip. Up and down its enormous length we fly,

searching for a seat. But every window is blocked
with hot simmering faces of children, streaked with
dust and jam : chubby hands ooze with fruit. A
hurried glance inside reveals hopeless vistas of reeking
babies, and steaming bottles, and dishevelled mothers :
and here and there, through measureless litter of
parcels, the haggard face of a buried father looks out
with the eyes of a weary Titan, staggering on to his
goal, yet hardly able to bear the too vast orb of his
fate. Where on earth can we get in ? Guards shout :
whistles blow. To and fro we rush. Not a seat for
a fly to be found anywhere ! Distinctions between
First Class and Third Class have long ceased to exist.
At the last second, as the train moves, we desperately
plump ourselves on to the knees of three stout ladies,
scattering squalling children, hugging our rugs, faintly
ejaculating apologies for any babies that we may have
sat down upon in our haste : and we are off. A kindly
Bishop travelling one such summer day apologized
for fatigue in the evening, on the ground that it was
slightly tiring to hand out one set of babies at every
station the train stopped at, and to hand a new set in.
That had been his unceasing occupation all the
way from London to Grantham.

And this is only one specimen of the thousand
thousand other trains that are performing the like
feat. The whole country is on the move. Everywhere it is happening at once. Far away in Switzerland, the white glaciers are turning black under the
inroad of parsons, even as the white tablecloths in
the Rhone Valley go solid black with the swarming

flies. At home, stout middle-class gents sleep thick on the floor at respectable Hydros. Coaches and brakes discharge and take up the herds that flock to Lake and Waterfall. Up on the high heather-fells, the blackcock scud, with frightened chuckle, over the shoulder of the hill, as 'Arry, in the character of "Excelsior," poised on the crag, points the forward way with his umbrella, and calls to M'ria ; and M'ria giggles and shrieks back to 'Arry. Down there, by the Beach, the wide indifferent sea tolerantly smiles at the thin spider-legs of boys and girls that paddle endlessly ; and the sands are dark with the rounded shapes of fathers and mothers, perspiring on their backs ; and the light tinkle of the banjo lends a quiver to the sunlight.

It is Nature that we have all come out to see. We have flung away our sordid commercial robes ; we have ceased from our petty bustle and our mean routine ; we have flung ourselves upon the deep bosom of Nature, to steep ourselves in her calm, to feed on her changeless and eternal peace. That is what we call it. That is what we came for. That is why we are here, with our cockney cries, with our heavy waists, with our limp 'bus-grown limbs, with our curiously ugly white faces, chucked out, in laughing swarms, wherever earth has hidden away, far from prying eyes, holy spaces of sleeping waters and of silent hills. We have come to drink of Nature's draughts. Do we get them ?

Hardly ! We trippers wreck the very thing that we pursue. With our restless feet we muddy the waters at which we stoop to drink. It is impossible to combine the hubbub of a trip with " the silence that is in the starry sky," the sleep that is " among the lonely hills." Something must be lost, wherever we go. Nature is coy: and shrinks from this boisterous wooing. She only speaks her full mind to those who can be alone with her : and she cannot be hurried. Her speech is slow-distilled. You must wait long upon her dumb moods before they break. It takes time to lean an ear to fairy-waterbreaks, if you really desire the beauty born of murmuring sound to pass into your face. This is not the sort of thing that can be managed in the interval while the rowdy coach is waiting for you to have " done " the waterfall. No ! In the agonies of handing plump Mrs. Brown up to the famous spot for a view, you lose, for the time, the sense of " winds austere and pure " blowing over " grey recumbent stones in desert places on the naked wine-dark moor." The inner heart of the thing—that which Wordsworth saw and knew and told—is inevitably gone. You must surrender it, if the trip is to be. This is the sacrifice asked. Whenever the trip comes in, Wordsworth goes out.

I remember preaching this to an Oxford Reading Party at Bettws long ago. I told them simply to give up three famous spots, and above all, one known as the " Fairy Glen." This was the tripper's due : let him have it. " Go not near it yourself. For you it is lost while he has it. Give it up freely and gladly ! " But the doctrine was too hard. They saw, daily, exquisite photographs of the place—a dream-like vision of waters slipping down between high walls of mystic rock, under a veil of birch and bracken. They really must go. At last I relaxed. "Go," I cried, "and be undone." They were. For the moment that we got there, we saw, in the very heart of the fairy shrine, a stout lady waving an umbrella and calling for help. We rushed to her side. We saw an old fat gentleman on his back kicking. We hoisted him up. We looked with anxiety into his face. Was it apoplexy? Was it some strange seizure? Oh no! The old lady thanked us for our trouble: and said "her old man could never get up again if he once got upon his back." He was simply kicking there, like an old sheep, helpless and inane. We fled in tumult from the scene. The charm was broken; the vision had fled. "There!" I said, "I told you so! Those are the only fairies that you will ever find in this Glen. That is what you wanted to see so much. But the Fairy Glen and fat gents kicking on their backs won't go together."

What, then, is to be done? Well! First, we of the Wordsworth band must avoid all sniffing and snorting. It is no earthly use to vex the air with peevish complainings, and idle protests. Our towns have got to get loose: at all costs, they must trip. Against this necessity, we shall be as futile in our resistance as Mrs. Partington with her mop. The throngs whom we have huddled into congested barracks, have the right to escape: and to scatter: and to breathe: and to move about: and to enjoy. They must do it: they shall do it: nothing shall be allowed to stand in their way: every road shall be thrown open: every device shall be put to use, by which they may be shot abroad with ever larger freedom. We, with our Wordsworths in our hands, are to wave our hats round our heads, and cheer them on in their thousands. We are to be glad that they are coming down like the wolf on our pretty fold: like the blind black locusts on the summer green. Hurrah! Hurrah! There is room for more! All Liverpool one day, strewn over our sweet highlands: all Birmingham another, rollicking down our still mountain streams: all Leeds plunging into our lone tarn, where once the wind swept to and fro by itself with the long low wail as of a crying child. Hurrah! Nothing could be better! Let this good sacrificial heart be in us: and, then, we shall have our reward. For we shall discover the merciful and providential law which sets its limits on the Atlantic Ocean and, also, compels all trippers to confine themselves to fixed routes. Certain lines are laid down for them, decreed by secret compact between the hotel-keepers and the writers of guide-books. To these certified spots, they are regularly conveyed. Down these appointed roads the innocent troops travel. They never break out: they never venture afield: they move like merry puppets pulled by strings. Every motion that they make is calculable: and can be foreseen, and guarded against. Avoid those few chosen spots, consecrated to them: and not a trace will you find of them. Not an 'Arry will be heard to cry; not a giggle of M'ria's will reach you. Sheer off a few yards from the beaten tracks, and you will find yourself in uplands as lonely and still as they were in

the day when the morning stars sang together. You
can wander at will : and not even guess that, down
there in the dip, all London is streaming past, with
lunch-baskets and bottled beer. You may lie there,
by the hour, in the purple heather : and hawks will
hang above your head : and grouse will cluck : and
hills will sleep : and the deep silence will brood : and
the only sound that stirs will be the far-away murmur
of the brooks that run among the hills. While all this
is yours for ever, do you dare to lift your querulous
howls, because you have to forgo the few and limited
opportunities for delight, which those others are
contented to possess ? They take their little : and are
perfectly satisfied. They have left you all the rest.
Who are you, that you should complain of a bargain,
which is so largely in your favour ?

The tripper shall trip. He is the one triumph of
our modern day. Never before has the whole world
tripped, as it trips now. We have lost the secret of
great Art ; we have been beaten, in a thousand ways,
by Greek and Roman ; by Mediævalism and the
Renaissance. We own it humbly. But, at least, we
can trip. We have laid the earth open : we have
searched it nook and corner : we have given everyone
the chance of going everywhere : we have perfected
the democratic holiday. This is our unique achievement. As we remember it, we lift up our heads, and
forget our shame. And, even if the tripper loses,
and must lose, half of what he goes out to find : if it is
impossible for him, for the very reason that he is a
tripper, to enter into the secret of nature's brooding

peace, or to catch the mountains in their primeval
sleep: yet does he not get something of what he
seeks ? Half may be lost: but yet half may remain:
and is not half a loaf better than no bread ? Even
in his scurrying haste, he sees what the town could
never show him. He has a glimpse of it. He wonders
what it is that looks up at him from those shining
waters. For a moment, here and there, he is dumb,
as he catches the woods at play. On some still evening,
before the gong clangs for table d'hôte, the new
moon rises over a bare crag, and holds him in its
breathless silence. Something queer is at work in
him. He never felt quite like that in Edgware Road
on a Sunday. A magic hangs over his holiday: a
charm has stolen into his soul, from brook or sea, from
hill or shore. Ever after, as he recalls it, his heart is
lightened, even as the Poet's heart that danced with
the memory of the dancing daffodils. He is initiated
into the shadowy skirts of the mystery. He has been
in Arcady. He cannot win all: the finer rapture is
denied him by the very conditions under which he
sets himself to secure it: but it is not for nothing
that he has passed under the shadow of Helvellyn.
Skiddaw and Snowdon were not too proud to help
him. They lent themselves to the humble task.
They could not utter to him the deep things that
they reserve for the more disciplined worshippers:
but they are good-natured, as all giants are. They
did what they could for him. They showed themselves
to him under flying gleams, or peeped out upon him
through scudding mists, in broad and simple ways

that he could easily take in. They gambolled for his delight: and he understood: and laughed: and thanked them: and, therefore, the sight of them availed to set his chords to a little higher tune than before. He went back to join his clinging bee-bunch: but a " bolt had been shot back somewhere in his breast ": and he was not unaware, now, of a strange world, of measureless and mysterious meaning, lying close round him, on the fringe of which he had stood and into which he yet might be enabled to enter, in the freedom of a great release.

XXVIII

PAGAN PUMPKINS

The recoil from Harvest Homes has been the result of their peculiar success. Why should all the great epochs of the Christian year be overshadowed by the Feast of St. Pumpkin ? So we wailed. We had broken our hearts over the meagre group of worshippers whom, by strenuous efforts, we got into Church for Good Friday. As for Ascension Day, we had almost despaired. No hunting could bring a flock together. Yet lo ! and behold ! we have only to wave a potato round our head, and the Church is packed from end to end. Why should people be so thrilled to see us wade through vegetables to the lectern : or emerge in the leafy pulpit like a Jack-in-the-Green ? Why should they love to see us blink through a forest of carrots, like an owl in an ivy-bush ? What does it all come to ? What spiritual significance goes with it ? Is there anything Christian about it at all ? Look at the people who come swarming in. They are rank outsiders. They have no notion of living the Christian Life, or cherishing its Creed. There are all the familiar loafers from the public-house, with their faces hardly distinguishable, in colour and expression, from the tomatoes glistening near them. Why are they so keen ? Is it more than the old Pagan instinct, which looked for a God who sent rain and sun and fruitful seasons ? Is our respectable old rector, as he peers out over the sheaves of barley-corn, any better than a medicine-man beating a tom-tom over the rice offerings of some poor blind heathen blacks ? Is it not an irony, that only on this one night in the year, can the whole Parish unite in brotherly companionship, and shake hands, and sing hymns, and recognize its common life ? So great is the power of the Pumpkin ! It is irritating : it is disgusting. We cannot, it would seem, put our hearts out : we cannot rise to the sway of the common emotion : except through vegetables. Nothing appeals but potatoes. What value has a united effort if it is limited to that " watery " level ? The whole affair is only a genial social gathering. Why then lug in a religious service ? A good dance in a barn would serve the purpose as well if not better.

So we clergy are apt to go grumbling to ourselves, as we threaten to break up the popular Harvest Home : and mutter darkly about reviving the Rogation Days. Yet I would venture to plead that the very grounds on which we criticize our Harvest Homes, form their true justification.

" They are Half-Pagan Ceremonials," we say. Yes ! And that is their merit. Our Catholic Faith, just because it is the true and full religion of Humanity, draws up into it all that makes us human : all that has ever been truly characteristic of man. It drives its roots down into that soil out of which all our developed life has emerged. It has memories that go back to the primal days, when man first knew the security of peaceful days, and was thankful for the freedom to build his homestead, and to store his fruit in safe barns, and to till his fields in good hope that he would live to gather in his harvest. Then it was that he felt the dim presence of a Fatherhood brooding over him. Then it was that he first lifted up holy hands, bringing gifts of first-fruits in thank-offering to his God. All this is ours still. It is not lost, or forgotten—the early religion of the Lares and Penates: of the household, and the homestead: of the fields and crops. It stirs and wakes within us, as it is gathered up into the Thanksgiving made for ever by Christ, the Master of the House, over the fruits of the earth, over the bread and wine. We are one with the wide Heathen world. We are its true priests, doing for it what it does but imperfectly for itself. Whom they all half ignorantly worship, Him do we show forth.

Let us, then, dig deep! Let us evoke the primal elemental emotions, which are the stuff of all religion: and are transfigured into new glory in ours. I never felt the joy of Harvest Home more fully than when, in Bishop Hornby's parish, close on the old Roman Wall, in a Church which had Roman Monoliths for all its Nave pillars, we drew out of the churchyard into the Church a real old Roman Altar, and crowned it with fruit and flowers, just as some Roman Legionary had done some sixteen hundred years ago. There it stood, baptized into Christianity, yet charged with its ancient purpose, still bearing its witness to a good God who sent fruitful seasons, filling our hearts with joy and gladness.

It is a day then to gather in all that was delicate
and tender and sweet and pure in poor dead Paganism.
And that is why it is right to call in all those dim outsiders who lie so far away from our spiritual mysteries.
They cannot yet understand our secret : but they may
know something of those deep stirrings which first
fed the religious movement. They find something
friendly and near, in these jolly vegetables. They
can recognize in them their strange dependence on
some power beyond and behind. Religion comes
home to them, through the potatoes and the asparagus.
They can get as far as that. It is something that they
should not fall outside the utmost boundaries of
religion. It may be the beginning of more. Anyhow,
let us appeal to them where they are, as they stand.

And so, again, as to the Brotherhood. If we are
never conscious of our social co-operate unity except
through the pumpkin, then let us, at least, recognize
it there, where we can. Here, for once a year, we
are all brothers, within the Church walls. And our
brotherhood lies in our secular work : in our social
interdependence : in our work for our daily bread :
in our common store of corn, and hay, and fruit : in
the labour of our hands in the fields. Well, that is a
good bond. That is worth a bit of thanks, and a bit
of thought.

What a fair opportunity for speech on social obliga-
tion, on social hopes, on social equity ! This is the
very day in all the year on which to bring out the law
of work, and the dignity of labour. This is the day
on which to learn and to teach what the Apostle meant

by declaring " If any man will not work, neither shall
he eat." This is the day to open out the promise of
God to those who desire to eat, in joyful security, of
the labour of their hands, each under his vine and his
fig-tree. " Oh ! well is thee and happy shalt thou be."
This is the day to disclose all the wide width and range
of that vast brotherhood of bread which knits the
whole earth to us by our need for food from far away
beyond our own shores. This is the day to speak of
the disasters of unemployment : and of all that is
contained for man's well-being, in the deep prayer,
" Give us this day our daily Bread." This is the day
on which to touch on the economic principles which
govern the co-operation of Human Society in a
common welfare. This is the day to enlarge our
vision of the new dawn of Peace in a land of Righteousness, whence sorrow has fled away.

XXIX

THE DOLDRUMS

Do you know what it is to be in the Doldrums ? I
learned through a voyage to South Africa. After
rounding the Canaries, you rush along in a big trade
wind that rises every day to do its work : culminates
about five o'clock when your weaker flesh begins to
tremble and to murmur " I hope the waves won't get
much bigger " : and, then, dies off and goes to bed.
It is regular as the clock. After passing the Line (is it?),
a like wind rises, and blows, and sinks each day at the
same time : only it blows the other way. Your good
ship roars through every strand in indignation at these
obstructive tactics, and ploughs and plunges on,
burying its nose in the billows slung against its onset.
And, just between the two, after the North-Wester
has dropped, and before the South-Easter begins,
there are two days of dismal suspense, when the
breeze knocks about to and fro, in aimless, sulky
indecision, and everything is hung up, and a dull
sense of inconsequence, and of impotence, and of
querulous, peevish, cross-purposing occupies the empty
foolish hours. That is the Doldrums. Your masterful liner, of course, drives its relentless course smash
through it, and laughs at the windy futilities of the
aimless weather. But the old sailing-ships must have

had a miserable time of incompetence: and they
have embodied their misery in this historic word,
which they have handed down for the use of all
generations who know well the curse of their melancholy word, " The Doldrums."

Is it not " The Doldrums " in which we so often
find ourselves, politically and socially ? Everything
flags. Everything is in suspense. Nothing moves.
Yet nobody quite knows why. There were winds, felt
and urgent, which blew with all their power our way.
An immense volume of springing energy swung us
along. We dreamed social dreams. Things seemed
possible, and near. There was, on every side, a
gathering of force, a sweep of emotion, an intellectual
onrush, a pressure of ideals, which appeared to hold
the secret of victory. It is still there: nothing has
happened to controvert or reverse it: yet it is all
spent. It is weary. It hangs back. It dies off. It
withdraws. It does no work. It is gone. And, over
against it, there seemed to be rising a deep passionate
resistance: a counter-pressure: an intense recoil: a
forward onset of antagonistic ideas: a vehement
reversal of current hopes. Up against this, we were
driving. And, at least, in the collision, in the struggle
for pre-eminence, there would be strenuous life. A
drama would be enacted. An issue would emerge
Something would be doing.

But, as we are, neither force is quite in action
Nothing is real. The movement of advance is held
up. The movement of recoil is uncertain and aimless. Both are half-hearted. Both are waiting for a

new move and a new moment. Both " hang in their stays."

There was once, for instance, an enthusiastic effort to deal bravely with the ancient menace of " the Trade." At last, we would show what the true Temperance Policy might mean. This is irretrievably wrecked: it is given short shrift: this is done insolently, and recklessly. And lo ! and behold ! Nobody minds. A paralysis falls upon us. The force engaged disappears, without a struggle. Where are we ? What next ? What have we done ? What are we going to do ? Nobody knows. Nobody troubles. We leave it alone.

National Education, again, gets into one of its proverbial tangles. An heroic impulse suddenly seizes us. We will really settle it up. So it would seem: but a moment's shock knocks everything to smithereens. Out goes the steam. There is no counter-policy. Nothing is proposed. We simply and foolishly lapse back into the old incredible position: and there we leave it. What next ? Whither are we travelling ? Who can say ? For the moment, there is no travelling anywhere. We have no plan: no proposal: no intention: no ideal. There is no driving power in any one direction.

Socialism looks so like coming on with a rush. Yet, somehow, we sit with unemployment untouched. Everything is in suspense, until the Report comes out. Oh ! that blessed Report ! If only it will supply us with an idea, with a policy ! In our barrenness, we stake our all on its fertility. But how improbable

s

is that fertility! Who knows whether the Report itself will not be the child of the Doldrums? When it is born, will it not bear the impress of the period of its incubation? Will it not suffer from our uncertainties, from our impotence, from our futilities?

Tariff Reform scatters brave braggart words to every wind. It waves gallant banners. But has it any deep reality behind it? Does it not suffer strange collapses whenever it ought to get to work? Does it face the job that it has undertaken? Does not all its bravery disappear in every challenging discussion in the House of Commons? It has made its criticisms. It has flaunted formulæ. But whenever strenuous action is needed, does it know what it is in for?

The Doldrums! We are all caught in the Doldrums. We can feel what these splendid ships, with their sails superbly set, felt, as they blobbed up and down, and heavily heaved, and wearily rolled, and groaned through all their tired timbers, and ever seemed to be on the edge of a forward movement, and ever lay back unaccountably logged in the same trough of senseless sea, waiting for something to happen that would not come. It was stupid to be so helpless: but it could not be helped. They were in the Doldrums.

Ah! Those Doldrums! They have got hold, too, of our spiritual Ship. We run up its white cloud of sails. We fly all its flags. We talk the great language about our Church, and the People, and Democracy, and all that they could mean to each other. We

believe it. We are sure of it. Every scrap of reason is
for us. The logic of the Incarnation is irresistible.
Jesus Christ is the only Life of Humanity, the King
and Lord of flesh and blood. And His witness in the
Church is the spirit of prophecy: and what is there
that we dare not prophetically anticipate of a nation
over whom Christ was the one Master? We ring out
our faith. We give the call. Why does not the great
breeze rise, and fill our canvas? Why only these
fitful fretful puffs of air, that come and go, and rattle
a shroud or two, and then scud off over the sulky
seas without avail, without result? It is the Doldrums! It is a dreary transitional stage. It is a gap
between two epochs. One age is dead: the other is
not born. We must wait a bit yet.

But, after all, the Doldrums are but an interval:
they have a limit: they must pass. If we hold on,
the dull flagging of the laggard sails is bound to end.
And there will be roaring winds, and rushing keels,
and plunging bows, and the white wake astern, and
the push, and the press, and the steady drive forward,
whether it be battling up against the opposing stream,
or racing with the racing seas.

So, for that hour, we grimly look out, and watch for
horizons, and note the omens of movement. At last
the moment will come when the signal is given: and
the voice will say, "Prophesy, son of man: prophesy,
and say, 'Come from the four winds, to breathe,
and breathe on these dead things, that they may
live!'"

The new Hope will bear down upon us. The new

energies will have us in their grip. There will be a stir : and a start : and a voice under the stars : and all these waiting ships of ours, now stuck fast in idle, sodden waters, will shake themselves together, and be off out of sight, seeking fresh ports in unknown lands, risking the great adventure that keeps the old seas young.

XXX

A DREAM

"THE LAKE ISLE OF INNISFREE

"I will arise and go now, and go to Innisfree,
    And a small cabin build there, of clay and wattles made ;
Nine bean rows will I have there, a hive for the honey-bee,
    And live alone in the bee-loud glade.

"And I shall have some peace there, for peace comes dropping slow,
    Dropping from the veils of the morning to where the cricket
      sings.
There midnight's all a-glimmer, and noon a purple glow,
    And evening full of the linnet's wings.

"I will arise and go now, for always night and day
    I hear lake water lapping with low sounds by the shore ;
While I stand on the roadway, or on the pavements grey,
    I hear it in the deep heart's core."

W. B. YEATS.

I HAD a dream: and in my dream I dreamed that the haunting magic of these lines held in it a test by which life was to be proved. It brought the spirit of the Celt to bear upon our gross Saxon conventionalism. It broke in upon our dull assemblies with the challenge of an Eternal Pilgrimage. So I dreamed that I was meant to carry the music of the poem with me wherever I went: and, just as Shelley startled the stagnant coach-load by his sudden and earnest invitation to the stout lady at his side:

"For God's sake, let us sit upon the ground,
    And tell sad stories of the death of kings " ;

261

so I was suddenly to bring this test to bear upon any meeting, or drawing-room party, or conference, or gathering, in which I might find myself: and was to whisper abruptly in the midst:

> " I will arise and go now : and go to Innisfree."

As I uttered it, a new atmosphere would swiftly come over the scene : a new perspective would be felt. It would be seen, at once, how far the particular occasion, on which the test was used, would be able to respond with a congenial reaction, or how far it would stand condemned by its hopeless impotence to meet the challenge. I seemed, in my dream, to be looking in, through door and window, at the people gathered, for some reason, inside : and watching their behaviour, as they lifted their heads from dreary occupations, or turned round from listening to interminable speeches : and caught, with startled ears, the whisper creeping round—

> " I will arise and go now, and go to Innisfree :
> And live alone in the bee-loud glade."

Will they recognize the call ? Will they become aware of the far horizons, and of the brooding peace, where the lake water laps with low sounds upon the shore ? Will their stolid business, which had seemed to them to absorb the attention of the entire universe by its enormous bulk, suddenly shrink before their eyes into a very little thing ? Will their hurry and their haste after gold and honour shrivel up into contemptible futility, as they recall the nine bean-

rows, and the one hive for the honey-bee? Will all
the noise of a tumultuous commerce become as
nothing, and die away out of their ears, to leave only
the memory of the linnet's wings aflutter in the live
evening? Will the big world drop away from them
for one blessed moment, as once again they remember
how peace comes dropping slow from the veils of the
morning? Or will they repudiate, with Anglo-Saxon
indignation, the silly interruption of the Celt? Will
they send a Beadle at once to clear the Court? Will
they gather up their foolish old hearts into a yet
stiffer and stupider solemnity, as they turn themselves
again, from this frivolous interruption, to the
ridiculous business in which they were engaged? So
the judgment will work itself out: and we shall all
know what we are made of.

How good it would be, now and again, if the chairman of a stuffy committee, which had been getting
crosser and crosser every minute, as it passed on
through item after item of an endless agenda paper,
and tempers were fretful, and six rival amendments
had all got tangled up in one another, and it began
to look as if they would sit there till Domesday—were
to rise, and, in a quiet voice, to announce:

" I will arise and go now, and go to Innisfree,
    And a small cabin build there, of clay and wattles made."

It would give just that wholesome relief: that wider
outlook: which were so sorely needed. All the
amendments would drop at once to the ground: and
we should rush out into the open air, and whoop for

joy. It would not matter to us in the least what we had, or had not, carried. We should feel that there was only one thing that mattered—and that was to have

" Nine bean-rows [in the garden], and a hive for the honey-bee."

Or it might be a Mansion House meeting, and the Lord Mayor of London would just have invited the Venerable the Archdeacon of Timbuktu to address the dull leaden-eyed rows of torpid ladies who are the despair of all orators : and then, just while the Archdeacon was clearing his throat, and before he was off on his first period, a thin sound like a gnat's song would thrill piercingly round, and every soul in the room would hear it said :

" I will arise and go now, and go to Innisfree."

And, in a moment, Mayor, and Mansion House, and Archdeacon would have vanished to Timbuktu, and we should only hear the bees in the glade, and see the beans in their nine rows, instead of those melancholy rows of stuffy velvet chairs.

Would it be possible, again, to sneak in to Capel Court, and, at some pause of the yells of the bears in the Kaffir Market, a clear cry, like the note of a thrush, might spring out—

" I will arise and go now, for always, night and day,
    I hear lake water lapping in low sounds on the shore " ?

And the greed would die out of their savage eyes : and the wolfish passion would slink away abashed : while bear and bull stood caught in some sweet subtle trance, and became aware that all else was vanity except the peace that droppeth slow from the veils of the morning.

It might even be possible to find an opportunity at some comfortable Matins at 11 in the great West, while the congregation sit there with a stolid " Dearly-Beloved " look in their cold faces, solid and plump in cushioned pomp, to let the low, quiet voice steal round from pew to pew, murmuring, as the heavy sermon drones on its dismal length, " Why do I sit here ? Why am I not far, far away ? Will this never end ? I shall die if it goes on any longer. I have an idea. I will arise and go now, and go to Innisfree."

Ah ! and what of those tired bored ladies in Hyde Park, driven by relentless fate round and round the terrible circuit, with cards to drop on their way home ; and always cards : and calls : and calls : and cards : what if, to them, the deliverance came, and a new hope dawned, and each said to the other—

" I will arise and go now, and go to Innisfree,
    And a small cabin build there, of clay and wattles made " ?

If we could, now and again, stop a middle-aged gentleman in Piccadilly, on his way to his club to sit in the bow window, and grumble and swear at the world he sees through it, and softly, cunningly whisper our secret " I will arise " ; would the old boy's blurred heart not stir, and his liver forget its congestion, and his toes shake off their gout : and would not those big leather chairs look ridiculous to him, and all the flunkies silly : and would he not know what life was meant for, and what an old ass he had been to make such a mess of it ?

All healthy life responds to this challenge. By rising to it, it refuses to become the slave of its own handiwork. It is ever being tempted to imprison itself inside this vast Civilization, which it has piled up for itself. It is enveloped by such tremendous masses of stuff, which it has itself made, that, at last, it resigns itself to becoming the creature of its own creation. It falls inside the system. It accepts its own conventions as inevitable laws. It yields itself, a passive serf, to the tyranny of self-imposed conditions. It is from this stupid and treacherous betrayal of its own lordship, that the cry of the Celt recalls it. " This civilization is your own," it cries : " therefore, you are bigger than it can ever be. Your life overlaps it. Your spirit passes out beyond it. You can drop it all behind you : you can shed it off like an old garment. You can forget it. Your way of escape is always open. You can laugh at it : you can see what a poor thing it is : you are its maker : and it is but a tiresome toy, after all. Break it up, if you are bored with it. Get up, and go far away from all this money-grubbing business which those burly Saxons are taking so seriously. It is all a bad joke. There is a whole world outside it, far better and sweeter. Come along ! Don't sit there, plodding and doddering all day ! Why not come with us ?

' I will arise and go now, and go to Innisfree.' "

Even if we go on grubbing hard at our work, it is

good to remember the magic words, and say them over to ourselves, while we sit at our silly jobs. We shall do them all the better if we recognize how silly they are. We must be able to see round our work in the world, even as we surrender ourselves to its necessities. We must be able to remember what a little thing it all is, and to laugh gently at the solemn earnestness with which we all have to set about it. What a relief, as we close our morning study of the ponderous leaders in " The Times," big with portentous issues and dignified lamentations, to murmur to ourselves : " After all, there is always Innisfree, with nine bean rows and a honey-hive. When all else comes to an end, and society crumbles to pieces under the Socialistic aggressions of West Ham, there will, still, be lake water lapping on a low shore, and the evening will yet be alive with linnets' wings."

We can nurse and cherish this remembrance, without leaving our seat in the ridiculous Bank where we bend so absorbingly over the absurd ledgers. We can chuckle at ourselves, as we sit in strenuous Committees, convinced that the heavens will fall, if they are not sitting. We can keep tempers sweet, and lives sound, even while we toil and moil, if we will but keep our spirits free to find wings, at any moment that they choose, and be off alone to the bee-loud glade at Innisfree.

XXXI

SAINTS AND HEROES AND MARTYRS IN LONDON

LONDON is the School of Saints. No one could doubt this, who habitually travels on the top of a 'bus, and watches the long, enormous trail of London traffic, crawling and oozing, and tumbling, and bulging along the tortuous streets. What courtesy it needs, to steer it through! What spiritual discipline! What detachment! What self-mastery! What sweetness of temper! What urbanity of speech! And, yet, your 'bus driver never fails you. Amid the turbid throng, that bustles and jostles round him, he retains the mind of an Angel and wears the smile of Paradise. Yet could any life be more wildly aggravating? To stand blocked at the crossings, while the interminable things go by, that out of sheer perversity have set themselves to traverse your path! To pull up at the bidding of the merciless bell, at every minute in which you had whipped up your nags for a little clear run! To be checked, just as you start afresh, on account of one old fat lady, who might just as well have got in half a second before, when you were standing still! To be arrested by the conductor for no apparent reason at all! To be bullied by lady riders on bicycles, who slide also under your horses' noses, and challenge you to kill them if you dare! To be always

268

sent on, when you want to stop ; and stopped when
you want to go on ! Why ! it would drive a Saint
wild. It would distract a St. Anthony. It would
wreck the nerves of St. Francis. But your 'bus driver
is in secure possession of his soul. Inside the 'bus,
you, yourself, in your rude, impulsive way, gnash
your teeth, if you have any, in impotent rage at the
provocations of delay ; you tear out your remaining
hairs in handfuls, and strew them on the floor, in
passionate protest. But nothing disturbs the quiet
serenity of the empurpled countenance on the box.
At the worst, a little mild chaff falls from his lips on
to the head of some irritating conductor of a rival
'bus, or he kindly suggests to the inordinate Peeler
who holds us up for apparent hours at a crossing,
that he had better make haste, for the Missis is
expecting him home to tea. But the good humour
of it is unbroken ; the broad tolerance that has
learned to gauge all the infirmities of human nature,
beams from his buried eyes over the ruddy fullness of his face. Not a pucker spoils the smooth-
ness of the cherubic brow, as " he rides the
whirlwind and directs the storm." The voice,
though a little thick in tone, is rich with compassion.
" Lor ! bless yer 'eart ! what's the good of making a
fuss ! " That is the confirmed expression that breaks
from out of every feature. And his magnificent
serenity spreads itself over all the minor men, in carts
and cabs, who take their cue from the majestic figure
up aloft. Is it not amazing how easily it all moves ?
Up in the narrow lanes of the City, the enormous

vans block themselves in, and get stuck three deep, in impossible corners ; nobody can imagine how ever they can get in, and still less how they can ever hope to get out again. Yet the burly drivers sit there, rapt in lonely meditation for hours, without a sign of discontent, without a word of reproach. Perhaps, at the stormy hour of five, when everything ought to be getting away at once, a faint hum, as of gnats on a summer eve, begins to break the solemn silence ; and now and again a strong word passes, that reminds us that, after all, we are still human. But, taking it all round, it is a superb display of self-control, and of benignant good temper. And on many a 'bus driver's shoulder you can almost see the sprouting of an angel's wings. It is a refreshing tribute to the goodness of the Londoner. God bless him !

London sets its Saints to drive 'buses ; that is why we do not find them in Church. So we have discovered. High uplifted into that serene air, they hover over us, benignant in benediction ; bound " not by Paul's sad girdle," indeed, but by a black leather strap round their portly persons into their solitary seat. There they brood, detached and rapt. But London's heroes, where are they ? Ah ! here is a darker tale. She breeds heroes only to break them. For who can doubt the heroic breed of those indescribable hobbledehoys, who carry the News on rushing bikes ? Has the earth ever seen a finer display of nerve than is given by this strange and tattered crew ? Sitting meekly behind our Saints outside the 'bus, we

simply freeze with terror as we watch them scud, at
full speed, through the roaring traffic of the crowded
streets.   No pigeon threads its way more deftly
through the huddled stems of trees ; but then, trees,
at least, can be counted upon to stand still, while our
wild courser has to steer his desperate way through a
moving mob of wheels that jibs, and sways, and jerks,
and rolls, under every conceivable impulse, as incalculable as the breeze—a mob that is never in the
same position for two seconds together.   Through it,
he plunges at headlong speed, skirting the edge of
swift destruction at every turn.   He dives, as it would
seem to our excited imagination, under the very heels
of the horses ; he disappears beneath the wheels, he
slides between the grinding poles, he slithers past
a crunching van, he slips between the jaws of death,
and vanishes, and emerges again, and twists, and
wriggles, and scrapes, and ducks, and is gone.   It is
breathlessly amazing.   For he is shockingly equipped
for such a dare-devil enterprise.   He rides an old
broken down machine, sheeted in mud.   He has to go
at it in all weathers, with the slime on the cobbles as
slippery as grease.   On his back swings a bulging sack,
stuffed with " Pink 'Uns," of some fearsome type,
giving the name of all the winners.   As he flies, his
gang of smaller pirates on the watch for their ally,
pounce on him, and seize lumps of this pink matter
from out of his sack, destroying all possibility of a
calculated balance.   Yet he never falls ; but apparently, carries on intricate financial transactions
with his pals, in mid flight.   There is courage in this,

beyond parallel. Who dare talk of race deterioration, while we can still produce any number of boys capable of ventures that would have turned Nelson green ? And the skilfulness of it ! And the splendid force ! And yet every one of them is being hopelessly ruined for life. This hero of heroes will find himself, shortly, cast off, useless, aimless, parasitic, without a craft, without a chance, without hope ahead. The thrill is over, the race is run, he is a miserable loafer for life. Is not that wasteful ? Is not that a scandal ? Was there nothing there for us to use and value, when he was capable of that superb achievement on his flying bike ? But he, who rode the wheel for us, is broken under the wheel of that blind fate, unto which we commit him to his inevitable ruin.

Saints ! Yes ! We have got them, hung up aloft in their straps. And heroes. They swarm all round us on bikes. What about martyrs ? Well, perhaps you will say that they are thick in garret and workshop, working their fingers to the bone as still they

> " Stitch, Stitch, Stitch
> In Poverty, Hunger, and Dirt."

Yes ! But " the noble army " that we have in our eye is of a less tragic, but none the less patient, type. They are those who, for our convenience, and in order to give mechanical swiftness to our hurrying needs, are specialized into some pinched and paralysing routine. There are men who simply stand in halls and door-ways day after day, because somebody must

be there. They do nothing whatever. There is
nothing on earth that they can possibly do. Only
something disastrous, it is supposed, would happen if
they were not there. So the years pass : and they
exist as sheer unmitigated negations of all life's purposes. They are symbols of the inane. Their use is
to be, and do, nothing. Any demand for positive
functional activity would be their death. The crowds
of people who have something to do, eddy round them ;
but they stand aloof, or sit locked up in glass boxes, in
the belief that some day the occasion may conceivably
turn up when they might possibly be wanted. Suns
rise and set. Moons wax and wane. Still they wait
for the moment which will make them intelligible.
It never comes. In the meantime, civilization requires them, as it requires the two buttons above the
tail of our coats. They must be there, or all is lost.
Martyrs, these. And each new advance of civilized
order produces a new form of this martyrdom. The
Tube, for instance, has created that noble-minded
and dignified old gentleman who, with immense
moral dignity, sits all day long at the entrance, just
to see that we drop our tickets into the box. That
is his whole concern with the universe. At slow
intervals, he makes one motion which releases our
fugitive scraps, and they flutter down into some un-
plumbed abyss. That is the solitary break into the
monotony. What interest can he find in his craft ?
" Fling yourself into your work ! " we preachers cry
from all our pulpits. How is he to do it ? What is
there to receive him, when he flings ? Can he strive

T

after any perfection in the art of watching our bits
of paper fall ? Will he be able to say, at the end of
the day " Ah ! there was no one could do that job
like me ! I had somehow caught the trick of it. I
couldn't be beat ! " He has surrendered all hopes of
distinction. He is detached from earthly ambition.
His serious face takes on the look of some timeless
vacancy. He might die there, in his chair, and no
one would notice any difference. The tickets would
flutter in. We should hurry past. The earth would
roll on. Poor old chap ! Yet he looks happy enough.
It is all right. Martyrdom is not so bad, after all.

XXXII

SOME PERSONAL MEMORIES

ALFRED LYTTELTON

r is rare, indeed, for the pages of the Press to beat
ith the pulse of intimate passion, such as was to be
lt in the records that tried to tell why Alfred
yttelton was so wonderfully beloved. Men could
ɔt find words to express their emotion : they were
ɔt ashamed to show how deeply they were stirred.
'hey wrote what would seem to outsiders words of
xaggeration : and yet, even the outsider as he read
ɩem, knew that the words were below the mark of
hat was really meant. Alfred Lyttelton had a most
ngular charm, a sympathetic magic. There was
•mething distinctive in the tone of the voice, in
ɩe look of the eyes. He was unforgettable. He
on hearts straight away. He had, as Lord Curzon
id in "The Times," an endearing manner which
as in itself almost a caress. And, then, his athletic
chievements had about them the glamour and the
ory of some supreme perfection. " His Cricket is
ce Champagne," said W. G. Grace, in a fit of un-
onted poetic enthusiasm. Everything that he did
ɩd this exaltation about it. The Cambridge Eleven,
: which Edward Lyttelton was Captain, and Alfred
icket-keeper, with A. G. Steel bowling balls that

were unplayable, was like nothing that the world ha
ever seen before or since. Our own special memor
of him would be of an evening in the Hall in Exete
College, thirty-two years ago, when he stood up, i
his fresh beautiful manhood, erect, compact, aler
to speak to Undergraduates on behalf of the Whit
Cross League. Could anything have been mor
manly, more gracious, more winning ? He spoke o
the help of companionship in University life, cor
trasting it with the strain of lonely lodgings in a bi
city. " You stand in some wide Quadrangle," he saic
" looking round on every window aglow in the evening
and you know that there is not a room behind thos
lighted windows in which you would not be receive
with a shout of welcome." So he spoke, as if it wer
obviously true : unconscious that he was describir
what was the normal experience, only, of an Alfre
Lyttelton. He could speak on such a topic with th
perfect certainty and confidence of a man who kne
how to come through the fire. " What a delightf
fellow that young Gladstone is," said Ruskin, afte
his historic visit to Hawarden, at which Alfred ha
charmed him into a promise that he would introdu
him to Carlyle. " Yes ! delightful," we said, " he
a young Lyttelton, not a young Gladstone." " Oh !
cried Ruskin, with a look of real relief, " that will be
much more fortunate name to introduce to the Master.
Then, again, we recall now over his grave the trag
wonder of that first marriage—the amazing fascinatic
of the tiny little lady, whose very being was a livir
flame : who enthralled and bewitched the world

who moved about encircled by a crowd of rejected lovers who remained her adoring friends: who gave herself wholly to him who won her soul: who left those overwhelming records of her young wedded life: and who died within the year, to leave an incomparable memory as of a vision that had come and gone in a moment's glory. There was never anything quite like her. And the pathos of her love hung about him to the last.

He was the most loyal and devoted of all Mr. Balfour's henchmen: and one of his closest friends. It was a cruel misfortune which forced him, on his very first experience as a Cabinet Minister, to appear as the official defender of an intolerable Labour Policy. The thing itself had to go: but the attack on it was, no doubt, fierce in the extreme. On him who had always enjoyed the love of everybody, its full fury fell. It stung him to the quick: and its excesses roused the sportsman in him to defy what seemed to him to be against the rules of the game. It took a long time for the cloud of the memory to lift.

His last public words were filled with the spirit of Social Service. To this, he and his wife had ever given their very best. She had most nobly worked for the cause of Sweated Women both on the Industrial Law Committee and by her Dramas, in the best of which she gave an enkindling picture of Father Dolling among the Dockers.

So he moved to the last, in grace and joy, along the high planes of life, alive if ever man was in every nerve of his glad being: until the shadow fell, and the silence took him. But he knew in whom he had believed—Christ his living Lord and Master. And he that believeth on Him shall never die, but hath now and always, everlasting life.

GEORGE WILLIAM KITCHIN

By the passing of George William Kitchin, Dean of Durham, we lost from among us a man who never grew old, however many his years on earth. He was young-minded, and young-hearted, to the last. It was impossible not to be fond of him. He was so obviously made in a good mould. He did not surprise. He was of the ordinary make of man. His mental note was direct, straightforward, practical common sense. He took things at their plain value: and handled them most effectively. But, to this strong common sense, he brought the delightful simplicity of a character which was utterly free from all tangle and perplexities: and a winning personal charm such as belongs to a nature of singular openness and gentleness. He passed the deep problems of life by. They did not enter into his mind or interest. He saw very steadily what life asked him to do: and he did it with a free and glad heart. He was eminently companionable: with a perfect temper, and a mood that nothing could upset or fuss or ruffle. This enabled him to do exceedingly bold things in politics without offence. He entertained Michael Davitt at the Deanery in Winchester, for a social meeting, at a time when passion ran very high, without losing the confidence or outraging the affection of the most

Tory members of his Chapter. On the famous occasion of his outspokenness in the Boer War, he rather gave himself away to a political Judge, who was not likely to miss his opportunity: and Durham took a long time to forgive him. But he was, naturally, a man with whom no one could ever be angry: and this, in spite of his frank and fearless expression of very strong political opinions. He went to Durham to bring unity into a distracted Chapter, and to develop University life in its invasion of the great industrial North. No man could possibly have been more fitted for the double task: but, after a year of zealous work, full of promise, a slight stroke, that came and went, left him not quite the man that he had been. He had not all the old spring, and alertness: and, though he carried through his task, it was with some touch of diminished power. He left a high record of excellent work done at every step of his career: and, to his friends, the memory of a very lovable man, whose presence always brought brightness and delight: and who made them believe, with a fuller confidence, in the primal value that belongs to goodness of heart.

OCTAVIA HILL

Octavia Hill left behind her a noble and impressive memory. Her face and presence had a high dignity of their own. She spoke without any attempt at effect, but with a most eloquent simplicity. She was cast in a fine mould, with a certain massiveness of character. She belonged to a generation of higher

caste than our own : and was felt to be authoritative
and alone. She dated from the days of F. D. Maurice :
and it was always delightful to think of her splendid
sanity associated with the dreams and visions of John
Ruskin. There used to be an old story, which was
probably true, of the day when, after years of work
at the rough Court purchased for her by Ruskin's
money, she thought that she might take him to see
the heaven that had been made out of the horror in
which she had begun : and that the only result was
to send Ruskin back home quite sick with disgust at
what he had been invited to see. She laid fast hold
of some few life-giving principles : and worked them
out to the end. She trained a fine band of the best
women-workers we possess, who were enthusiastically
loyal to her teaching, and carried into effect her
experiences. The only trouble lay in this—that the
awful scale of the Housing problem demanded larger
and more organized action than any voluntary
organization could possibly bring into play. Miss
Hill showed, in special districts, what could be done
by the force of personal influence introduced into
business relationship, in the way of evoking, from
within, the higher standard of living. But these
districts could not be more than illustrations of what
was needed. Our vast cities were growing far faster
than the spaces that we could recover and remedy.
Municipality or State could alone cope with matters
of this enormous range. The voluntary effort that
first discovers, by brave experiment, the true nature
of the remedy, has, then, by virtue of its very success,

to see its work passed over to the Official System which alone is wide enough to cover the ground. That was why Miss Hill's work had lost a little of its special interest. It had proved its case. It had converted the world.

She herself did other work, and had other interests, all of the same high and pure type. The Kyrle Society has always done so nobly what it has attempted that one wonders why it has not done much more. She cared deeply for all that gave amenity and relief and beauty to the life of the poor. Her name is fragrant with good.

J. M. LUDLOW

Those members of the Christian Social Union who used to creep in to our monthly meetings would often see there, in the early days of our London Branch, a bent figure sitting, with the face of one who had come out of other and more heroic days. There was a nobility in the prophetic head which made the rest of us look very cheap. And, now and again, when some pink youthful cheerful Pessimist, such as Mr. Masterman, had plunged us all into the abyss of despair, the old man would rise, and shake with the passion of old days that for ever haunted him with their wickedness and woe, and bid us cheer up. "You young fellows have never seen the Hungry 'Forties." That is what would be the burden of his cry. "You don't know what men and women have had to suffer." And, then, he would bear his witness to the upward movement that he had seen with his own eyes. Things were bad enough, God knows ! still ; but they were a long way better than what he could recall. And, above all, he signalized the change of temper that had opened out possibilities now of which, in those black days, they could not have dreamed. The old man was J. M. Ludlow. And, as he gave us this comforting report, which sent us back to our work with some life and assurance, we took it from him just because he was, obviously, no spinner of smooth phrases. The fire gleamed still in his eyes, so that they shone with the passionate light which is only to be seen in men who have known Maurice. He quivered with an underground volcanic vehemence which no years or grey hairs could tame. He was devoured by a great zeal for Justice. We felt that we were listening to the man whom Maurice found it so hard to hold in—the man who had written the articles in the " Christian Socialist," the Journal of the Association of London Workers into which the band of Christian Socialists were putting all their force. Mr. Masterman has described them in his Life of Maurice :—

" They call upon Christianity to come out from its present position, cramped in between the four walls of its churches or chapels, and forbidden to go forth into the wide world conquering and to conquer ; ' to assert God's rightful domination over every process, and trade, and industry, over every act of our common life ' ; and ' to embody in due forms of organization every truth of that Faith committed to its charge.' They see society drifting rudderless on the sea of competition. They call for a fight against all the armies of mammon. They reveal in all these fiery pages the sense of an actual and visible combat against the forces of evil. They challenge the affirmations of John Stuart Mill with the proclamations of the Book of Deuteronomy. They find harvest labourers, hired at a penny a day, with their wages refused ; and receiving instead a penny halfpenny for three weeks' labour. They confront such courses with the judgment in the Epistle of St. James against those who kept back the hire of the reapers by fraud. ' People of England,' they ask, ' choose between these two gospels.' "

.   .   .   .

" Their attitude towards politics is revealed in the comments upon the Ministerial crisis of 1851. ' The people are sick of party cries and party leaders,' writes Mr. Ludlow, ' sick of Parliamentary interference altogether.' They despise the Whigs. They thoroughly distrust the Manchester party as an embodiment of competitive selfishness. They find the Peelites a clever coterie with no followers, and they will not hear of a return of the Protectionists. ' The people were disposed to give the new men a fair trial, but a bread tax they would not submit to. Come what might they would not allow the food of England to be taxed for the raising of landlords' rents and the swelling of farmers' incomes.'

" And throughout all they are conscious of the perilous condition of the body politic. ' I think of the four judgments of Ezekiel,' runs one leading article, ' again I repeat it, we have had famine, pestilence, we have noisome beasts ; again I ask, does the sword alone remain ? ' "

Ludlow had been in Paris, and had felt the ardours of 1848. He was out with Kingsley on the historic Charter Day. It took all his devoted loyalty to Maurice to bear the rebuffs with which the Master met his democratic fervour. Even the organization of the Co-operative efforts had to be done in spite of Maurice, rather than with his help. But, for all that, the power of Maurice had entered into Ludlow's soul. You might know it by the sudden passion that would rise if anyone rashly said "Kingsley and Maurice." "Maurice and Kingsley, if you please!" would be the abrupt correction, said with a haste that told how keenly he felt for the supremacy of his prophet. It was to and through Ludlow that Maurice entered on his deepest spiritual work. Ludlow constantly prompted the thoughts and discussions which became the Gospel delivered by Maurice. A deep strong noble soul, he retained to the last his democratic faith in the people, his passionate pity for the poor and down-trodden, his fiery cry for Righteousness. He never flagged in his work for justice and equity. He held fast to his belief that in God the Father, through the Power of His Christ, lay the strength and hope of the world's salvation. He will never be forgotten by those who saw, in his presence among them, the living bond that bound them to the brave men of old.

JOHN WORDSWORTH

John Wordsworth, Bishop of Salisbury, was cast in a big mould. He had the strong type of his parentage visibly and vividly expressed in his entire personality. The power of the North was in him: dogged, fearless, independent. It was impossible to make him afraid. If he had been told by his doctor to hunt, he would have gone at it the next day, as if he was not bound to fall off at every fence. He was a great scholar, who went his own way, and carried weight wherever he went. No one could mistake his great qualities. Whatever he put out, counted. He had the simplicity of a great scholar : he was absorbed in the intellectual problems with which he had to deal : and common life and affairs had to fall into line, as they could. He once confessed that his own style lacked charm : and that was true. He had no fascination : no eloquence : no obvious humour. But he was thoroughly natural : he gave himself no airs. He knew where his strength lay, and he put it out rightly and effectively, when it was wanted. It was a valuable thing to possess a Bishop who had a European reputation. And then, he was so human : so typical : so entirely a Wordsworth. This made him a delight to those who knew and loved him. Everything about him had a character of its own. It witnessed to the vigorous Westmorland stock. It had the note of the soil : of the good earth : of true flesh and blood. It illustrated the strong qualities of the dalesman. It told us the story of the immortal poet. We laughed over many characteristic peculiarities. We remembered the frankness with which he said, at the close of a debate in the old days on the well-worn subject of how to influence our pupils, " It is wise to speak to freshmen in their first Term before they have learned to know us and to despise us." But, in all our laughter, we had high respect for a character that found distinction by its very individuality, and for a scholarship that had in it the hall-mark of real humanity.

J. B. PATON

The most lovable of the great Nonconformist Leaders was Dr. J. B. Paton. There was nobody like him. He had the fire of the prophet and the heart of a child. His dear old face revealed everything that passed through his mind, with a vividness that sometimes provoked a smile, but a smile that was always charged with affection : and sometimes startled by the sudden flame of righteous passion, or the light of a great inspiration. He was absolutely tireless in hope, and work, and suggestion. Always, he was breaking in upon our lethargies with some new and tremendous plan for saving all the world, or for uniting all the Churches. It might sometimes not quite be " war," but it was always magnificent. And in all his special later work, whether in Lingfield Colonies of Labour, or in Continuation Classes, or in the Home Reading Union, or in Schemes on behalf of the Unemployed, he was splendidly practical and effective. He was a delight to catch sight of, in the thick of Ludgate Hill, with comforter flying, and crammed bag, stuffed with papers and plans, as he would stop to greet one with brimming eyes, and an overflowing smile, and a kindly human voice with the touch of the trumpet of God in it. He wrote me a most tender letter from his bed, as he drew towards his last illness, full of youth, and hope, and love, and sacrifice. He had heaven in his soul. He was delighted at Rawnsley saluting him as " Churchman of all the Churches." He prided himself on being a great

Churchman, in temper and spirit : and he had a special theory about the ideal Church, in its connexion with the Kingdom of Heaven, by which he denied to it the mingling of good and evil, which is generally believed to be represented by the Parable of the Wheat and the Tares. But, whatever may be said of his exegesis here, he was profoundly loyal to his Vision of a pure and holy Church : and was ready to work with all good Christians for the Cause of the Master, and in the service of man. His deep human sympathies drew him to the side of all who were weak and broken : and he devoted heart and soul to the welfare and the salvation of the children. He was a most noble and gentle-hearted old man, who moved everyone to love him.

JOSEPHINE BUTLER

About twenty-eight years ago, in passing up Holborn, a face looked at me out of a hurrying hansom, which arrested and frightened me. It was framed on pure and noble and beautiful lines : but it was smitten, and bitten into, as by some East wind, that blighted it into grey sadness. It had seen that which took all colour and joy out of it. I felt as the children who saw Dante pass as a shadow through the sunny square : and whispered " He has been in Hell." The face gave a look (I thought) of recognition before it had swiftly gone : and, after I had recovered my memory, I knew that it was Josephine Butler. A day or two later, a message reached me from her, to warn me that a tremendous storm was about to break, and that all friends of the Cause must be prepared for the emergency. It was something to do with Mr. Stead ; so the message implied.

Shortly after, all European civilization shook with the convulsive horror of the disclosures made by Mr. Stead in the pamphlet, " The Maiden Tribute." And, then, I knew that I had seen, that day in Holborn, Mrs. Butler in the thick of that terrible work that she had undertaken for God. She was passing through her martyrdom. The splendid beauty of her face, so spiritual in its high and clear outlines, bore the mark of that death upon it to which she stood daily and hourly committed. There was no hell on earth into which she would not willingly travel, if, by sacrifice of herself, she could reach a hand of help to those poor children whom nothing short of such sacrifice could touch. The sorrow of it passed into her being. She had the look of the world's grim tragedy in her eyes. She had dared to take the measure of the black infamy of sin : and the terrible knowledge had left its cruel mark upon a soul of strange and singular purity.

Men could never be the same again, after they had seen and known Josephine Butler. A new sense of what passionate pity could mean was brought home to them : and an awe fell on them, as they became aware of the woman's power to lay down all that was most dear and precious in life, through the grace of Jesus Christ, for the weak, and the broken, and the fallen. She was driven on and on, along the way of her Calvary, by the poignant memory of her own child, in her beauty and grace, swept out of her arms into the night. It is the children, the girl-children, whom she must spend herself to save.

Into this life-long task, she flung the passion of a dauntless faith. She had the vision: and she obeyed it. Nothing could make her falter, or compromise. And is it not to her, above all, that we owe our deliverance from the ever-menacing nightmare of those incriminated Acts ? There was a time when it was always possible that all our city life would be brought under their evil handling. Their supporters were loud and confident. Those who might be expected to oppose them closed their ears and shut their eyes, lest they should be themselves defiled by touching defilement. Science and experience appeared to lend all their weight to the extension. Only those who clung fast to first principles, and who held desperately to the Truth as it is in Christ, had the force and courage to organize resistance. It is extraordinary to recognize how much the menace has past. And that this is so, we owe to Mrs. Butler's unswerving faith more than to any other cause. We have lived through to see the day dawn when the Army itself will repudiate the degrading protection.

She was of us: yet she found among Churchmen, often, her most obstinate opponents: and, moreover, these good women and holy sisters, who were given to rescue work, were frequently the last to understand her wrath against the dreadful Acts. But, always, she had with her the loyal-hearted help of her husband, George Butler, Canon of Winchester, and also of his two gallant brothers, Montagu Butler,

U

Master of Trinity College, Cambridge, and Arthur,
Headmaster of Haileybury School, and Fellow of
Oriel. She had suffered greatly from a weak and
broken bodily health. She had passed, in her later
years, into a quiet retreat in the twilight, until the
big world had almost forgotten her name: and only
the few knew how strong was her spirit in the old
cause: and how real her help. She was like no one
else. There are men alive who will say that they
owe their souls to her inspiration: and who felt at
her death that the earth had been emptied of the
purest and strongest spirit that it had been their
privilege and joy to have known.

KATHLEEN LYTTELTON

Kathleen Lyttelton, widow of Arthur, Bishop of
Southampton, wore life with a certain royalty of
mien. Her masculine intelligence, her moral force, her
dauntless simplicity of character, her splendid presence
her large sweeping motions, her glorious colouring
her confident freedom of air, her fine masterfulness
made her an inspiration. She especially drew the
young to her by her splendid strength of mind and
warmth of sympathy. To those of her own standing
she was the best companion in the world. She made
herself your comrade, in all the breadth and fullness
of the term. She held very clear views: and her
convictions were strongly liberal: and she stated
them firmly, and enjoyed keen discussion and argument
She could be hot in argument: but she was always
entirely rational, and peculiarly " manly," in the

reasons that she would use. About Women's Suffrage she had an almost religious ardour. She could not help distrusting a little the moral condition of those who hesitated here. But she was frank, transparent, open-hearted, with a largeness of soul that saved her from intolerance. She was a superb musician : and the sight of her seated, in her masterful ease, at the piano had a singular beauty and charm. She was active in all Social causes : and especially in those that affected the work and lives of women. An admirable speaker, she was a familiar figure at gatherings and conferences that dealt with Women's labour. She had to win her money : and laboured steadily in reviewing books for the " Guardian," and had covered, in this way, the whole field of fiction. She left a splendid memory to those who loved her. She passed into the quiet places where he waits with whom she had enjoyed the very perfection of wedded union.

C. L. MARSON

In Dr. Driver, the Church succeeded in using a man at his best to the full. She gave him just the post in which he could most nobly do the exact work for which he was fitted. Into it he could throw all his power. In the same week in which he died, another man passed away whose exceptional gifts the Church never discovered how to place and use. C. L. Marson died, very suddenly at last, after a time of illness, at Hambridge, his vicarage in Somersetshire. It is difficult to say quite how much of the blame lay with her or with him. He certainly did not make it easy for her. He could not hold back his quips, however disconcerting they might be. His humour was instinctively ironic, and he was rash in its exercise. He would never allow himself to pander to his own interests. So he puzzled : and vexed : and frightened. He could not resist the fun of a Bishop's gaiters. He added to the gaiety of nations at his own expense. But it remains that he was never given his fair chance : he was never really put to use. He had varied reading, and a brilliant power of putting to service all that he had read. His literary capacity was quite excellent : and he had swift insight, a critical skill, and delightful humour, and a peculiar distinction of touch. He loved God's Poor with all his soul. He cared for the dog that was down. He got inside the heart of human nature. He abhorred convention and respectability and gloss. He loved his broken Londoner instinctively. He learned slowly to love his country-folk. He had, just before he died, put together a little series of fascinating " Silhouettes," in which he had caught all the familiar village types with delicious grace. He got to understand, and to revere them. He dug up their songs, and their dances, and their secrets, and their joys. Yet he was never meant to be left in the country. He had capacities which belonged to the central laboratories of life. He could have made a mark on the spiritual thought of the time. As it was, he has left us the imperishable delight of " Huppim and Muppim and Ard," and a beautiful little book, a storehouse of delicate learning, on the Psalms at Work. He had friends who understood

him, and loved him dearly. He ought, somehow, to
have been given a fuller opportunity.

GENERAL BOOTH

General Booth carried through a most amazing
achievement. His courage never faltered: his force
never flagged. Right to the end of his long life, he
remained the supreme inspiration, the sole driving
power, the absolute master, of a world-wide Organization for the succour of fallen Humanity. He compelled
the world at large to accept and to honour him.
Nothing had looked less likely. But it was done.
And, in spite of searching and unanswered criticism
on his methods of Help, and of Finance, he never
slackened, never withdrew, never changed, never
shook. His forcefulness went straight forward. And
his enormous army of workers, under very trying
strain, stood resolutely by him, and tolerated his
intense autocracy. He had a certain vigour of speech:
and a good rough humour. But nothing that he said
explained his power. The secret of that lay in his
entire concentration upon his task: and in his absolute
confidence in his power to push it through. He had
quite extraordinary powers of organization and of
management: and immense financial ability. He
held the threads together of the whole enormous
business: and he held on tenaciously to his single
purpose. He had deep compassion for the poor, and
a sure trust in the God whom he loved to serve. But
he had not any peculiar touch on the spiritual nerve.
He was not a religious prophet. Mrs. Booth was of

another order altogether. She was a profound
spiritual enthusiast. She spoke words that were
alive. She saw visions. She had the instincts of the
prophet. They formed a strange contrast. There
was a moment when the chief officers of the Church
of England offered to the General terms of a working
alliance. The proposal was made by Archbishop
Benson and George Wilkinson, Bishop of Truro.
They asked that the General, who should be left
perfectly free to carry on his Mission on his own
lines, should pass on to the various Religious bodies
those converts who claimed to belong to them, for
permanent establishment in their recovered life.
But he could not do it. It would have broken up the
military organization on which he so strongly relied.
A curious instance of his relationship to the Church
came up on the occasion of the Queen's visit to St.
Paul's at the celebration of the second Jubilee in
1897. The tickets for the Nonconformist Bodies,
which admitted to seats on the Western steps, were
sent to them to distribute as they thought fit. They
sent an allotted portion to the Salvation Army, but
they were returned to the Dean and Chapter, on the
ground that the Salvationists were not Nonconformists.
" Do you mean," we said to the Colonel who came,
" that you would come if you received a direct
invitation from us ? " " Most certainly," he answered.
So the invitation was at once given and accepted.
The death of the supreme master, originator, and
administrator, in whose remarkable personality lay
the secret of the whole movement, raised a

tremendous question. He staked all on the effective
force of a central autocracy. The crucial peril of
such a method lies in the difficulty of transmission.
All historical evidence is dead against it. That is
the criticism passed by History on a system which
beguiles by its obvious immediate efficiency. Yet
the Salvation Army has, from first to last, defied
every assumption of a democratic age. And the
Bramwell Booths possess the wonder of their parents.
And their workers are a body of angels. So we must
wait and see and learn.

MOTHER CECILE

Mother Cecile, of the Community of the
Resurrection in Grahamstown, was, certainly, one of
the most remarkable women of our generation.
She went out, as quite a girl, to lead a small religious
community, under the direction of Bishop Webb.
From him she learned the depth and majesty and
splendour of the full belief in the Incarnation. From
him, too, she learned to sweep the whole field of
human endowment, in its width and in its wealth,
in within the horizon covered by the Catholic Creed.
He had the large vision: the brave and venturous
outlook. She passed across with him from Bloem-
fontein to Grahamstown, on his translation to that
See. And, there, she established the work which
made her fame. School after school, at every grade
of the social scale, was developed under her
Napoleonic organization. And, always, she made
straight for the finest excellence in the work to be

done: for proved and tried efficiency: for the scientific standard. Always, she justified her undertaking before the bar of public criticism. She won the confidence of the men of business, the men of mark, the men of education ; and, above all, of the great Minister of Education in Cape Colony, Dr. Muir.

To her, he turned for the training of Elementary teachers, for Government Schools. So well did she respond to this demand, that he called upon her to supply the training wanted for teachers in Secondary Schools. So the immense and important work grew ; building was added to building ; and, still more was required. She had come home, to make an appeal for £20,000 more, to meet the public demands made on her services. But her visit home was not only to make this appeal. She was ordered home for a serious operation. The doctors at first thought it too perilous to attempt. She was put under treatment, which for a time seemed to do wonders. She could work hard for the cause: she was charged with all her old splendid vitality: she talked with all her familiar power and capacity, and charm. At last, under the strain, perhaps, of a sudden disappointment, with its sequent call upon her resourcefulness for a fresh effort, the evil broke out with menace: and it was decided to be necessary to risk the deferred operation. Even then, it looked as if all had gone well. But, a few days later, she sank, under the strain, and peacefully passed away.

She was a woman of splendid gifts. Her mind had

a range and a freedom which enabled her to take in an entire situation. She had fastened on the South African problem with tenacity: her experience had been deep and prolonged: her imagination admitted her into the inside of the racial secrets. She had gained a profound impression of the Dutch character. She felt their worth, their moral weight, their deep-seated domestic qualities. Above all, she recognized in them the essential factors in the stability and reality of South African citizenship. They must be won to loyalty; or England's hold on the Colony is lost. And she felt it vital that they should be admitted to their share in anything that England could give to the enrichment of social life. We had that which would help them. And they must be persuaded that we should place this at their disposal, just as much as to our own folk. She abhorred anything that symbolized English things for the English: anything that made an English ring: anything that, however unintentionally, was closed to the Dutch. Only by free sharing in a common treasure did she look to see the races fused into a united State.

So it was that she laboured to open her doors to Dutch girls: to let them partake of all the opportunities of higher education offered under the Grahamstown Training. She admitted them to take all they could of our religious spirit: while she gave the free entry to their own religious pastors: or made it perfectly easy for them to go outside her establishment for instruction and worship. She won her way. She gained their confidence: she laid herself alongside the interests of the Government : she toiled to prove that her work had social value for the Society at large. So she dreamed and schemed, to the very end. She was, no doubt, intensely committed to her own undertaking : and, perhaps, found it difficult to estimate what was being done elsewhere. But such achievements as hers are hardly ever carried through without this idealistic absorption in the task set. And certainly, she attained : and she knit to herself the hearts of all who served under her, by bonds that could never be broken : and she drew love out of all her children : and she fascinated : and she commanded : and triumphed. None who came under her influence can ever forget it. They will thank God, until their dying day, that they have felt the touch of her friendship.

LORD ROBERTS

" Within the sound of the guns." That is where Lord Roberts died. And, in this, he took with him the heart of the nation. For we are all, for the first time in our Island Story, within the sound of the guns. They are nearer than they were at Waterloo : and they carry further. To be there, " within the sound of the guns," was his natural place. He could not rest until he found himself there. And, then, to die was simple enough. Nothing could be more pathetic, more dramatic, more stirring. Always he possessed the magic of personality. Never was the " touch " more vivid and more effective than in this swift and tragic death. It was the true heroic end.

He had seen his beloved Indian troops. He had been up to England's firing line. What more could he do, at eighty, than die then and there ? He was a fighting soldier, to the very tips of his fingers. He had the genius for strategic action. He loved his men : and passionately desired for them the chance of clean and honourable living. He worshipped Christ, his King. He won hearts in that indescribable manner by which hearts are to be won. " Why is it that Roberts holds the Army in India, as no other man does ? " So some one asked. And the answer was " Just you see him come on the ground at a Review : and you will know. That rushing gallop with which he arrives— bewitching the world with noble horsemanship. That reining in of his horse at the appointed spot. It is irresistible. The Army is at his feet." I felt a little of what this meant as I saw him come caracoling out of the north corner of St. Paul's Churchyard, on his noble white Arab, at the head of all the Colonial Contingents, on the day of the Queen's Jubilee. It was a sight to sweep the imagination. His moment of moments came when, at the close of that awful week of blackness, when the very ground under our feet was breaking as the news fell upon us of Colenso, Spion Kop, Magersfontein, every heart in England turned to one man, every mouth in England framed one name : and, with the shadow of his only son's death upon him, he went out, carrying in his hand the fate of England and its Empire. Never, surely, did any one man so gather up into himself the soul of a nation. He saved the day. That was enough. As in Afghanistan, so in South Africa, he left difficulties behind him, which his own brilliant stroke had disguised even from himself. But, anyhow, he had worked the change : he had reversed the situation. The rest could be done by others. He had won so high a place in the National regard, by his untiring and splendid patriotism, that he had become sacrosanct : and to criticize him in any way was to be convicted of a crime. So we have learned. But no such criticism was ever intended to qualify the devotion and the honour and the affection which England owes to one of the noblest and purest men who has given his life to her unstinted service, and has shown how high a heroism lies in the simplicity of a dedicated life, given wholly to its country, and its God.

ALBERT DE MUN

Amid the tumult of the war, while the France that he so passionately loved was fighting for its life, Count Albert de Mun passed into the silence. He was writing to the last, breathing courage into his countrymen, and defiance to their foes. He came out of the very heart of that Catholic piety which has in it the high tradition of consummated Grace. It bewitched the world by its historic record in the " Récit d'une Sœur." He gave it delicate and brilliant expression. He had that spiritual distinction and charm which we in England associate with the personality of Lord Halifax. But, also, he was a champion of that appeal to the Democracy which took the form of Catholic Socialism. Twenty years ago it had swing and move-

ment in it.   It held, annually, large and important
Conferences, and it was backed by great ecclesiastical
names.   It had its tongue set free against Capitalism,
by the fact that the great Capitalist Bourgeoisie was
so largely Voltairian, Secular, Anti-Clerical.   It stood,
en bloc, for enmity to the Church.   And the Church,
therefore, saw no reason for moderating its criticism
of its commercial methods.   On the other hand, it
was handicapped by the fact that the current Socialism
of the working classes was Marxian and anti-Christian.
Hence it despaired of Christianizing its spirit :   and
could only offer its own Socialism as an antagonistic
alternative.   It went in largely for model Factories,
for Co-operative Banks, for Workers' Guilds.   It was
full of inspiration.   Somehow, under the unfortunate
rule of the last Pope, these efforts have been in retreat.
The suspicion of Modernism, which beclouded the
" Sillon," effected much all round.   But the Count
de Mun was once its chief spokesman, and secured
for it its proper place in the recognized activities of
the Church.   With him, passes away the memory of
a beautiful group of saintly lives, who touched, as
only Frenchmen and Frenchwomen can, something
of what we feel to be perfection.

XXXIII

ALL THE YEAR ROUND

WINTER

SKATING! We really have seen it again. That has been the great event of the winter. It was rapidly becoming a tragedy that boys should grow up in England who had never seen a man skate, and who had no traditions and memories and associations of the magic of the ice. Rich folk could crowd out to remote valleys in Switzerland and revel in the old fascinations: but the great multitude might live and die without ever beholding the triumph of life over death—the triumph by which man turns the very deadness of Nature into the elixir of a new joy. Once again we saw it, the delightful sight of the glimmering figures against the brisk grey of the morning or the blue grey of the afternoon, with all the wonder that a touch of red in cloak or hat gave to the bewitching scene. And there was the dint, and glint, and ring of the steel, and the dry low hum of innumerable skates; and the old exaggerated poses, and the fantastic figurings, and the wild rush of hurricane hockey. And there was the man just arrived at the outside edge, so rapturously proud; and the swift fall on the back of the head, and the ice so amazingly hard ; and the old sore on the hip which told of adventures that had come to grief. How well we remembered the great days in the 'Seventies, when all the meadows were full of black ice as hard as nails, and the river was frozen hard, and little Mr. Plumb, of Exeter, gave us the first fascinating sight we had ever had of Canadian vine-leaves. Now at least there has been a week put back into the human imagination which will keep the thought alive of what skating means, if we are to have, once again, the long sterile interval. Just think : if this week had not come, English boys might have lost all power of entering into one of the finest and purest pieces of English poetry that our literature possesses. Wordsworth hardly ever showed his power of idealizing common life more finely than in the splendid imaginative passage in " The Prelude " on his boyish skating. It would have been a disastrous thing for our literature if we had had to bolt off to Grindelwald or Mentana in order to discover what our poet meant :

> " And in the frosty season, when the sun
> Was set, and visible for many a mile
> The cottage windows blazed through twilight gloom,
> I heeded not their summons : happy time
> It was indeed for all of us—for me
> It was a time of rapture ! Clear and loud
> The village clock tolled six,—I wheeled about,
> Proud and exulting like an untired horse
> That cares not for his home. All shod with steel,
> We hissed along the polished ice in games
> Confederate, imitative of the chase
> And woodland pleasures,—the resounding horn,
> The pack loud chiming, and the hunted hare.

So through the darkness and the cold we flew,
And not a voice was idle ; with the din
Smitten, the precipices rang aloud ;
The leafless trees and every icy crag
Tinkled like iron ; while far distant hills
Into the tumult sent an alien sound
Of melancholy not unnoticed, while the stars
Eastward were sparkling clear, and in the west
The orange sky of evening died away.
Not seldom from the uproar I retired
Into a silent bay, or sportively
Glanced sideway, leaving the tumultuous throng,
To cut across the reflex of a star
That fled, and, flying still before me, gleamed
Upon the glassy plain ; and oftentimes,
When we had given our bodies to the wind,
And all the shadowy banks on either side
Came sweeping through the darkness, spinning still
The rapid line of motion, then at once
Have I, reclining back upon my heels,
Stopped short ; yet still the solitary cliffs
Wheeled by me—even as if the earth had rolled
With visible motion her diurnal round !
Behind me did they stretch in solemn train,
Feebler and feebler, and I stood and watched
Till all was tranquil as a dreamless sleep."

THE BIRDS OF SPRING

Spring has come, with its noise of birds. For them
it is a time of " sturm und drang." They bustle, and
jostle, and tweet and twitter, and rush and tumble
and scud. The garden throbs with their loud flutter-
ings. And it is a real relief to learn from our supreme
Instructor on all live matters such as Nature, or
Music, or the Argentina Beef Trust, " the penny
'Times,'" that this fuss and fret is not all the mere

flummery of courting. It is not all to be put down to the count of 'Arry and Eliza at 'appy 'Ampstead. It is better than that. The superb careering of the wood pigeon in early Spring is no attempt to impress the eye and fascinate the heart of a future lady pigeon. It is due to sheer joy in daring and beautiful motion. It is the outbreak of spontaneous vitality. So the " Times " assures us. The wood pigeon does it off its own head, because it just loves it. That is exactly what it looks like : and it was always a blow to learn that it was done with an eye to something else—out of a vain desire to win and woo. We wanted it to represent the rollicking sense of the " joie de vivre." It is exactly what we should like to do ourselves when we are happy. Indeed, we mean to try some day. It looks so easy, if once you let yourself go from the roof of a good barn. So we shall now watch it again, with fresh delight, and leave Mrs. Wood-pigeon entirely out of the reckoning. Who knows whether Dr. Liddon did not entirely misjudge the corn-crake to whose dismal creaking croak he listened, and said, " That is the noise, dear friend, with which he won the heart of Mrs. Corn-crake, I gather"? Not a bit of it! It has always had in it the gurgling chuckle of complete self-satisfaction. Simply to make that strange sound inside was delightful enough in itself. It comforted like a snore in the smoking room after a good shoot. It tickled the innards. It rattled like a bad pun. It had a sense of joke in its absurdity. It was as comforting as a laugh or a sneeze. That was all it was. Hang Mrs. Corncrake!

x

THE CRY OF THE SPRING

If only the cruel wind will give it a chance, the earth is ready to shout with joy. It looks as if it could hardly hold it in. Yet its shout is delivered in silence. We feel it to be there: but no sound arrives. "The Heavens laugh with us in our Jubilee." Yet the laugh never comes: it vanishes into the low chuckle of a flying thrush. There is always this promise in Nature's face. She is ever on the edge of something that is never fulfilled. She wants to shout: but we have to do it for her.

> "Shout round me, let me hear thy shouts,
>   Thou happy shepherd boy."

Exactly! She must find a shepherd-boy to utter what she means. He does just what she desires. He shouts: shouts long and loud: fills the air with his shouts. And, in that blessed noise, she finds herself. Every tree and bush and blade of grass shake all over in a tumult of joy at the shout that man makes on their behalf. This brooding silence of the listening earth is always a strange mystery to us. Speech seems so very near. Yet is always withheld. You feel it trembling trouble most of all in a dear dog's eyes. Yet even then its fate is on it, and it cannot attain. That is why it is so right for us to whoop aloud while we walk abroad in the Spring. That is our high priestly part. That is what heaven and earth wait for us to do. Man is "the Word." Life is in the Word. Life rises from level to level, through grad-

after grade : and still something is wanting : until man speaks : and the earth and the heaven are set at rest. Only the speech had better confine itself to a whoop of sheer joy. For, as soon as he goes much beyond that, his speech begins to trouble the peace that it has made.

EASTER-TIDE

It was in a garden that Easter began : and the faithful earth can never forget it. It breaks out into a Garden over all its happy surface. Field and hedge, and wood, hurry up to do their best. There are flowers in every corner : and all of them are babbling about a Garden. They cannot keep still. Their merry voices go ringing on, repeating the old tale. It was in a Garden that it all happened. Death ended : life was reborn. The flowers know what it has meant to lie bound in the iron winter, with the colours all wiped out, and everything as silent and grim as the grave. And, then, the Spring stirred. The call came. Out they leaped, and sang aloud : and all the world is alive with splendid colour. Every year it shall be as if a garden has burst its borders, and outgrown its walls, and has set itself to see whether it cannot make the entire round earth to become one garden, for the sake of Easter joy. How pleasant and lawful it is to play with happy associations like these ! Yet how firm and austere is the steady historical outline of our real Easter story ! This charm and stir of Spring has been enough to set a swarm of Mysteries going—Mysteries of Thammuz,

Mysteries of Dionysius, Mysteries of Mithras, Mysteries of the Maid who was swept by so swift a stroke out of the Sicilian meadows. But for the Jewish imagination, the fact is the real thing that matters, and the human historical interest is altogether paramount. Not a glance is allowed to left or to right. No glamour of mythical fancy is allowed to blur the sharp clear lines. When the natural analogy is introduced, it is kept tight and fast to the rigid identity of the law: and not a loophole is offered through which the human and the natural elements may obscurely mingle and be confounded. " Except a corn of wheat die, it abideth alone: but if it die it bringeth forth much fruit." The parallelism with the Resurrection is exact and complete: yet the phenomenon of Nature and the phenomenon of Humanity stand steadily apart. There is no tendency whatever to confuse the dividing lines. The symbolism is found in the double layer of fact, in the exact repetition of the one underlying law: not in the play of fancy or emotion. The historicity of the story holds the heart entirely. It is all given in the intimate and familiar voice that utters " Mary ": and in the direct and immediate response of personal loyalty—" Rabboni: my Master." The concentrated passion of this recovered intimacy absorbs into itself every conceivable interest. There is no possibility of letting feeling loose to play about with pretty figures of the Spring. It is the moral and spiritual crisis of man's new birth into Eternal Life. This is enough. This is all that can be thought of. Everything, but this, drops away. The Drama is purely spiritual: and human. Yet, though it owes nothing to Nature's analogies, and though it goes its own way without a reference to anything outside the actual facts, nevertheless Christianity can sweep up, in its stride, without even stopping to notice it, all these natural figurative symbols, all these delicate associations of the Spring. Absorbed though it be in the Drama of Salvation, in the reality of Christ risen from the Dead, it is true that the Spring is all about the Christ, as He rises ; and we can see our own resurrection music taking form and colour in the garden of earth, and can recognize, with clear heads and hearts, how all the Sons of God are shouting for joy over the splendour of God's new Creation.

SPRING IN LONDON

"Sumer is icumen in ! Sing cuccu ! " No ! It is not true. It cannot be true. It is impossible. No earth in which we, and Mr. Perks, are living can conceivably be as beautiful as it looks this Spring. It is no real flesh and blood world. It is a dream. It is a lyrical cry. It is a bird's song. It is an outburst of passion. It is a magical vision. It is Paradise regained. Did you ever see such green in the grass, there above all, where, at the East-end of the water in St. James's Park, those wicked old Stockbrokers with the immense yellow bills waddle across the sward? And the bluebells hover about, like sudden breaths, delicate as thought. And the tulips let it all come out unashamed like love, in a glorious unbroken dauntless shout.

We have never remembered how beautiful it always is as the miracle of spring startles us with its ecstasy. Look ! how the flowers are all laughing ! What can it be that they are laughing at ? Surely, it is at the absurdity of imagining that a few hundred yards off, well within sight of all the singing birds, there is positively going on a House of Commons : and a stuffy old gentleman is bringing in a Bill, and really thinks it worth while to explain its several provisions to rows of weary green benches who have heard it all before. And there, in the other big room, a noble lord is making a motion. Conceive it ! He had much better lay an egg, at once. It would be far more appropriate and congenial in a fairy world like this. It would show that he appreciated the situation. As it is, he is hopelessly out of the picture. For the Earth has no trouble or sorrow : there is nothing to set right : there is nothing more wanted. It is simply perfect. It is light as a bubble blown by fancy. It is sweet as children's laughter. It floats there, in its blessed halo of green, clean and clear, as a flying vision caught in the mysterious depths of a crystal ball. So fair ! So frail ! It cannot last. Yet somehow, for one happy moment it is true that we have stepped inside the dreadful gate while the angel with the drawn sword kindly looked the other way : here we are in Eden. It is our own again : it has never been lost. But, before we can capture it, there has been a hiss in the grass : and a black shadow that slips away through the trees : and it is all over ! Gone for this year ! But that five minutes will be back again next Spring! It always recurs anew. It always surprises. Thank God that we did just manage to see it this time, before it passed. That sight of Eden in St. James's Park, within a few yards of Buckingham Palace, is enough to carry us through the year: though, already, the World has broken in upon us with a roar of 'buses. And that admirable man in the House of Commons is at it again, I do believe, just as if nothing had happened: and that excellent Peer has carried his motion, and never once felt that it ought to have been an egg. So we must go home: and sigh: and never forget.

ENGLAND IN SUNSHINE

We have seen the sun. That is what has been so bewildering. It was determined to show what it could do if it tried. We had been grumbling and groaning for many a long week. We had begun to doubt whether there was such a thing in the vast heaven as this real live sun. We were drowned in despair. When, in a moment, stung by some taunt of ours of more than usual bitterness, he pulled himself together, and obliged. For two delicious weeks he did nothing else but shine and shine, as if he could never give us enough of it. The whole sky was full of light. And still, the wind was cool: and no sultry heat spoiled the delicate and airy illumination. The world was light. And, then, we saw England. Had we ever seen it before? Had we ever guessed what lay there asleep, under the habitual disguise of grey? Surely, no one could have dreamed of the loveliness

that, now, woke up and laughed for sheer joy in the
glory of light. It was a supreme revelation. The
whole land glowed through and through with its
delighted response. It was bathed and steeped in
beauty. Every nook and corner brimmed over with
loveliness shaken down, pressed together, running
over. Never was such green before seen as the grass :
or such mottled sunlight in the orchard : or such
sheen on the sleeping waters : or such brooding
wonder on the heavy-headed woods. And the splendour of the flowers in every cottage garden : and the
rollicking abundance of the ramblers that flung themselves about in tumbling festoons : and the magic of
the lawns : and the grey churches loved in our dreams
all there, nestling under the elms, just as we should
have prayed for them to look : and the ruddy comfort and square faces of Georgian houses, dozing over
flowery borders, as if they were lapped over with
contentment and ease. Was there ever such a Country,
this side of Paradise ? Is there anything comparable
to the bewitchment of an English countryside, when
once the sun is really shining ? As we look and look,
and drink our fill, and almost beseech the beautiful
vision to stop ere it exceed our capacity to enjoy it,
we begin to know why, at the first, " the morning
stars sang together : and all the sons of God shouted
for joy." These astounding days had to end. The
sun has returned to his normal in-and-out business.
But we can thank him, now, as he flickers about, for
that supreme effort of his which can never be forgotten. He has given us a standard by which to

measure his power and goodness. Once, at any rate, we saw, by his grace, what England is. And the memory of it can never pass away. She may grizzle up again : and frown : and swear. The smile may go out of her face : and the old dour greyness blot out the light. But it will never be forgotten how she laughed up at us in the day of her glory.

MID-SUMMER

The usual miracle came and went. It is dreadful how quickly the first incredible magic of Spring passes. It is always quite new. Nothing like it has ever happened before. It is an annual act of creation, wholly unanticipated, and unparalleled. Like Melchisedec, it has had no father or mother. It simply is. And, then, like Melchisedec, it withdraws with the like celerity. It is gone. In its place is the sober old Summer Earth, plump and full as a Dowager, with heavy lumps of bunched foliage and massive depths of solemn green. The blue festoons of the elm nod in drowsy blobs. All is as it ever will be. The gay freak, that glistened and broke, will hide itself away until next May.

And, after all, as we grow old, these blue dowager elms, with their bunched toques, are full of solace. They have a comfortable fat thickness about them : and they clump so well together. Under them, the arched shadows grow positively black : and there is a sense of recessed splendour. England is altogether beautiful ; and that is enough.

LONDON IN THE SUMMER

On some glorious day in June, when the breeze blows fresh, and the sky is clean, London has a way of beating every other town hollow in sheer unadulterated beauty. There is a wealth in her flowers, a splendour in her grass, a depth in her verdure, and a brightness in her plane-trees, that is her own alone. Her 'buses, in shimmering colours, glow and move like the living creatures in Ezekiel. St. James's Park spreads secret lawns under bowery groves : and there are visions of strange birds that preen their white breasts with enormous yellow bills : and think of nothing at all. And, then, there is the crowning wonder of the immortal river, racing in full flow beneath its bridges, buoyant, eddying, immense, with no touch of age to tame its undying motion, for all the sorrow and sighing that have clouded its shores. Undimmed and undaunted, it swings to and fro in rhythmic tides that put to shame all fears for England. How can any city lose its hope with such a river to roll along its Parliament House, and to water its white walls ? The sun dances and dazzles over all its brimming face. The wind flickers it into hurrying ripples : the brown barges slide : the curve of the Embankment swerves under the delicate grey dignity of Somerset House towards the far-shining Cross of St. Paul's, fresh-washed and triumphant. Spires glisten, and domes brood : and the wide heaven laughs over all. Somehow, the black shadows have disappeared : and the sins have been shamed into hiding: and the sorrows and the sighings have vanished away: and there seem to be no more tears. Have we, after all, really built Jerusalem? To-morrow, we shall know better. But, to-day, at any rate, "Earth hath not anything to show more fair."

HARVEST

Through the heart of happy England, the August train glides like a live thought. It carries no haggard commercial crowd bent on business. It is full from end to end of gathered families, papa, and mamma, and the four big children, and the baby. They are one large bundle of wraps, and baskets and spades, and buckets. They are off to some bright Paradise, white and flushed and expectant: or they are returning, brown-legged, and ruddy, and hung round with bottles full of sea treasure. And, as they slide along as in a dream, on either side of them, for mile after mile, spreads the golden harvest. It is as new a surprise every year, as the song of a nightingale, or Westminster Abbey. We jump up at the sight of it, and gasp, and cry, and shout, and sing. We enthusiastically point it out to glum and total strangers. Who ever saw it before? Who ever will see anything like it again? It is so golden: that is the wonder. Look at the golden splendour of the brown wheat! And the shimmering glamorous gold of the quivering oats! And the fairy gold of the bearded barley! And the stooks, with their golden heads laid close together! And the floor of gold on which they stand, in their golden rows! And the gold of the tossing straw romping itself over the ledges of the thresher that hums through all the loaded air and fills it with the passing peace of infinite satisfaction. The blessed ranks of golden corn bend and sway under the delight of the leaping wind, and the deeper colours come and go, ruddy and purple-shadowed: and, still, as the tasselled heads shake against the sky line, they fling out a glitter of golden glory, which holds in it all the secret of the laughing sun. There is gold far away there in squares on the uplands: and gold lying deep under the shadows of the woodlands: and gold that rises and falls over endless spaces of curving downs. Until, at last, as the sun sinks, it finds that there is nothing better to do than to turn all to gold, and to mix the gold of the glad fields with the gold of the flushed skies; and the glory floods in at the windows of our dusty carriages, and we ourselves, with our rosy babies and brown-legged children, are caught up into a golden haze and receive our transfiguration. And then! Look! As soon as day is gone, somehow, unawares, there has slipped into the quiet heaven the thin curve of the golden harvest moon! Once or twice this year, in spite of all that the rain could do, we have seen this sight: we have been given the vision. And, once again, we know, in our very heart of hearts, that there is nothing so splendid as the colour of Harvest, and no country on earth so fair as England. Our holiday has not failed, if only we have caught the shout of Harvest, golden-throated, trumpet-tongued, ascending up to that high City with the golden streets, where "the cherubic

host touch their immortal harps of golden wires."
And this golden glory, this splendour of wealth—
what is it ? Just Bread ? Plain, simple, homely
Bread. Bread, the elemental necessity of every man,
woman, and child, in the land. Bread, the common
daily food of rich and poor alike. Bread, the staff of
all ordinary life : " bread that strengtheneth the
heart " of all that is most human, and child-like, and
fraternal. Bread, the bond of fellowship, which
whoso eats is our brother. Bread, that knits humanity
together in one unfailing need—the touch of common
nature which makes the whole world kin. Bread,
which is the primal want in every cottage, and in
every slum. Bread, the commonest thing known :
that is at our side at every meal : that we feel for
with anxious fingers wherever we miss it : without
which we cannot even begin. Bread is our true wealth.
Bread is our glory. All over the glowing golden face
of the earth, we see how noble is the width and
honour of the prayer which pleads " Give us this
day our daily bread."

THE RAIN

" Heigh ho ! the Wind and the Rain ! For the
rain it raineth every day ! " How Shakespeare goes
at once to the heart of the matter ! He hits the nail
straight on the head. Nothing could be better said.
And there is nothing more to be said about it. " The
rain, it raineth every day ! " There you are ! What
more do you want ? That is exactly it. That is
what we all are feeling. The great heart of humanity

is summed up in a single line. The oppression that
lies so heavy upon it is just this—that it rains every
day. If only it would leave out a day here or there!
If only it would keep up an air of expectation and
surprise! If only now and again it would startle us
by leaving off! But no! It has got a sort of dull,
stupid, lifeless, ox-like mind of its own: and, having
begun, it just goes on. It sees no reason for varying.
Why stop? Why do anything else? One day is the
same as another. If it rains on one day, it may just
as well rain on all. So the poor, blind, silly thing goes
doggedly on. It rains every day. And, that being
so, we are reduced to saying "Heigh ho!" That is
what the poet so lucidly asserts. He can sing about
other things with exuberant abundance of fancy and
l nguage, as we know. But about the rain, he limits
himself strictly to "Heigh ho!" It is not original:
it is not suggestive: it leads to nothing. No! Nor
does the rain. We look gloomily out of window:
and, as we gaze at the relentless downpour, nothing
else comes up into our mind but "Heigh ho!" Our
imagination refuses to work. Our thoughts are
blocked. We can do nothing but sigh. We are too
feeble to initiate any action. We can't go out. We
are tired to death of sticking in. What on earth can
we do? "Heigh ho!" So we sigh: with heavy
wits. "Heigh ho!" So we monotonously repeat,
" I never knew such beastly weather. When on earth
is it going to stop?" "Heigh ho!" "The rain, it
raineth every day!" So we once more take up our
book: and go fast asleep. It was a stroke of genius,

which so caught the spirit of the rain. If Shakespeare
had tried to say more about it, he would have ruined
it. There is nothing more that will ever be said about
the rainy day: but " Heigh ho! the wind and the
rain!" Stop at that. You will never get further.
Every sad face looking through the wet, streaming
panes is saying it over and over again. " Heigh ho!"

OCTOBER

" Years begin in October." That is the great and
undeniable truth that broke in upon us from the lips
of J. K. S. Why did we not discover it before?
" Years die in July." That is so right. The spell of
work is over. The whole Epic Cycle of our Year's
Labour rounds itself to a close. We pack up: and
run off: and are free of the yoke: and lie at ease:
or play with fury. Anyhow, there is a lapse. And,
then, there is that still grey morning with the light
frost on the grass, and the slight sting in the air: and
we know it. It is " the dawn of the year." October
is near: and we must find our way back to the office
and the stool. We must take up the old job. It all
lies ahead of us again, laid out in its steady sequences,
with its ordered breaks at Christmas and Easter. We
can see it from start to finish. We are familiar with
its rhythmic movements. It has a certain air of
completeness, a beginning, a middle, and an end. We
can plan it out, and prepare for its regular crises.
" Years begin in October." The real years. The
Christian year is another matter. That makes its
start in black November. The Secular and Ceremonial

year is yet another affair. That has got a wholly
artificial moment to begin in. It drops in as a casual
echo to our Christmas refrain. " A Merry Christmas."
That is right enough. And, then, we have to tie on
to it a wish that carries us no further. It can only
succeed in varying the epithet. " A Happy New
Year." What a power there might have been thrown
into our lives, if the three Beginnings of the Year
had been united into one supreme impression ! What
resolutions we could have made, if they had had in
them and behind them the combined pressure of the
Religious, the Secular, and the Real, New Year ! It
is so impossible to form resolutions in October. Yet
that is the only moment when they might make a
difference. For by Christmas or January, our year
has already determined its drift. Shall we try, then ?
Shall we look ahead over the whole period before us,
and detect what it is likely to lack, and bring into
play what it most requires ? Here is October. We
have our chance. It is the Dawn of the Year.

AUTUMN

Are those three perfect days in Spring fairer or
not than the three perfect days in Autumn ? Who
can judge between vision and vision ? We have had
three Autumn days this year at their very fairest ;
and while their magic is upon us, we find it impossible
to believe that anything on earth can be more beautiful.
They are still and noiseless as a dream : they are limpid
as a crystal. The light blue sky basks over the woodlands as if it held them in a trance. And every leaf

and every fibre is a golden glory. The brown and
bronze of the bracken glows through the film of the
glittering birches. The whole earth is alive with the
splendour of colour. And there is as yet no sense of
death about it. Nothing clammy: or corrupt.
Only the sudden flush, as if the time had come to say
good-bye. Is it only youth that can afford to love
Autumn ? Must the old, as Wordsworth bids us,
cling ever to the joys of the spring ?

> " In youth we love the darksome lawn
> Brushed by the owlet's wing,
> Then twilight is preferred to dawn,
> And Autumn to the Spring.
>
> .   .   .   .   .
>
> Still as we nearer draw to life's dark goal,
> Be hopeful Spring the favourite of the soul."

Yet even the old may let their eyes feast on this
tender and gracious hour, when the earth turns,
brooding, to her quiet rest, before the wild West
winds have begun to drive before them " yellow and
black and pale and hectic red," their " pestilent-
stricken multitude " of dead leaves. Very good it is
to have been alive : very dear is the earth which has
been so kind a home : very gentle the creeping whisper
that bids us leave it all, and rise, and go. We have
loved, even though now we must lose what we have
loved. The vanishing hours are all the dearer because
they must pass. For

> " Ah ! the very reason why
> I love them is because they die ! "

Y

Works by Dr. Scott Holland.

PERSONAL STUDIES. 4th Edition. 6s.

VITAL VALUES. 3s. 6d.

THE FIBRES OF FAITH. 1s. 6d. net.

BROOKE FOSS WESTCOTT, Bishop of Durham. (*Little Biographies.*) 2d. net.

GEORGE HOWARD WILKINSON, Bishop of St. Andrews, Primus of the Scottish Episcopal Church. (*Little Biographies.*) 2d. net.

Standard Biographical Works.

ONE LOOK BACK. By the Rt. Hon. G. W. E. RUSSELL. 10s. 6d. net.

THE LIFE OF ARCHBISHOP SHELDON. By the Rev. Canon VERNON STALEY. 10s. 6d. net.

"I REMEMBER." By the Rev. Canon HORSLEY. 2nd Edition. 7s. 6d. net.

CHARLES EDWARD BROOKE. A Memoir by the Rev. Canon A. G. DEEDES, with introduction by VISCOUNT HALIFAX. 5s. net.

THE LIFE AND TIMES OF MRS. SHERWOOD. By F. J. HARVEY DARTON. 2nd Edition. 16s. net.

WILLIAM DALRYMPLE MACLAGAN, Archbishop of York. By F. D. HOW. 2nd Edition. 16s. net.

FATHER DOLLING. A Memoir. By JOSEPH CLAYTON. 5th Edition. 2s. net. Paper, 1s. net.

FATHER STANTON, OF ST. ALBAN'S, HOLBORN. A Memoir. By JOSEPH CLAYTON. 4th Edition. 2s. net. Paper, 1s.

Travel.

THE LAND OF OPEN DOORS. By J. BURGON BICKERSTETH ; being letters from Western Canada. With foreword by the Rt. Hon. EARL GREY. 7s. 6d. net.

A BISHOP AMONGST BANANAS. By the Rt. Rev. HERBERT BURY, Bishop of Northern and Central Europe ; with Preface by the Bishop of London. 6s.

A SHEPHERD OF THE VELD : BRANSBY LEWIS KEY, Bishop of St. John's, Kaffraria. By GODFREY CALLAWAY. 2nd Edition. 2s. 6d. net.

Sociology and Philosophy.

CONSCIENCE : Its Origin and Authority. By the Rev. G. L. RICHARDSON, B.D. 5s. net. (*Just ready.*)

MARRIAGE AND THE SEX PROBLEM. By Professor F. W. FOERSTER, of Zurich ; translated by Dr. MEYRICK BOOTH. 2nd Edition. 5s. net.

PERSONALITY AND WOMANHOOD. By R. M. WILLS, with a Preface by Canon RANDOLPH. 5s. net.

ON PERSONAL SERVICE. By a Headmaster ; with a Preface by the Secretary of the Cavendish Association. 2s. 6d. net.

Architecture.

TOWERS AND SPIRES. By E. TYRRELL GREEN, M.A. 10s. 6d. net.

PORCHES AND FONTS. By J. C. WALL. 10s. 6d. net.

Messrs. WELLS GARDNER, DARTON & CO., LTD., issue the following Catalogues, which they will be pleased to send, post free, on application.

1. A Catalogue of General Literature.
2. Books suitable for Presents and Prizes.
3. A Catalogue of Religous Works.
4. School Books for Scholars and Teachers.
5. Amusement for all the Year Round. (A list of Plays and Entertainments for Home and School.)